Opium of the People

OPIUM
OF THE PEOPLE

*The Christian religion
in the U.S.S.R.*

by

MICHAEL
BOURDEAUX

'Die Religion . . . ist das Opium des Volkes'
(Karl Marx, *Kritik der Hegelschen Rechtsphilosophie*)

MOWBRAYS

LONDON & OXFORD

© 1965 by Michael Bourdeaux
First published in mcmlxv
by Faber and Faber Limited
This edition published by
A. R. Mowbray & Co Ltd
Oxford, 1977
Printed in Great Britain by
Lowe and Brydone Printers Limited
Thetford, Norfolk

ISBN 0 264 66420 5

Keston Book No. 9

To
GILLIAN
and
KAREN JANE

Keston College

(Centre for the Study of Religion and Communism)

Opium of the People, Michael Bourdeaux's first book, is now reprinted as the ninth in the loosely-linked series of Keston Books. This series, and the work of Keston College in general, are instrumental in presenting to the public the facts of religious life in the Soviet Union and Eastern Europe.

Keston College has a growing programme supporting and publicising the cause of believers in communist countries. It helps the churches in the West to pray, to be informed and to express their concern in the most practical ways.

Keston has various publications, including the Keston News Service and a journal, *Religion in Communist Lands*.

To learn more about our work, please write to:

Keston College,
Heathfield Road,
Keston,
Kent BR2 6BA.

Contents

Illustrations

Acknowledgements

My thanks are due to the following:

to Darton, Longman & Todd Ltd. for permission to reprint the extract from *The Russian Religious Renaissance of the Twentieth Century*, by N. Zernov;

to Penguin Books Ltd. for permission to reprint the extract from *The Orthodox Church* by Timothy Ware;

to Rupert Hart-Davis Ltd. for permission to reprint the extract from *Conversations with Stalin* by M. Djilas;

to Victor Gollancz Ltd. for permission to reprint two extracts from *One Day in the Life of Ivan Denisovich* by Alexander Solzhenitsyn;

to the Faith Press Ltd. for permission to reprint the extract from *Theological Study in the Russian and Bulgarian Churches Under Communist Rule* by A. Johansen;

to Macmillan & Co. Ltd. for permission to reprint two extracts from *Religion in the Soviet Union* by W. Kolarz;

to the Hogarth Press Ltd. for permission to reprint the extract from *A Journey into Russia* by L. van der Post.

Preface to the Second Edition

"With the increasing possibility of travel to Communist countries and the greater cultural contact between East and West, it has at last become possible to know Soviet life at first hand. This does not mean that it is now easy to be objective about it, but at least one can try to understand. Christianity in the Soviet Union is, and seems likely to remain, especially difficult to see in its true perspective, because of the hostile attitude which the Government takes towards it and the resulting impossibility of having free contacts with those who practise it. Much of this book, however, is an attempt to record the attitudes of ordinary people, both believers and atheists, towards the faith, and is the result of meetings with Russians on several visits I have made to the U.S.S.R. since 1959. During a year's residence I met reactions which were often different from those which most members of delegations and the majority of tourists encounter. I apologize for all the instances where my judgments are too subjective."

This was the first paragraph of my original Preface written twelve years ago. It was a gratifying moment when my present publishers suggested reprinting this, my first book, but at the same time I felt anxious as I took it off the shelf and began to re-read it after so many years. I was sure I would feel angry at the immature value-judgments (for which it had been criticized at the time) and choked by the urge to update every page. Since the original was written in 1964 a vast new corpus of evidence has become available, leading to several books and a spate of articles. In particular, Soviet Christians have begun to speak forthrightly and voluminously for themselves in a way which is foreshadowed in the last chapter.

However, I ended by approving a reprint of the original text *in toto* (with the correction of three or four factual mistakes) and adding some "Notes to the Second Edition", since the text, in a curious way, seemed to me as relevant to 1977 as to 1965—and to interweave one's present judgments among past impressions would have

13

spoiled the flavour of the original. Where I really do disagree with what I formerly said, I have made this clear in the "Notes to the Second Edition".

MICHAEL BOURDEAUX

Keston College,
Keston, Kent

December 1976

CHAPTER I

Our Radiant Russia

U
ntil recently interest in the Russian Church was considered to be an esoteric pursuit. Many still think it is, though with the latest ecumenical developments this must soon change. The strangeness is in the isolation which was hardly broken by the settling among us of a few *émigré* communities after 1917. The separation is one of centuries, not of miles, and the setting up of the Iron Curtain did little more than seal off a door which had already been effectively closed since the Middle Ages.

It does not lie within the scope of this book to remedy the absence of a comprehensive modern history of Russian Christianity in English.[1] It is impossible, however, to understand the situation of Christianity in the U.S.S.R. if we see it in isolation from the thousand years which preceded it. If I were to fit these into a single chapter there would be room for little more than a table of dates and names, so instead I want to record the reflections which occurred to me as I travelled around the Soviet Union to view its Christian monuments. I have made no attempt to write a connected history, but have noted in chronological order the events of abiding importance for understanding Christian Russia of the twentieth century.

THE KIEVAN PERIOD

I had already been in the Soviet Union for several months before I at last reached Kiev, but the capital of the Ukraine was from one point of view the goal of my whole stay. The TU-104 in which I was flying north from Odessa banked sharply on to its wing-tip and suddenly a pageant of golden domes thrusting upwards from green woods appeared, laced along the bank of the broad, sandy Dnieper. Never did I regret the restriction on aerial photography more than then.

[1] See Notes for Further Reading, p. 240

From this vantage point one could see why Kiev became the first great city of Russia, a nodal point in the eastward expansion of the Slavs after the eighth century. Here, where a broad strip of fertile land intersects a navigable river, an overland trade route led from west to east, from Central Europe through a corridor between the Carpathians and the Pripet marshes to the measureless steppe beyond, across which merchants brought back the riches of the East. The river was even more important, for it was the spinal cord of medieval Russia, a vital stage in the route between the Baltic and the Black Sea, linking the productive regions of what is now the Ukraine to Constantinople, the 'city of the world's desire'. Every year at the end of the long Russian winter a fleet of small craft would set off on the journey southward towards the Black Sea. Laden with corn, furs, wax and honey, they would return before the next winter with cargoes of Byzantine silks, gold, wine and fruit which would bring joy and colour to the approaching cold, dark nights.

By the tenth century the nations of Europe were already being bound together in a common Christian culture which was becoming synonymous with civilization. Russia was subject to more oriental influences than the countries of Western Europe, but her commercial ties to the capital of the Byzantine Empire made a conversion to Christianity a probability from the first.

This was not accomplished without some wavering and unpleasantness, for in 860, a little over a hundred years before the final conversion, the Russian fleet attacked Constantinople. The imperious and delightful reply to this petty annoyance from the barbarians of the north was an attempt, temporarily successful, to convert them to Christianity. Those with vested interests in the old pagan religion doubtless inspired a forceful return to the ways of their ancestors, but the bridgehead thus made was never completely destroyed and the new faith grappled for a firmer foothold in preparation for the official conversion in 988– or 989, as recent historical scholarship suggests.

A monastic view of the early history of the Eastern Slavs is found in the *Russian Primary Chronicle*, compiled over a period of time and going up to the early twelfth century. It gives us a stylized but most interesting account of the actual event. The Grand Prince Vladimir sent his envoys to spy out the great religions of the world, Christianity (both Eastern and Roman), Islam and Judaism, before deciding which one to adopt for his own land. He heard their testimonies in his council chamber, rejecting each religion in turn (Islam, for example, because 'It is the Russians' joy to drink; this we cannot forgo') until he finally selected Greek Christianity. An ambassador had brought word from Constantinople of the overwhelming beauty and splendour of worship in the great Cathedral of St. Sophia, reporting that there heaven was enshrined and nothing on earth could equal it.

This story makes it clear that it was above all the aesthetic attraction of the Greek Church which made its impact on the Russians. This has been a dominant factor in Russian Christianity ever since.

The conversion changed the whole character of Kievan civilization. The racially disparate elements of a trading community were welded together under one Christian ruler. The divergence between Eastern Orthodox and Latin Christianity was not yet cemented into the schism it later became; and Russia at this early period entered more closely into the community of European Christian nations than at any point in her subsequent history.

The autobiography of Vladimir Monomakh, who ruled from 1113–25, shows the depth to which the Christian ethos had already penetrated the educated mind. Through his relatives he was closely connected with both Byzantium and Western Europe. His mother was a Byzantine princess, his sister married Henry IV of Germany, ruler of the Holy Roman Empire, and his wife was Gytha, daughter of the English king, Harold II, who was killed at the Battle of Hastings. It is intriguing to read how this busy ruler conscientiously applied Christian criteria to the problems of exercising authority. All pursuits, he shows, whether mundane or important, can be permeated by the spirit of Christ and made valuable in the sight of God.

Russia was able to take over intact from Byzantium a corpus of Christian literature and music, a perfected tradition of art and architecture, a system of morality, which together comprised a whole aesthetic of civilization. This can be seen in its purest form in the Cathedral of St. Sophia in Kiev—not in the exterior, which is sadly masked by a late seventeenth-century restoration in the so-called 'Cossack' baroque style, but in its magnificent interior. Contemplating the 'Christ Pantocrator' mosaic in the central cupola or the 'Bogomater Oranta' (Praying Virgin) in the apse, one is transported in spirit to Constantinople or Thessalonika. Among the abundant medieval frescoes the most remarkable is a series in the western towers dating from the eleventh century, which illustrates festival and hunting scenes in the Hippodrome of Constantinople. The Emperor and his consort look on, while below, depicted in a highly realistic

17

way, are cavorting acrobats and actors. Two play pipes, one a psaltery, another a 'domra' (an early form of balalaika), while a dancer reels with something of the abandon of one of Matisse's revellers. Beside them two others prepare for a wrestling match, one of whom has a look of unashamed insolence on his face. In the background a clown is trying to climb a greasy pole, but he seems to be finding it too much for him.

St. Sophia was damaged only slightly by the Germans in the Second World War, but an even more ancient Christian site suffered considerably. The *Kievo-Pecherskaya Lavra* (Monastery of the Caves) is the most venerable of the four Russian Orthodox monasteries dignified by the title of 'Lavra' (from a Greek word meaning 'street' which came to be applied first to a row of monastic cells and then to a whole community of especial importance or size). It flourished from the very first days after the official conversion of Russia to Christianity. There is even a hint in the *Sermon on Law and Grace* by Ilarion, the first Russian Metropolitan of Kiev who wrote about half-way through the eleventh century, that there may have been monks here before 989. The situation of the monastery on the high right bank of the Dnieper is superb, but the Government has not yet begun to do anything to repair the savage destruction of the last war. One church is in ruins, with a wall gaping open like a wound to reveal a superb fresco exposed to the elements.

Though Kiev could, at times, evoke for me the glories of its history, it also saddened me to see the way in which the past has been betrayed. Nothing underlines this more readily than a great church which has been perverted from the worship for which its founders built and embellished it. I have had this feeling in the Cathedral of St. Sophia in Istanbul and I was constantly experiencing it in the Soviet Union where most of the finest and oldest churches have been converted into museums. In Kiev's St. Sophia the atmosphere still felt heavy with the prayer of past generations; the cessation of religious activities since 1934 seemed an apostasy from all that is best in Russia's history. When I was at the Monastery of the Caves in June 1960, about thirty monks still occupied a very small part of the huge area covered by the conventual buildings (these were by no means totally destroyed in the war). Since then even they have been evacuated on the pretext that their quarters were no longer safe. The labyrinthine caves beneath—from which the monastery takes its name and where many former inmates are buried—are supposed to have undermined the superstructure. Apparently the good citizens who now occupy their quarters are immune from such dangers.

Over the whole course of history Russia has been more impervious to external influences than any other European nation of comparable importance. Yet when she has adopted something which originated beyond her frontiers, she has done so with a prodigious enthusiasm which at the same time rapidly and completely russified what was taken over. The end-product then seems more national than many indigenous manifestations. So it was with the infusion of Byronic romanticism early in the nineteenth century. Even more notably was it true of the adoption of Communism. Most certainly of all can we say this of Russian Christianity. No other country has ever had quite this sense of individual mission, of being the sole repository of the true faith. This belief was at its most intense in the later, Muscovite, period, yet there is something of it to be found earlier, too, in the theological arguments of Metropolitan Ilarion and in the thought of others who contributed to the inflaming of Russian national consciousness. Indeed even the way in which the Russians ingested Christianity in the first few years after the conversion was remarkable.

In what were the great cities of medieval Russia we find notable churches, the origins of which are traceable to the eleventh century and which often preserve their primitive form almost intact. Travelling around the cities which once formed the northern confines of Kievan Russia—Novgorod, Pskov, Vladimir, Suzdal—one is constantly amazed that Byzantine Christianity spread so far with such rapidity, leaving its indelible imprint on all the towns which it touched.

Some people may find the sky-line of Novgorod, indented with countless onion-shaped domes of every height and volume, the most moving reminder of Russia's past. The best view is from a boat on Lake Ilmen. For others, the imposing height and squareness of the Dmitrievsky Cathedral·in Vladimir might evoke the same sensations, its starkness relieved by the ornate and beautiful bas-reliefs on the upper part of its walls. But for me there is one building which, above all others, brings to mind the splendour and glories of Russia's medieval civilization. This is the Church of the Pokrov on the River Nerl.

To reach it one has to travel by bus from Vladimir to Bogolyubovo and then walk to it across the fields, for the church stands in absolute isolation. From the bluff on which the village of Bogolyubovo is situated one can see it in the distance below, a white speck standing out against green alluvial meadows. I suppose that in winter the snow must make it invisible.

It is an exaggeration to say that one follows a path towards it. Rather one makes one's way hopefully along the river bank, though when the river is in flood in spring and autumn it can be a hazardous walk; sometimes, at the height of the thaw, the way is quite impassable. Even when conditions are not very favourable, the sight of the church ahead growing larger before one's eyes with each perilous step constantly beckons one forward. At last one is safe, standing on a firm platform of grass, washed at its foot by the waters of the Nerl where they flow into the Klyazma.

On closer inspection the exterior of the Pokrov Church fulfils the promise it had held from a distance. On a sunny spring day its dazzling whiteness is emphasized by the proximity of three or four trees with their new light-green foliage, which never seem to obscure the building, no matter from what angle one looks at it. On a really still day the ensemble is completed by a reflection of the church in the water which copies the minutest detail of the original.

A person who does not like having his illusions shattered should not go inside and see the absolutely bare interior, its white walls denuded of frescoes, without even an iconostasis to hide the bare expanse of floor where the altar should be. This is not the result of an atheistic campaign, but merely of the long lapse of time which has removed the necessity, even the possibility, of its being used for worship. It is indeed only at this point that one begins to wonder just why the church was built at all.

If one goes outside again to look at the setting of the church, one may well guess the answer. In fact its position is a symbol of the region's past and of the philosophy of its builders, the earliest Christians of the Suzdal princedom. It is a direct illustration of the axiom that the rivers were the highways of Old Russia. The Church of the Pokrov was situated at the eastern gateway to the Vladimir-Suzdal territory and it stood out to visitors like a triumphal arch on a Roman road. Envoys and merchants on the last stage of their journey from the Orient would sail up the Volga and along the Klyazma. When they saw the glint of the white stone they would know that their long expedition was reaching its end. Those who had made the voyage before would be reminded of the power of the great prince whose palace was already visible on the hill beyond at Bogolyubovo, and of the great Christian town of Vladimir which lay beyond it. The church may have been intended as a missionary gesture towards those many pagans who sailed past it, while emissaries from other Christian lands and Russians returning to their homes may well have stopped at it to offer prayers of thanksgiving for a journey safely completed.

Tradition has it that the foundation of the church was laid in 1164 to commemorate a victory over the Volga Bulgars and that the stone was brought here by the captured as part of their tribute. It was consecrated on the feast of the 'Pokrov', a local holy day which celebrated the special protection (hence the name) which the Virgin afforded to the citizens of the princedom.

The church as it now stands is so perfect that one is almost shocked to read about excavations which have proved that what we now see is little more than the nucleus of a much more grandiose building. The church originally stood on a platform which one reached by a broad flight of steps and a great colonnaded gallery surrounded it on three sides. Nevertheless, the Pokrov on the Nerl as we see it today is a synthesis of Byzantine and national elements, showing the deep root Christianity had already taken in the land and even suggesting, in the Gothic elongation of its windows, how close Russia at this time stood to Western Europe.

THE RISE OF MOSCOW

This contact with the main stream of European civilization was summarily broken off by the invasion of the Golden Horde. The final subjugation did not occur until 1240 under the leadership of Batu, nephew of Jenghiz Khan, but that was merely the last and most terrible of a series of incursions westward from the steppe which had been threatening Kiev already in the days of her greatest brilliance in the eleventh and twelfth centuries. The situation of the city had from the first been extremely vulnerable, as there was not sufficient natural protection from the east. Internecine strife among various branches of the princely family had jeopardized the unity of the land and Kiev became increasingly unable to defend herself.

The Tartar yoke did not have the dire effect on Russian institutions which might have been expected, and the most significant result was the squeezing of the centre of civilization farther to the north. Thousands of Russians retreated for safety into the distant, frozen and impenetrable forests. This is the main reason why the capital city today is situated in a more northerly latitude than any other town of comparable size and why there are so many large concentrations of population even farther towards the Pole. Even the proud city of Novgorod submitted to the Mongol invader, though this was part of Alexander Nevsky's realistic policy to save it from destruction.

The Tartars did not directly persecute the Church, but their domination had the effect of debilitating all native culture. The Russians who migrated to the north, however, maintained the vitality of Christianity and were ready to inject vigour into the new Russia when the country had been rid of the invader. Among such beacons in a period of darkness none shines brighter or is better known to us than St. Sergius of Radonezh, the greatest national saint of Russia.

His life is evoked by a visit to his shrine in the *Troitse-Sergieva Lavra* (Holy Trinity Monastery) at Zagorsk, about forty-five miles north of Moscow. It is still the greatest place of pilgrimage in the Soviet Union, and one to which thousands of foreign tourists used to be guided annually. My own impressions of it from the visits I paid will be described in Chapter III, but I would like to say a few words about St. Sergius himself at this point, because of the immense importance of his spiritual influence on Russian Christianity.

The strange phenomenon in St. Sergius's life was that although he shunned the world, he was coerced into playing an active part in politics. Rarely can a man so totally lacking in personal ambition have been catapulted in this way right into the centre of his country's affairs. He tried to avoid even the society of the cloister, and in the company of his brother alone (who later deserted him for a more conventional form of monastic life) he lived as a hermit in the most savagely primitive conditions deep in the forest north of Moscow, a town which was only now beginning to have any significance. He was joined by a few others who came unbidden, but rapidly fell under the spell of his personality and then remained with him to share his solitude. The settlement quickly grew—against the will of its founder —to huge proportions and he was not pleased to find that it had become a magnet for various itinerant workmen, mendicants and hangers-on who were not primarily drawn by the monastic vocation. To relieve overcrowding in the new community St. Sergius sent some of his most reliable followers to start new colonies, of which some forty were started in his own lifetime and another fifty in the second

22

generation. This movement established monasticism in the north as the Monastery of the Caves had done in the south four hundred years before.

The part St. Sergius played in the public life of his country was scarcely of less importance. His fame became so widespread that the Patriarch of Byzantium wrote to him, inviting him to become Metropolitan of the Russian Church, an offer which he refused on the grounds that this would finally wreck the type of life which he had set out to lead. Nevertheless, military leaders would pay visits to him in his monastery to gain advice about their coming campaigns. It was on his assurance of victory that Dmitry Donskoi set out for the decisive battle of Kulikovo against the Tartars in 1380, and he persuaded a certain Oleg of Ryazan, who betrayed the Russian cause in this campaign, to renounce his treason in order to spend the rest of his days as a law-abiding and peace-loving man.

Sergius, who set out to accomplish nothing other than deeds of spiritual heroism, became the patron saint of Russian monasticism, but he has also been called 'the builder of Russia'.[1] This he certainly was in the religious sphere. In political life he inspired those who were striving to throw off the Tartar yoke, and of no less significance was the way in which his followers opened up vast areas of north-east Russia for trade and development.

This is all bound up with the emergence of Moscow as the capital of post-Mongol Russia. It is curious, as one scans the magnificent contour of the Kremlin, to think that the city owes its dominance to Russia's humiliation by a hated foreign invader. It is also curious to find that the best comprehensive view of this complex of buildings can be obtained from the precincts of the British Embassy. This vantage point is separated from the Kremlin by the river's width, so that an unimpeded view of its whole length spreads out before one, allowing one to take in the contrasting outlines of the various buildings. The classical elegance of the *Oruzheinaya Palata* (Armoury) and the Great Kremlin Palace is softened by their warm buff colouring and offset by the riot of golden and lead-coloured onion domes to their right, while the whole group is enclosed lower down the slope by a forbidding wall of mellowed red brick, guarded by squat pepper-pot towers. On the Red Square side of the Kremlin the fortifications are too high and the surrounding buildings too closely packed to allow any comparable view and the area inside is too vast for a visitor to be

---

[1] The title of Nicolas Zernov's book on St. Sergius.

able to gain an overall impression from any one place. But when one stands in the square, which is enclosed by the finest of the cathedrals and overshadowed by the soaring Bell-Tower of Ivan the Great, one has an unforgettable feeling of being walled in by Russian history.

Just as it physically dominates the centre of a huge city, so the Kremlin holds sway over a vast empire. Anyone looking at it from the angle I have described must be struck by the way in which it compresses into one architectural whole the images of God's and man's power. Though this may strike a note of bitter irony today, its historical significance should not be overlooked.

Economics, ecclesiastical theory and the desire for imperial expansion contributed equally to the steep rise in the importance of Moscow in the fifteenth century. During this time Ivan III expanded Russian frontiers as far as the Lithuanian border in the north-west and to that of the Crimean Tartar khanate in the south, and in the process finally rid the country of any further threat from the Golden Horde. The Church justified imperial ambition with the most elaborate political and ecclesiastical theorizing. The old title of Grand Prince seemed inadequate for the holder of supreme temporal power after all these successes, so the Church evolved a theory which represented the Prince of Muscovy as the successor of the Byzantine emperors and the supreme plenipotentiary of the Orthodox Church on earth. Hence he was invested with the titles of Autocrat (*Samoderzhets*) and Cæsar (*Tsar*). This was justified by some astute reasoning. The Greek Orthodox Church had signed away its birthright by agreeing to union with the Roman Church (ephemeral though this proved to be) at the Council of Florence in 1439. The Turkish capture of Constantinople, the 'second Rome', in 1453 was regarded as speedy retribution for this apostasy. This left Moscow as the 'third Rome' and sole repository of the true Christian faith. This doctrine was already fully developed in the lifetime of Basil III, Ivan III's successor, when the monk Philotheus wrote to him in these terms:

'The first Rome collapsed owing to its heresies, the second Rome fell a victim to the Turks, but a new and third Rome has sprung up in the north, illuminating the whole universe like a sun. . . . The first and the second Rome have fallen, but the third will stand till the end of history, for it is the last Rome. Moscow has no successor; a fourth Rome there will not be.'

Church and State were welded together into a unit of overwhelming power. The material standing of the Church was greatly increased by the victory of Joseph, Prior of the monastery of Volokolamsk, over his rival, Nil Sorsky. The clash between these two men summed up a dual tendency in the Russian Church: the idea on the one hand of becoming rich and gaining power in order to control the affairs of the world and have ample resources for the distribution of money to those who most needed it; and on the other of renouncing the world and its wealth, using only the power of prayer to extend the influence of the Church. Nil spent many years on Mount Athos, where he learnt his ideals of abnegation. He did not become a public figure until 1503, when he was already seventy years old, but in that year he stood before Russia and before Joseph of Volokolamsk and accused monasticism in his country of following the course of perdition because of its emphasis on possessions. In the dispute Joseph's ideals won the day and Nil preferred to retire again into obscurity for the remaining five years of his life rather than pursue an ugly public wrangle. His defeat, however, was symptomatic of the course which Russian Christianity was following. His ideals reappeared from time to time, but their influence never became dominant.

I wanted to see Volokolamsk and applied for permission to travel there by train.[1] The great monastery, which was once a symbol of the immense power and wealth of the Russian Church, is only eighty miles west of Moscow, but I was unfortunately refused permission to go there on the grounds that 'there is nothing interesting to see: the Germans destroyed it'.

The Russian Church appointed its own patriarch in 1589, thereby acquiring the fullest dignity of an autocephalous Church, not only in fact, as it had been for over a hundred years, but in name also. A ceremony which neatly epitomized the relationship between the temporal and spiritual power used to occur on Palm Sunday. The Tsar would lead a procession, holding by the reins a donkey on which the Patriarch himself would be seated, enacting the part of Jesus Christ at the triumphal entry into Jerusalem. The State was thus represented as being subservient to the Church.

Russian ideas on the place of the Tsar never went as far as Byzantine theories. The Emperor, for the Greeks, was an icon of Christ, so the main throne in his palace was occupied only by a Gospel. Such

---

[1] All foreigners must obtain special permission to go more than forty kilometres out of Moscow. Some places even within this demarcation are closed. On the whole tourists find it much easier to travel where they wish than foreign residents in Moscow.

ideas never penetrated Russia. The Tsar, Russians believed, was the spiritual leader of all Eastern Christians, but was not represented as the ruler of the world.

There is always a danger that when Church and State become completely intertwined the tradition of the former will ossify. Instead of perpetually renewing itself in the power of the Holy Spirit, the Church becomes intent on holding fast to the exalted position which it occupies, with all its trappings of magnificence and wealth. This is what happened to the Russian Orthodox Church between the fifteenth and eighteenth centuries and the diehard conservatism of these years was one of the main factors in setting up a situation which made the Revolution possible.

It is this period of inbreeding, when the ritual splendour of coronations and funerals was untouched by any breath of change from the outside, which is called to mind by a visit to the great cathedrals of the Kremlin. The Russians are the finest restorers in the world. As one contemplates the intricate and wonderfully preserved wood-carving of Ivan the Terrible's throne in the Uspensky Cathedral or looks around at the overwhelming profusion of frescoes covering every inch of wall-space and now glowing again with all the richness and subtlety of their original colouring, it is as if one had suddenly been transported back four hundred years in time. Only an occasional man among the many visitors who fails to remove his cap and is scowled on by other Soviet citizens disturbs the illusion, which might otherwise lead one to expect the imminent arrival of the patriarch at the head of a dazzling procession.

Russia's isolation from Europe could scarcely have happened at a more unfortunate time in history. These were the centuries when the western and central part of the continent were transformed from a feudal society into one on the verge of the Industrial Revolution. Though a late-comer to the society of Christian nations, Kievan Russia had been a bright light in Europe. A pall of darkness descended with the Mongol invasion which was not dissipated with the restoring of Russian civilization. During the years of the Renaissance and the Reformation scarcely a chink of light penetrated Russia from the outside and when Peter the Great came to the throne, the Church, in company with all other institutions, was the most medieval in Europe.

The one man who could have done something about this was Maxim Grek, but he was the victim of reactionary powers stronger than he and his fate finally shut the doors on the outside world. In the sixteenth century he was the only link between the three worlds of Renaissance Italy, post-Byzantine Greece and Muscovite Russia. In successive stages of his career he was a Greek exile in Italy, avidly devouring Venetian and Florentine culture; a Dominican friar in Florence, influenced by the sermons of Savonarola; an Orthodox monk on Mount Athos; and a Greek missionary in Russia. He may have gone there originally at the invitation of Basil III, but while there he set out to reconcile Moscow to the jurisdiction of Constantinople.

By the time of his arrival in Russia, Maxim not unnaturally had a highly cosmopolitan outlook, but a gruesome hint at the obscurity of the world into which he had penetrated can be gleaned from the fact that he was the first to announce the discovery of America, nearly fifty years after the event. Basil III asked him to translate certain Biblical exegetical texts from Greek into Slavonic. In 1525 he was arrested and tried for heresy in the translations he had made. It is hardly surprising that his work was not always accurate, considering that before he arrived he knew not a word of Russian or Old Church Slavonic (the ecclesiastical language); he had made a Latin rendering of the Greek texts and someone else put them into Slavonic. After his trial he was sent under duress to the monastery of Volokolamsk, then hounded from one place to another before being retried six years later. This time the Metropolitan of Moscow, Daniel, vilely accused him of black magic and various political intrigues. He was convicted and imprisoned at Tver for the next twenty years of his life, until a slightly more enlightened régime allowed him to spend his last few years in the sympathetic surroundings of the *Troitse-Sergieva Lavra*. He died there in 1556, and, strangely enough, was eventually canonized by the Russian Church.

THE GREAT SCHISM

A visit to the Pokrovsky Cathedral, which stands beside the Rogozhskoye Cemetery, far out in the eastern suburbs of Moscow, at least partially evokes the events of the seventeenth century. It is now the headquarters of the main group of Old Believers, the Church of the Belaya Krinitsa Concord.[1]

The cemetery itself is a green and exquisitely peaceful corner of

---

[1] Further information about this and other groups will be found in Chapter VII.

Moscow where one can sit for hours undisturbed, immersed in the atmosphere of the past. All the graves are carefully tended, so the warning notice which states, 'Any grave which is neglected will be handed over to the State', seems hardly to be necessary. Many now have tall shrubs growing from within their railed confines and it is therefore impossible to get a view of the whole area. Simple post-Revolutionary graves contrast sharply with the profusion of monumental masonry above the older ones. The new ones mostly have crosses made out of old bedsteads or other oddments of scrap metal, frequently with a photograph of the person buried there stuck on to the home-made construction.

The cathedral itself is a treasure-house of the most precious works of art. The Old Believers recognize no icons more recent than the seventeenth century, and whereas most Orthodox churches have had to give over their most valuable treasures to State art galleries, they have kept theirs, including six magnificent works by Rublyov, the finest of all Russian icon painters.

I say that the Pokrovsky Cathedral partially evokes the events of the seventeenth century because to attend a service here and listen to the spare, unharmonized chanting carries one back more surely into the world of Old Russia than anything else in Moscow, but at the same time the peace of the cemetery and the opulence of the interior of the cathedral mask the fearful ordeals which the Old Believers have had to undergo throughout their history.

The name 'Old Believer' is a misleading translation of their Russian title, which means 'devotee of the old rite'. One has to appreciate the fanatical devotion of the Russian Christian to everything traditional in order to understand what brought about the schism between the Old Believers and the main branch of the Orthodox Church in the seventeenth century. Old Believers are not schismatics in the truest sense: they are the ones who have clung to the detail of tradition more tenaciously than other Orthodox Christians. The schism is usually referred to by its Russian name of *Raskol*.

The main protagonists in the *Raskol* were the Archpriest Avvakum[1] and Nikon, the Patriarch to whom he owed allegiance, but the issue was complicated by the intervention and enigmatic personality of Tsar Alexei Mikhailovich. It is easy, if one has a mind conditioned by modern Protestantism, to misread the conflict as one which was concerned only with trivialities, but in the context of the mystical

[1] A Russian form of the Biblical name Habakkuk.

28

doctrine of Moscow as the Third Rome holding fast to a faith which was indivisible, the tragedy was not only understandable, but inevitable.

Avvakum, the founder of the Old Believers' Church, conducted a pastoral ministry which had about it the deep spiritual quality which we find in the work of his exact English contemporary, Richard Baxter; and like him, he was drawn into violent ecclesiastical disputes in which he would much rather have had no part. His autobiography is one of the great works of Russian literature, impregnated with the warmth and humanity of the author. During the darkest days of his exile in the frozen wastes he constantly showed the deepest compassion for his wife and managed even to treat his domestic animals almost as if they were human. When one of his hens which had provided two eggs a day for his children fell ill, he sang a prayer over it, sprinkled it with holy water and censed it. On a more serious note, he faced great issues with complete honesty and brought his principles to bear in every situation which he encountered.

Nikon, whom Tsar Alexei Mikhailovich elevated to the Patriarchate in 1652, is an enigmatic figure compared with Avvakum. He did not accept office without a long period of hesitation, which may just possibly have been a gambit to strengthen his position *vis-à-vis* the Tsar. He undoubtedly enjoyed the power which he could wield in his new position, but was not a bludgeoning reformer and had many of the people of Moscow with him, as well as the Tsar. The latter was feeling at this time an increasing responsibility towards Constantinople, whose people were crying out for his help in ridding them of the Turkish oppressor. The basic idea behind Nikon's reforms was to bring the Russian Church back to some of the Byzantine rituals from which it had deviated. The Tsar agreed to these, believing this would make a *rapprochement* between the two Churches and enable joint rites to begin again.

This hope was never fulfilled, and Nikon had badly underestimated the offence that his reforms were going to cause to the common illiterate people throughout the land. Nikon demanded that the faithful should cross themselves with the first three fingers joined, representing the Trinity, while the old custom was to use index finger and thumb (symbolic of the two natures of Christ, leaving the three folded fingers to represent the Trinity). It is ironical that the sign used by both parties symbolized the same idea in a different way. There were other liturgical points at issue, too—the orthography of the name

'Jesus', the exclusion of a word from the Creed—as well as several ritual details.

The issue was further complicated by the relationship which existed between Avvakum and the Tsar. In the initial clash between Nikon and his adversaries, all the recalcitrant church leaders except Avvakum were removed from office and excommunicated, so he became the natural rallying-point for the opposition. As a protest against what had happened to his sympathizers he kept a vigil service in a barn—which was not strictly against canon law, but which violently flouted tradition. Because of this it was decided that Avvakum should be defrocked in front of the Tsar and the Patriarch and then exiled to a camp on the River Lena in Siberia. But in a dramatic scene the Tsar changed his mind; in the middle of the service he was seen to walk over to Nikon, following which the order was given not to proceed with the unfrocking and it was announced that Avvakum should be exiled only to Tobolsk, less than half the distance away.

Avvakum had previously had some influence at court and it is evident that a close personal relationship existed between him and the Tsar. This and the surprising turn of events at the service had led him to go into exile in 1655 with an expectant heart, believing that all the traditional tenets of the old faith would triumph in the end. Eventually, in 1664, the Tsar sent for him and received him as a long-lost friend. In reply to the Tsar's gentle and courteous greeting, Avvakum replied: 'As God lives, so does my soul, my lord; the future will be according to the will of God.' The Tsar correctly construed this as meaning that Avvakum would not yield an inch; he sighed softly and turned away, but did not change his mind about the issues at stake.

The schism was now inevitable, though none of the contestants could have foreseen the terrible consequences it would have. The Old Believers were formally excommunicated three years later and ahead of them lay the path of martyrdom. The title of this chapter is taken from a sentence by Avvakum himself, which runs in full: 'Satan has obtained our radiant Russia from God so that she may become crimson with the blood of martyrs.'

When a council in Moscow decided to ferret out the Old Believers the intended victims anticipated the persecutions that would follow and before the end of the seventeenth century there were thirty-two recorded cases of mass suicides, terrible self-immolations inside burning buildings in which at least twenty thousand people perished. The last case of a suicide on account of the *Raskol* occurred in 1897. It is exceedingly difficult for the non-Russian to appreciate the state of mind which lay behind such violent acts, but there are two artistic creations which bring the fanaticism of the Old Believers to life. The first is Mussorgsky's opera *Khovanshchina*, which ends in one of these mass self-immolations (though the composer himself did not reach this stage in the composition and Rimsky-Korsakov completed the manuscript). The other is a fine, though underestimated, documentary novel by Melnikov-Pechersky, called *In the Forests*,[1] which describes with great understanding the lives of the Old Believers in the Trans-Volga region. Both these works go further towards explaining the state of mind of the Old Believers than the analyses of history books.

Schism breeds schism, and the Old Believers never were a united faction. If one walks today from the Rogozhskoye Cemetery to the Pokrovsky Cathedral one passes two other small churches, each belonging to a different sect of Old Believers and each claiming to be the sole true survivor of old Russian Christendom. All, however, revere Avvakum as a saint. If devotion and single-mindedness be the criteria, there is no one in the history of Russian Christianity who deserves canonization more.

PETER THE GREAT

To travel from Moscow to Leningrad is, as no visitor fails to notice, to move from one world to another. Just as the Kremlin dominates the capital both politically and physically, so does the smooth-flowing River Neva dominate the city of Peter the Great. Its current flows resolutely westwards, issuing into the Gulf of Finland and the Baltic Sea, and from the day of its foundation in 1703 the city's gaze has followed the line of its watercourse.

From 1617 until the beginning of the eighteenth century, the Swedes had been in possession of the whole coastal strip from Estonia round to Finland, both countries being under her suzerainty. Peter the Great campaigned to break through this wall (to 'force a window into Europe', as it was described); and even before the conclusion of a peace treaty he shored up his gains in the most decisive manner possible by building a new fortified city on the delta of the Neva, employing about forty thousand men to accomplish the work in the shortest time. Anyone else would probably have been content to leave a chain of well-manned garrisons to ensure the

[1] Available in a French translation.

permanence of his new conquests, but Peter the Great forged on the desolate marches a new capital which was to bear his name. The site he had chosen was so strategic that within fifty years about nine-tenths of all Russian foreign trade was passing through the port, and the allied growth of industry saw the population rise to almost two and a half million by the outbreak of the Revolution.

Leningrad's nickname, 'Venice of the North', seems to me misplaced. The warm bustle and chaotic intricacy of the streets in the southern town is in no way reproduced in Leningrad's severe, classical elegance and the sober demeanour of her citizens as they walk along the banks of the Neva. I doubt whether any planned city could ever acquire the spontaneous warmth which we associate with the medieval towns of Western Europe. I have seen many tourists in raptures saying that Leningrad is the most beautiful city in the world, but there are others who find it, unlike its people, cold. I incline more to the second view. The air of faded magnificence about all except a few of the finest palaces is slightly depressing, and I have the feeling that there is no continuity between those who built the centre of the city and the present generation. Strangely enough, in Moscow where there are so many churches dominating the centre I did not feel this.

I wonder whether my impression of the old St. Petersburg in its heyday as capital would have been so very different. There seems to be a conflict between the imitative grandiose style of architecture and the northern landscape around it. The city does not appear to have grown up naturally from its surroundings in the way that Novgorod or Vladimir has.

The cathedral in the Fortress of St. Peter and Paul was built by an Italian, Tresini, over a period of eight years from 1713 to 1721 and has a very Roman Catholic look; similarly, the other great churches of Leningrad were either built by foreign architects or designed by Russians in direct imitation of Western European models. The St. Isaac's and Kazan Cathedrals, though built a century later, continue the westernizing tendency. St. Isaac's was built by a Frenchman, Montferrand. Outside it imitates St. Peter's, Rome, with a huge dome surmounting the façade of a classical temple; the inside, adorned with stone of every colour, has been aptly dubbed 'the geological museum' by the Intourist guides. The Kazan Cathedral, though built by a Russian, reproduces the colonnade of St. Peter's, while the main portal is a copy of Ghiberti's Baptistery Door. It ought to be called 'the gate of Hell' to distinguish it from its Florentine counterpart,

Church of the Pokrov on the Nerl

since it now gives entry to the Soviet Union's greatest shrine of atheism, euphemistically named 'the Museum of the History of Religion'.[1]

I have dwelt on this at length because I believe that Leningrad reflects the ethos of the Russian eighteenth century and gives us a key to a partial understanding of church life between 1700 and the Revolution.

The achievement of Peter the Great was that he realized, in the course of his travels in Western Europe, what would have to be done if Russia was to be brought abreast of the rest of the civilized world and that he did it. Although he tried to impose all kinds of foreign institutions, he never lost sight of the fact that his country had to be governed by Russians and not by foreigners imported to do the job. He tried never to sweep aside any part of the old Russia unless he felt himself able to replace it by something better. His ideals were not always fulfilled, but he did succeed single-handed in ridding Russia of her most dangerous enemies and in changing the course of the nation's history. He was huge in stature as well as being expansive in all his ideas—almost an incarnation of one of Russia's mythical heroes, the *bogatyrs*.

His private passions had a similarly colossal sweep. When he hated he exterminated. When he ate he indulged in the most tempestuous orgies which rarely stopped short of violent sexual debauch. If he lived and loved like one of the giants of old, few men of equal greatness and vision have descended to such depths of treachery and cruelty. In his youth he exasperated the Patriarch Adrian and other clerics in court circles by improvising elaborate mock rituals lampooning the Orthodox Church. He elected his old tutor Nikita Zotov Patriarch of the Church of Bacchus, provided him with a mitre of tin and incised on it a crude representation of the naked god astride a barrel. He and his friends parodied Orthodox singing and processions and for holy water sprinkled vodka. This burlesque church was begun on an impulse, but became an obsession to which Peter returned again and again throughout his life. Yet at the same time he saw himself as God's champion on earth. There is evidence to show he was not being facetious or insincere when he wrote home to the same Patriarch Adrian:

'We are in the Netherlands in good health and following God's word, thanks to God's blessing and your prayers. Being of Adam's

---

[1] Described on pp. 106–8.

33

line, we labour . . . in order that, having complete experience, we can, in the name of Jesus Christ, be conquerors, and liberators of the Christians. That, till my last breath, I shall not cease to desire.'[1]

It is not surprising that the main opposition to Peter's reforms came from the Orthodox hierarchy. An institutionalized Church is by its nature resistant to change, but nowhere more so than in Russia. Then, too, the private debauchery of one who was believed to be God's representative scandalized the Church. Peter accepted his own divine right as a convenient means of fortifying his position, but he could not tolerate that of the Patriarch because it gave the Church the moral right to judge his own actions.

The tension which grew up between the hierarchy and the young Tsar who guyed the Church's rituals later on developed into an open conflict. In 1698 the Patriarch headed a deputation to Peter, asking him to show clemency to the Moscow garrison infantry, the powerful *Streltsy*, who had rebelled against him. The Tsar refused to listen, saying the Church had no right to interfere in matters of military discipline. His aim was to drive a wedge between Church and State, which up to this time had acted as an organic whole. When the Patriarch Adrian died two years later, Peter postponed the election of a successor—a first step towards forging an absolute authority over the Church. No one could then have realized that the postponement would last for 217 years.

The Church submitted weakly to Peter's delaying tactics. It is unlikely that the Emperor could have accomplished such schemes at any other epoch in history, but at this time the Church was still weakened by the disaster of the *Raskol*, with many of its finest figures dead or in exile.

Peter appointed Stefan Yavorsky, Metropolitan of Ryazan, a learned Ukrainian whom he had quickly come to trust, as guardian of the vacant patriarchal throne and named him Exarch. Yavorsky fell out of favour before his death, but by then he had already carried out certain westernizing reforms in the Church which at least hinted at the action Peter was to take in 1721.

During his travels in Protestant countries Peter had been most impressed with what he believed to be the subordination of Church to State in those countries. He gave a brief to his new favourite, Bishop Theofan Prokopovich, asking him to draft a constitution for the

[1] Quoted by Stephen Graham, *Peter the Great*, 2nd ed., Ernest Benn, London, 1950, p. 94.

Church which would introduce an imitation of the German ecclesiastical synods. But whereas they existed to implement the religious desires of the people, their Russian counterpart—the Holy Governing Synod—was created to do the will of the Emperor and to replace everything the old Patriarchate had stood for.

Prokopovich's brain-child, the Ecclesiastical Regulation, was a strange document because it was so entirely alien to the whole tradition and outlook of the Church which it was destined to hold in its thrall. The new Synod was to be composed of bishops and other clerics in high office, but its members were chosen by Peter, not elected by the Church. This was the oath to which they had to swear: 'I acknowledge the Monarch of all Russia, our Gracious Lord, to be the final judge of this College'. A secular official called the Procurator was directly responsible for the Synod to the Emperor himself and had the right of veto on all its decisions.

All this was pushed through without a council of the Church being convened. A copy of the Regulation was merely sent to each of the bishops, which he had to sign and return on pain of exile. One by one the demoralized hierarchy obeyed and signed away the independence of the Church. The resulting situation endured up to 1917—a factor which must be borne in mind in assessing the significance of the Revolution in Russian Church history.

The Church had not been entirely out of contact with Western Europe in the seventeenth century, mainly because of the latinizing tendencies of Peter Mogila, Metropolitan of Kiev, and his followers. Some cultural influence also had seeped through in court circles via people of western sympathies, such as the *boyar* Fyodor Rtishchev, the monk Simyon Polotsky and Prince Basil Golitsyn. But all this hardly went the first step towards preparing the Church for the brutal westernizing policy of Peter the Great. He wrenched it out of its natural line of development, which is exactly what he did to most of the secular institutions he reformed. That is why for me, 250 years later, Leningrad still has the feel of an imported city, hanging on the edge of a vast empire. For most Russians it now carries, in fact as well as in name, the associations of Lenin, for this was the city of the Revolution. But I wonder if there are any Christians for whom it is the city of the Ecclesiastical Regulation, the city of the Holy Governing Synod, which used to meet in a building opposite St. Isaac's Cathedral.

THE NINETEENTH CENTURY

The history of the Russian Church in the later eighteenth and nineteenth centuries is both tantalizing and depressing: tantalizing, because there were certain signs of a spiritual revival and desire for reform; depressing, because these elements were in no way widespread or strong enough to harness the high charge of energy generated during the nineteenth century and released at the Revolution, and to conduct it into a channel more beneficial to Russia and to humanity.

To illustrate these opposing tendencies I would like to have contrasted the monastery at Optina Pustyn with almost any other church built in the nineteenth or early twentieth century except those in Leningrad which I have talked about. However, I found it impossible to visit Optina Pustyn, situated about a hundred miles south-west of Moscow at Kozelsk in the Kaluga Region, and was assured that there was no point in doing so because all active church life had long ago disappeared from it.

The astonishing upsurge of creative activity in the nineteenth century and the sudden emergence of Russia on the cultural map of Europe show the depths of the spiritual reserves which had been lying imprisoned for centuries. It was a period as remarkable as the fifteenth century in Italy, the sixteenth in England or the seventeenth in France, only in this instance the preparation for it was less and it was achieved more as a revolt against the prevailing political system than because of any co-operation or patronage such as occurred in the Italian Renaissance or the French *Grand Siècle*.

The Church, though its hands were tied by the iniquitous Ecclesiastical Regulation, seemed to be reawakening and it was not without influence on musical and literary developments. The monastery of Optina Pustyn, which was rebuilt in 1796 after many years of neglect, rapidly became famous throughout Russia as a place of spiritual refuge, thanks mainly to the succession of inspired *startsy* (elders of the monastic community) who lived there. Leonid (1768–1841), Makary (1788–1860), Amvrosy (1812–91), Yosif (d. 1911) and Anatoly (d. 1922) were the best-known of the *startsy*, but there were many others who received pilgrims from all over Russia, never turning away anyone who came seeking spiritual refreshment and redirection. It was notable that the elders did not attempt to divide off the spiritual from the practical aspect of human life; they were ready to give advice on how you should farm your strip of land or on what to do about the neighbour with whom you had been quarrelling for the last fifteen years.

A visit to Optina Pustyn became almost obligatory among the great literary figures. A host of minor writers, as well as Gogol, Tolstoy and Dostoevsky, made pilgrimages to it at some time in their lives. Tolstoy, who lived five days' walk away at Yasnaya Polyana, was a frequent visitor, and although by the end of his life he had been excommunicated, a few days before his death he wandered around outside without resolving to enter the monastery. Dostoevsky tells us what the elders were like, though people who knew Optina Pustyn well said that Father Zosima in *The Brothers Karamazov* is only partly modelled on the *starets* Amvrosy.

Optina Pustyn was in fact one of the spiritual founts of the Slavophil movement. This was an important religious and philosophical current in the Russian nineteenth century which influenced a number of great writers and thinkers. Its founder, Alexei Khomyakov (1804–60), was at the same time poet, philosopher and theologian, but it was in the field of theology that his most important work was accomplished. He saw the Orthodox Church as God's greatest gift to man, which Peter the Great had perverted and enslaved. He attacked both Catholicism and Protestantism and yet was able to present his faith to Western Europe in comprehensible terms, explaining the ideal of *sobornost* as an antidote to western individualism. Whole books have been written attempting to explain this term peculiar to Orthodoxy. The root meaning of the adjective *soborny* is 'gathered', but it has the double sense of 'catholic' or 'universal' and 'conciliar'. 'In the Church there is neither dictatorship nor individualism, but harmony and unanimity; men remain free but not isolated, for they are united in love, in faith, and in sacramental communion. In a council, this idea of harmony and free unanimity can be seen worked out in practice. In a true council no single member arbitrarily imposes his will upon the rest, but each consults with the others, and in this way they all freely achieve a "common mind".'[1]

Khomyakov's approach was quite different from the earlier chauvinistic dogmatism of 'Moscow the Third Rome', and his correspondence with William Palmer was the beginning of the intermittent

---

[1] Timothy Ware, *The Orthodox Church*, Penguin Books, London, 1963, p. 23.

contact between the Russian Orthodox and Anglican Churches which
has become somewhat more frequent in recent years.

The Slavophils, however, clashed with everything that Peter's reforms had stood for. Surrounded by a host of writers and thinkers
with westernizing tendencies of one sort or another, they alone had
the insight to penetrate to the heart of the political and religious
situation of the time. They could see a crisis looming between those
who believed in the self-sufficiency of man and the sovereignty of
God. They were alive to the acute danger caused by the rift between
the westernized upper stratum of society which had grown up under
the tutelage of a series of German tsars who had succeeded Peter and
was hardly at home in its own language or country, and the peasantry,
whose tap-roots gripped deep in the Russian soil.

Ecclesiastically, there were few events of note during the whole of
the nineteenth century, so that the official Church gives the impression
of being aloof from the conflict of ideas which tore Russia apart from
the middle of the century onwards. Many of the churches built in
Russian style in the nineteenth century reinforce this impression.
There are several minor ones in Moscow and Leningrad, and the one
in Tallinn in Estonia dominates the city as a symbol of an alien
ideology. I am thinking particularly, however, of one begun in the
last decade of the nineteenth century and completed in the first decade
of the twentieth.

It is situated in the Vladimir Region, in the town of Yuriev-
Polskoy, a three-hour bus journey across desolate country north-west
of Vladimir itself. I went there to see St. George's Cathedral, one of
the most elaborately ornamented of all early Russian churches, and
the last great work of architecture to be built before the Mongol
invasion. It was very impressive in itself, but the total effect was
completely spoiled by a monstrous red-brick church standing beside
it and completely overshadowing it. It reminded me strongly of the
hideous Historical Museum in Red Square. How could any church
authorities, I wondered, have been so completely insensitive as to
ruin the effect of one of Russia's most remarkable buildings? The
extreme traditionalism apparent in every facet of the more recent
edifice seemed to me worse in this setting than anything I knew in
Victorian Gothic. I saw it as a Christian aspidistra—standing erect in
its place, decorative, I suppose, to a certain taste and now wholly
useless since it had been closed down at the Revolution, shortly after
its completion. Even if this fate had not befallen it, I doubt whether it

could ever have fulfilled any useful purpose, since quite apart from St. George's Cathedral itself, the town was already provided with several churches (not a single one of which is now functioning).

The fact that Khomyakov's persuasive and reasonable theology was for many years out of favour and his writings on the subject not even passed for publication until nineteen years after his death is a further indication of the Church's rigid attitude in the nineteenth century. It was not, however, so totally uncompromising as this might lead one to believe, for Khomyakov's work gradually did gain recognition, and he is now regarded with great respect in Orthodox circles.

THE EVE OF THE REVOLUTION

A few churches built in the last years before the Revolution are more aesthetically pleasing than the one in Yuriev-Polskoy which I have described—St. Vladimir's Cathedral in Kiev, for example—but there is little in the architecture of the period to suggest the quickening of the Church's pulse which was such a feature of the pre-Revolutionary years.

Beneath the stultified ecclesiastical administration during the final days of the Empire there was a general but submerged revival, of which the fame of Optina Pustyn was an obvious manifestation. Christian dogma also became intellectually respectable again—a reaction against the revolutionary atheism which had triumphed in the eighteen-sixties and -seventies, despite the passionate voices of Dostoevsky and Khomyakov.

The symbolist movement in literature was influenced to a large extent by this revival of faith. The father of the movement was Vladimir Solovyov (1853–1900), a poet and philosopher, like Khomyakov. Solovyov's mystical experiences and apocalyptic vision inspired such poets as Alexander Blok (1880–1921), Andrei Bely (1880–1934) and Vyacheslav Ivanov (1886–1949). The conversion of members of the intelligentsia to Christianity prepared for a new Russian theology which was able to come to full flower only in exile after the Revolution with such figures as Berdyaev, Frank and Lossky.

The Church shared fully in the national trend towards reform which erupted in the revolution of 1905. As well as the political reforms gained in that year (the Duma was Russia's first elected deliberative body), there was an Imperial Decree granting religious freedom to all citizens. This was widely welcomed, and thirty-two St. Petersburg priests signed a letter published in their diocesan paper,[1] saying: 'The Church is at last acquitted of the heavy charge of violating and suppressing religious freedom. . . . The time has come for the Church to resume her proper influence in all spheres of national life, and this can be done by a return to the traditional canonical order, based on self-government and independence of the State.'

The hated ultra-reactionary, Pobedonostsev (1827–1907), who had been Procurator of the Holy Synod for twenty-five years, was forced to retire. The bishops, most of whom had been appointed under Pobedonostsev himself, voted almost unanimously that a general Council of the Church should be held to decide its future.

The Council was most carefully prepared. The diocesan bishops put their first recommendations into five large volumes, to which six new ones were added in 1906–7 by a special commission with both clerical and lay representation. However, the last Russian Tsar, Nicholas II, put off convening the Council because by this time he could see just how urgent the demand for reform was becoming and he feared the emancipation of the Church, which would undoubtedly have ensued. The bishops who protested at the way in which the Tsar was refusing to face the situation were compulsorily retired into monasteries, so by 1917 the state of affairs was again critical. The final period of violent reaction which precipitated the Revolution had prevented the Church from ordering its internal life as it had wished. If it had been able to do this freely from 1905 the situation of Christians in Communist countries would be very different today.

[1] *Tserkovny Vestnik* (Church Messenger), No. 11, 17th March 1905; quoted by N. Zernov, *The Russians and their Church*, S.P.C.K., London, 1954, p. 150.

CHAPTER II

The Rise of the Red Star

THE CHURCH AT THE REVOLUTION

The tendency to see the Russian Church either as the epitome of reactionary forces or as a beacon of enlightenment is nowhere more pronounced than in its relation to the Revolution. I have heard Russian *émigrés* say that in 1917 it was the one progressive force in a country which had shown itself totally unable to reform itself. For other people a mention of the Church at this time calls a single image to mind: Rasputin. Neither view even approximates to the truth. At a time when the atmosphere of the entire country was so emotionally charged, every individual, every political grouping, every aspiration, normally coloured some shade of grey could take on a deeper or a lighter hue almost overnight.

In attempting to assess the real situation,[1] let us first put aside the Rasputin legend. Contrary to popular belief, Rasputin was not a monk, he was not even an Orthodox cleric. This grimy, smelly, tousled man insinuated himself into inner circles of the Imperial Court as a *starets*, but like many so-called *startsy*, he was never ordained. He gained admission to the court and cemented his influence in the highest circles by using his supposed powers of healing and prediction. Tsar Nicholas II and his wife at first accepted him as the representative of their subjects, in whom they could hear the heart-beat of the common man. They offered vicariously to this illiterate peasant from Tobolsk a kindness which they were unable to pass on to others. Rasputin gradually gained an influence over the Empress's hæmophilic son and she came to believe that only his

[1] For much of this information I am deeply indebted to Nicolas Zernov, *The Russian Religious Renaissance of the Twentieth Century*, Darton, Longman and Todd, London, 1963, Ch. 2.

41

mysterious power could keep the boy alive. She adhered to this belief doggedly until the day Rasputin died.[1]

Even though his influence was so great, Rasputin was unable to keep Russia imprisoned in the Middle Ages as he might have wished to, and his fall was as dramatic as that of Nicholas II was undignified.[2] He was in no sense, however, a representative of the Russian Orthodox Church.

The tendency to see the Church as an instrument of darkness has of course been accentuated by Communist propaganda. It has obviously been to the Communists' advantage to denigrate the virtues of their opponents and they have never missed an opportunity to do this with vigour. There were, of course, defects in the organization as well as in the spirituality of the Russian Orthodox Church during the early years of this century (of which branch of the Christian Church at what time could this not be said?), but there were undoubtedly virtues too.

The worst shortcoming was the dichotomy—one might almost say the hostility—between the 'black' and the 'white' clergy. The former were monks and from their number the bishops were elected. The latter were the ordinary parochial clergy. According to the Sixth Ecumenical Council (688) bishops had to be celibate, while a compromise clause was introduced to allow for the marriage of the parish priest. Later it became obligatory for the parish priest to marry. From this a highly unsatisfactory system of two classes of clergy grew up in the Orthodox Church. No marriage was allowed after ordination (which introduced an almost intolerable burden into the lives of seminarists and at times led to a most unseemly and hasty scramble for brides), while the only time at which an upgrading from the 'white' to the 'black' class was possible was on the death of one's wife. There was one escape clause here: it was possible to become officially celibate by persuading one's wife to remove herself to a convent.

When a monk became a bishop he inherited the oversight of a vast

---

[1] In a programme on the rise of Soviet power called *The Titans*, B.B.C. television showed an unforgettable scrap of old film in which one sees Rasputin solemnly blessing an apple before giving it to the Tsar who accepts it gratefully and then starts to eat it. It is incredible to reflect that there was a cine-camera present at the palace at that moment, as if two worlds centuries apart had suddenly come together.

[2] An excellent portrait of Rasputin is to be found in the book by Alan Moorehead, *The Russian Revolution*, Collins and Hamish Hamilton, London, 1958, pp. 84–9, 116–20, 123–7.

diocese. Before the reforms of Peter the Great there were only eighteen dioceses in the whole of Russia, and although the number of bishops was later increased, the priest remained unfamiliar with his 'father in God' and the parish did not receive the annual visitation for confirmation which is such a familiar feature of English parish life. In the Orthodox Church 'chrismation' is performed by the parish priest immediately after baptism. He anoints various parts of the body with ointment, making the sign of the cross as a seal of the gift of the Holy Spirit, and this admits the child into full membership of the Church.

The 'white' clergy were eligible for promotion according to a graded scale. A junior priest or deacon was equal in rank to a lieutenant, a bishop to a general, and any member of the parochial clergy who was promoted from the lowest grade of a deacon (fourteenth) as high as the fourth became automatically a member of the *dvoryanstvo* (nobility). This usually carried with it neither the advantages nor the attendant jockeying for position which one might have expected. The clergy were imposed on as state registrars and they were expected to uphold and enforce government decrees. Until 1893 they were not paid by the State; and even after this the official stipends were mostly totally inadequate. As many as a third of all clergy received nothing for their official services at all. They had to depend for their living on the direct giving of the parishioners, supplemented by farming their own glebe land. Parish priests today in England may often be exhausted by trying to maintain a vast garden or psychologically depressed by allowing it to go to waste, but their Russian counterparts before the Revolution often had to become farmers in order to live.

In contrast to the English parochial system, there was no security of tenure and a priest could be removed from his living or even deprived of his orders by the decision of a bishop or the verdict of a consistory court. Hearings at these courts were held in the absence of the defendant and there was no right of appeal. Before a sermon could be preached, the consistory had to approve its text. Needless to say, the priest's public utterances were few as a result.

Most members of the clergy, 'black' as well as 'white', were the sons of clerical families and by the time of the Revolution the whole caste amounted to a total of some half a million in number. There were few born in this class who took up work or looked for wives outside it, while few entered it in order to become ordained. Before 1869 there were even legal difficulties in the change from one class to another. There was one great difficulty which dissuaded many outsiders from seeking ordination: they would not have received a theological education in a seminary or academy, where instruction was reserved in the main for the sons of the clergy. Although the education here was so antiquated and one-sided that westernized Russians looked on seminarists as uncouth and ignorant, at the same time it was most difficult to assimilate the learning necessary to perform the offices in church without having attended one. Clergy who wished to send their sons to secular institutions usually could not afford it.

A further limitation which the conditions of the Empire enforced on the Church was the lack of any form of self-government. At one time the parish had been allowed to elect its own minister, but this right was suspended; the parishes, in their turn, were not represented in the government of the church. The bishops were chosen and moved at will, often most capriciously, by the Procurator of the Holy Synod.

Despite the enslavement of the Orthodox Church under the old régime, there were many more positive features in its life. The seminaries imbued their inmates with a love of the Bible and of the Orthodox liturgy which was usually indelible. Moreover the outsiders' view of the backwardness of this kind of education was only partially justified and there were some outstanding intellectual products of the seminaries who succeeded in achieving greatness in the world of learning. Among these may be mentioned the historian, V. Klyuchevsky (1841–1911), and I. P. Pavlov (1849–1936), whose scientific work is of international renown.

Despite the subservience of the bishops to the Holy Synod and the fact that many of them would hardly have reached such high office under a democratic system, there were some in the nineteenth century who left their mark on the spiritual life of the nation, others who were scholars of note, and one or two who inspired the notable return to missionary commitment (for example, Innokenty Venyaminov of Alaska (1797–1879) and Nikolai Kasatkin of Japan (1836–1912)).

A parish priest often stood in much higher common esteem than my description may have implied. 'A Russian priest was usually neither a mystic nor an ascetic. Nevertheless, like a Levite of the Old Testament, he was a man set apart, dedicated to the service of God, bearing upon him the permanent seal of his special calling. He was the recognized leader of corporate worship whose presence made the local assembly of the faithful an organic part of the universal Church. The sacred character of his office was fully revealed during the divine services. Any element of familiarity disappeared at that time, and the priest was seen as the earthly image of the Heavenly High Priest. . . . Outside his liturgical function he was treated, like other Christians, on the merit of his spiritual achievement. The gift of prayer was particularly valued, more than eloquence or learning. Charity and humility were also considered special signs of grace. Those who had them were venerated, those who lacked them were pitied.'[1]

Looking at these more positive aspects of Russian church life gives one a slight indication of how much vitality there was which had not been sapped by Peter the Great's administrative reforms and helps to explain why the demand for change and renewal existed in the years 1905–17.[2]

CHRISTIANITY VERSUS MARXISM[3]

The Church was not so servile to tsarist power that its organization collapsed when the ruling family was overthrown and replaced by the Provisional Government on 2nd March 1917. On the contrary, the new Procurator of the Holy Synod, V. Lvov, hastened the preparations for the general Council of the Church which had been so long delayed, while at the same time he purged most of the reactionary, pro-tsarist elements. Twelve dignitaries were retired to monasteries, among them the Metropolitans of Moscow and Petrograd.

To prepare for the Council and to calm the ferment now existing at all levels of church life, the Synod authorized a series of elections. These gave both parishes and dioceses representational rights and some autonomy. Most bishops already in office had their appointments confirmed, but a few more reactionaries were ousted. The people elected two most interesting men to the vacant sees of Petrograd and Moscow. Vasily Kazansky, then an assistant bishop of the highest quality, became Metropolitan Venyamin of Petrograd (he was murdered in 1922). Bishop Tikhon (Belyavin) of Vilnius, the future patriarch, became Metropolitan of Moscow. The dioceses elected between them four hundred representatives to the Council; a further 164 were appointed by various bodies and of the total 314 were laymen. Decisions had to be finally ratified by the bishops, but

---

[1] Zernov, *The Russian Religious Renaissance of the Twentieth Century*, pp. 51–2.
[2] See pp. 39–40.
[3] See Notes for Further Reading (pp. 240–3) for the main works of reference on this period. I am especially indebted to Nikita Struve, *Les Chrétiens en U.R.S.S.*, Paris, 1963, chs. 2–5, for the rest of this chapter.

three-quarters of them had to vote twice against a given measure before it could be turned down. In between it would be referred back to the main assembly.

Already before the Council's first full session the Church had officially gained its freedom. This was signalized by the action of A. V. Kartashev (1875–1960) who was appointed Lvov's successor as Procurator of the Holy Synod, but immediately began successful negotiations to have his office renamed 'Minister of Confessions'.

On 16th August 1917 the Council met for its first public session in the Cathedral of Christ the Saviour, the largest church building in Moscow. On the previous day processions of witnesses from the local congregations had gathered on Red Square in preparation for this most solemn and portentous occasion. From the very opening the political news was disquieting. The agenda was vast and could hardly be tackled dispassionately, as the storm clouds of civil unrest were rapidly gathering. Nevertheless, the Council was showing a most balanced approach to the problems which confronted it and had just come to the most important item for discussion, the restoration of the Patriarchate, when the debate was interrupted by the Bolsheviks' bombardment of the Kremlin. On 28th October they crushed the final resistance there and occupied it. On the very same day, in an atmosphere of indescribable tension, the Council voted unanimously to restore the Patriarchate. The Church was now to regain the full status which it had lost with the abolition of this highest office under Peter the Great two hundred years before.

On 5th November the election itself was completed by drawing lots. The names of three candidates who had each received a large number of votes were put in an urn, and an old recluse renowned for his saintliness was called out to draw the name of the new Patriarch from it. The announcement that Metropolitan Tikhon of Moscow had been chosen was received with general acclaim in the knowledge that he was a most saintly man and a good administrator, even if he was not an outstanding scholar. He had had some experience of the Church abroad, as he had begun his episcopate in America.

On 21st November the Communists allowed the members of the Council and the general public to come into the Kremlin to the Uspensky Cathedral, the traditional place for the enthronement of Russian patriarchs. On this great occasion Bishop Ilarion Troitsky pronounced these words: 'The eagle of Petrine autocracy, shaped in the imitation of the West, had torn asunder the Patriarchate, that sacred heart of Russian Orthodoxy. The sacrilegious hand of the impious Peter pulled down the senior hierarch of the Russian Church from his traditional seat in the Uspensky Cathedral. The Council, by the authority given to it by God, has once more placed the Patriarch of Moscow in the chair, which belongs to him by inalienable right.'[1]

Not only has this 'right' not been exercised from that day to this, but the Cathedral, like all others in the Kremlin, has remained closed to Christian worship ever since. Not until well after the death of Stalin could a Christian in Moscow even visit it to see the patriarchal throne. At the zenith of its new life, the Church was plunged into a critical struggle for its very right to exist.

One does not need to look for elaborate philosophical reasons in the work of Karl Marx to explain why Communism so rapidly showed itself to be the deadly enemy of Christianity. Although Marx was of course always opposed to religion, in purely practical terms it was imperative for the Bolsheviks to repudiate the Church. It was a messianic age; a nation was aflame. In order to save their own lives, the Bolsheviks had to make an absolute claim for men's loyalties. They had to break the power of old Russia completely and at a stroke. If this meant throwing out some that was good alongside the old dross, this could not be avoided. Tsardom had already disappeared; the Provisional Government was broken; the people were divided into many factions; and Lenin saw the Church as the main remaining bastion of the old régime. It had to be destroyed at all costs. Lenin was convinced that man's destiny lay in his own hands, that although the common people had nothing to loose but their chains, they must have a Messiah to lead them into the new age when Marx's apocalyptic vision of the free society could be fulfilled. The Church, he believed, had always been an agent of reaction. It might have given the people consolation, an opium in which to drown the sorrows of the present in a vague narcotic cloud of hope, with its promises of a future life where suffering would be richly recompensed, but the need for it would vanish in the new society where misery would be eliminated.

In this context a violent clash of wills was inevitable, even though no one in 1917 could have foreseen just how disastrous and bloody the consequences would be.

Lenin acted more quickly than might have been predicted, before

[1] Quoted by Zernov, *The Russian Religious Renaissance of the Twentieth Century*, p. 198.

the Church had any chance to savour its new-found freedom. The decree which he promulgated in the first two months after the Revolution aimed at rupturing the spinal cord of the Church. On 4th December a law was passed which deprived the Church of all its property. A week later the seminaries were closed and their books impounded; before a further week was out Christian marriage had been replaced by a civil ceremony. On 23rd January 1918 a decree set out in detail the way in which the Church was to be separated from the State. Its total effects, acquired over centuries, were to be seized without any compensation whatsoever. No doubt if Lenin had felt himself stronger at this moment he would have outlawed all forms of Christian worship in an attempt to extirpate religion once and for all.

It has often been asked whether anything could have been done in 1917 to prevent the head-on clash of these two irreconcilable forces. The question, phrased in this way, answers itself: nothing. If the Church of England were suddenly deprived of all its property, one can hardly envisage the bench of Bishops immediately embarking on a programme of national reconstruction in collaboration with the new régime responsible for the seizure, even with the historical precedent of Russia in 1917 to go by. Long since has the social vision of the Church in Jerusalem vanished from the eyes and from the minds of Christendom: 'The whole body of believers was united in heart and soul. Not a man of them claimed any of his possessions as his own, but everything was held in common, while the apostles bore witness with great power to the resurrection of the Lord Jesus. They were all held in high esteem; for they had never a needy person among them, because all who had property in land or houses sold it, brought the proceeds of the sale, and laid the money at the feet of the apostles; it was then distributed to any who stood in need.'[1]

But in 1917 it would have been beyond human capability for the members of the dispossessed Church to see that beneath their hostile expressions many of the Bolsheviks concealed a genuine will to reform Russia for the good of her least fortunate citizens—or indeed that much of their social programme would in fact be implemented during the course of the next fifty years. No one should be surprised that Tikhon replied to the expropriation of the Church by excommunicating those responsible for the decrees (19th January 1918).

Lenin, for his part, could not possibly have known, even if he had cared, that in the days while the battle for possession of the Kremlin

---

[1] Acts of the Apostles 4. 32-5, (New English Bible).

Inside an Orthodox church: the altar is revealed to the faithful

was going on, the Church was trying to reform itself into a body which might have been able to harness the newly unleashed forces to work for the good of the people: an ultimate aim not so entirely dissimilar from that of the Communist Party itself. The balance of centuries which was against the Church at this time could not be counterpoised in a few days. In a country in the grip of revolution and bloodshed mutual tolerance and will to compromise were not to be expected. There were not many who agreed with the poet Alexander Blok's vision of Christ at the head of the Bolsheviks—and even his vision was uncertain.[1]

There were many conversions of eminent people to Christianity in the years just before and after the Revolution. Sergei Bulgakov (1871–1944), Professor of Political Economics at Moscow University, became a priest; Valentin Sventitsky, a controversial figure before the Revolution, became a preacher of great renown after it, though he was never a stable personality. However, instead of leading to a spiritual expansion and revitalizing of its own life, the new-found energy of the Church was sapped·in fighting for its existence. Patriarch Tikhon was hailed as a saviour and mobbed by enthusiastic crowds when he visited Petrograd in May 1918; but soon the words of the Communists were implemented by deeds. The new lights of Christianity, the converts from atheism or Marxism, were either snuffed out in martyrdom or, like Berdyaev, Frank and P. Struve, among a host of others, condemned to shine—albeit with great intensity—in Parisian exile.

THE CONFLICT UNFOLDS

As the history of the Russian Church's life-struggle from 1917 up to the present has been reasonably well documented, at least up to 1955, I would refer the reader to several titles mentioned in the Notes for Further Reading. Here I propose to begin by recounting the situation in the early years as seen through the eyes of one man and to follow this up with a brief résumé of the events he does not cover. His story,[2] which is not at all well known, is remarkable for its

---

[1] In his last poem *Dvenadtsat* (The Twelve).

[2] The information is taken from a paper delivered by Fr. Alagiagian at the Twelfth Missionary Congress, held in Burgos, by the *Instituto español de San Francisco Javier para Misiones extranjeras*, and published in *Misiones extranjeras*, 1960, the official record of the congress. An English translation appeared as 'The Present State of Christianity in the U.S.S.R.', *Pagan Missions*, Winter 1960 and Spring 1961 (organ of the Pia Unio Cleri, St. Columban's, Navan, Eire).

moderation—and for the fact that he escaped from the Soviet Union to tell it.

Peter Alagiagian was born in Armenia, which had for a long time been part of the Russian Empire and where the small Roman Catholic Church had been under severe stricture during the tsarist régime. He went to Rome to train for the priesthood, became a Jesuit and took advantage of the British occupation of the Caucasus after the Revolution to return to his own part of the world.

Shortly after his arrival in Georgia, the Soviet Navy made landings in this area in order to suppress the independent democratic governments of Georgia, Azerbaijan and Armenia which had been set up at the Revolution. The first act of the occupying troops was to pass on various proclamations from Moscow, including one guaranteeing religious liberty to all Soviet citizens: there would be no interference in religious affairs and all religions and all branches of the Christian faith would have completely equal rights in the eyes of the law. Fr. Alagiagian's natural reaction to this was one of restrained enthusiasm. It seemed that the special privileges and protection which the small branch of the Russian Orthodox Church in Georgia had enjoyed under the old régime were at an end and that this would inevitably benefit the Roman Catholics. Some converts were made; so Fr. Alagiagian prepared large-scale plans for his missionary activities, including founding an orphanage at Batumi for two hundred refugee children.

By this time the Soviets were following up their military conquest by terrorizing the local population in a typical attempt to reduce the people to servility. No one suffered worse than the Church. Its buildings and properties were seized and the Soviet authorities converted many churches and monasteries into dance-halls, cinemas or anti-God museums. Monks and nuns were turned loose on the streets without asylum or means of supporting themselves. Not only did priests not have the right to vote: they could not join a trade union and find alternative temporary work. Many were denied ration cards, and were thus given the alternative of seeing their wives and families starving on the streets or of sending them off to some commune for a full course of Communist indoctrination. No religious instruction was allowed in schools, but some parishes managed to keep their churches open. This was possible where twenty people could be found to sign a petition to keep their place of worship. Those who signed were brave men and women. They had to supply their names, addresses and places of work; they must have known that to sign might mean a death-warrant if pressure against religion should be further increased, yet many gladly took the risk for the sake of their faith.

One such group gave Fr. Alagiagian the possibility of continuing his work in Georgia, though on a very reduced scale.

Soon his parishioners were being threatened with losing their jobs if they continued to attend church. Many joined atheistic societies and stopped coming to worship, but continued praying in their own houses and seeing their priest in secret. Those who still practised their religion openly were further terrorized. Children were indoctrinated in the schools to such an extent that they were persuaded to form processions to the various places of worship on Sundays, break into the services carrying red flags and blasphemous emblems, and hurl insults at God, the meaning of which they themselves were scarcely old enough to understand. They were trained to inform the authorities of the activities of believing parents.

Here is an example which Fr. Alagiagian gives from his own experience of the way in which these children were indoctrinated. One day a woman came to see him and said:

' "Yesterday my eight-year-old son, Carlitos, came home breathless with fatigue and excitement. He told me that when school was ended the children were taken on an outing which lasted more than two hours. Then they were conducted to the public park and took part in physical exercises for more than half an hour. At the end of that time they were asked, 'Boys, are you hungry?' and they naturally said that they were famished. Then these fiendish bolshevists told them to ask God to give them their daily bread. This petition was repeated three times and then the children were asked if God had given them any bread. Then the bewildered youngsters were told that they could see for themselves that there was no God, for their prayers went unanswered. Then the same petition was made in the name of Lenin and immediately there appeared a truck-full of bread, cheese and fruit which was divided among the hungry children. 'You see now,' they were told, 'it is not God that provides bread but Lenin'." [1]

This episode is a striking illustration of the process by which Lenin, and later Stalin, were literally deified by the Party machine for the benefit of the popular imagination. An outstanding example of what I call the 'Lenin/God' or 'Stalin/God mythology' occurred on the occasion of Stalin's seventieth birthday, which conveniently coincided

[1] *Pagan Missions*, Winter 1960, p. 127.

with the Orthodox Christmas of 1949. The Soviet illustrated journal, *Ogonyok*, printed an impressive picture on its front page. It showed vast crowds milling in Red Square, illuminated from above and behind by a supernatural glow. It came from a huge star in the sky which gave off brilliant rays all emanating from its central point—the face of Stalin.[1]

Before many weeks under the new régime had passed, a Red Army soldier, bayonet at the ready, walked into Fr. Alagiagian's office to summon him to appear before the *Cheka* (secret police). Passing through three control-points at their headquarters, Fr. Alagiagian was taken to the inner recesses where he found all the other ministers of religion from the town of Batumi already gathered. A young Russian political commissar appeared and began a long and violent tirade against them. He threatened everyone with instant death by shooting or hanging if his orders were not carried out. He blamed the assembled company for organizing the riots which had occurred after the closing of the churches. The only way to save their own necks, he continued, was to pacify the people under their charge by emphasizing the Soviet law on religious liberty and saying that it would be implemented.

The result of the priests' carrying out such orders is still to be seen in the U.S.S.R.[2] That Fr. Alagiagian had the courage to stand up and speak his mind in such a situation and yet survived is remarkable. There were not many such instances. But after bravely opposing the political commissar, he was allowed to return home, together with the other priests who had been gathered there with him. He was allowed to continue his restricted religious activities, though he remained under close surveillance. His orphanage was closed down and the children who had been under his protection were turned loose on the streets.

Fearing for his life, the order to which Fr. Alagiagian belonged transferred him to Krasnodar, just north of the Caucasus. Here he was able to continue a modicum of parochial work. At this point his story, according to the published sources, becomes less clear, but it appears that he survived a short period in prison in 1925 and in the ensuing trial was found not guilty on seventeen counts of counter-revolutionary activity. Eventually in 1930 he was expelled from the

---

[1] Reproduced by Walter Kolarz, *Religion in the Soviet Union*, Macmillan, London, 1961, facing p. 21.
[2] cf., p. 157.

U.S.S.R. In the Second World War he became a chaplain in the Italian Army, had the misfortune to be captured by the Russians and spent twelve years in various prisons and concentration camps before being released in 1954. One hopes that Fr. Alagiagian will be able to write his autobiography and bring us up to date with a detailed account of these later experiences.

Fr. Alagiagian was geographically far removed from the centre of events during the first years after the Communists' seizure of power. Had he lived closer to Moscow or Leningrad, he undoubtedly would not have survived to tell his story. There were many thousands of priests, mainly Russian Orthodox, but of other denominations also, who could have recounted their experiences in much more horrific detail if they had lived to do so. Most of those who did survive have had their voices muted by the course of events, yet an amazing amount of material on the Church's suffering during these years has been collected by observers in the West.[1]

During the four years of the Civil War, which lasted until 1921, the Communists were unable to organize the enforcement of their decrees against the Church in the way they would have liked. Patriarch Tikhon retracted his anathema against the Communist Party[2] and on 25th September 1919 advised his clergy to take no active part in politics.

The increased stability which followed the end of the Civil War gave the Bolsheviks the opportunity of turning their attention to the Church again. They were no doubt goaded to do so by the famine which gripped the land in the winter of 1921–2. Desperately short of food for the people and of money with which to purchase it from abroad, the Government ordered that all religious objects of value, especially ornaments of gold and silver, should be seized from churches and the proceeds put into the national funds. Although Tikhon himself had encouraged his people to contribute voluntarily what they could of their possessions to the fund, he opposed the giving up of any object connected with the performance of the liturgy. In the resulting clashes of parishioners with Red Army soldiers, there were reported to be 1,414 instances of bloodshed.[3] On 10th May 1922 the Patriarch himself was put under house-arrest and suspended from his activities.

[1] See Notes for Further Reading (pp. 240–3).
[2] See p. 48.
[3] Nikita Struve, *Les Chrétiens en U.R.S.S.*, p. 32.

This is an important date in the Church's history. It inaugurated the worst persecutions Russian Christians had so far had to endure and marked the beginning of the activities of the 'Living Church', later called the Church of the *Obnovlentsy* (Renovators).

This Communist-inspired movement sought to force clerics to take oaths of loyalty to the régime. Those who refused suffered the fate of Metropolitan Venyamin of Petrograd, who on the night of 12th August 1922, after a heated trial, was shot with three of his associates. A week before this the Council of the Living Church had said of the Communist Party: 'The Council affirms that every honourable Christian should take his place among these warriors for humanitarian truth and use all means to realize in life the grand principles of the October Revolution.'[1]

By this time Tikhon had been removed to prison. His eclipse seemed to leave the Church open to the depredations of the Living Church movement, which soon gained control of all except five or six of the Moscow churches. However, the people were never behind it and its grip was broken when the Patriarch was freed from prison unexpectedly in June 1923. A document to which his signature was appended appeared in *Izvestia* on 28th June to coincide with his release. In it he expressed in abject terms his regret at the opposition he had formerly shown to the new régime and blamed it entirely on his social origins. He denied that he had ever been tortured in prison and declared his complete loyalty to the Soviet State.[2]

There can be few Christians who are entirely happy at this episode. Despite Tikhon's assurances that he had not been subjected to torture, one wonders what means were used to extract this confession and it is never pleasant to see a Christian publicly humiliating himself after making a courageous stand against evil. Some Christians in Russia, however, believed he knew exactly what he was doing—abasing himself for the good of his flock. Whatever his inner motives may have been, his release did secure the unity of the Orthodox Church in face of the challenge from the Living Church. These Communist agents found that the ground had been cut from beneath them, for the only reason for their existence was to show that they were the true Church, while the patriarchal faction was being justly persecuted by the authorities. Even though the Soviet Government continued to recog-

[1] Quoted by Paul Anderson, *People, Church and State in Modern Russia*, S.C.M., London, 1944, p. 64.
[2] A long extract from this declaration is printed in Struve, *Les Chrétiens en U.R.S.S.*, pp. 292-3.

nize the Living Church up to 1927, it had perhaps given away more than it intended by releasing Tikhon.

For a short while there was less persecution. The Government found it necessary to gain respectability in the eyes of foreign governments in order to secure better loans. Tikhon, however, was kept under close surveillance and his activities were extremely restricted. When he died on 7th April 1925 the Government did not allow the appointment of a successor.

After a period of internal dissension which the Government had deliberately induced, the Metropolitan Sergius Stragorodsky emerged as the most powerful figure. He had had a most interesting career up to this point. He was a theologian of note, whose work on the doctrine of salvation is still highly regarded today. He had been a missionary in Japan, chaplain of the Russian Embassy in Athens, rector of the Theological Academy in St. Petersburg and a bishop in the Orthodox Church of Finland, where he had introduced many valued practical reforms into his diocese before the Council of 1917. He was, then, a man with a great reputation, not, apparently, the sort to become pliable in Communist hands.

Sergius was given a new post with the strange title of 'Vice-*locum tenens* of the Patriarchal Throne'. His nominal superior, Metropolitan Pyotr Polyansky, exercised no actual power as *locum tenens* and was not replaced when he was sent to Siberia, where he died in 1936. Despite the pomp attending the re-introduction of the Patriarchate in 1917, the Church had kept its new-found dignity for only seven and a half years.

By 1926 pressure was beginning to build up against the Church once more. The League of Militant Atheists was formed to co-ordinate anti-religious propaganda and to speed the demise of the Church. Its members realized that although the quality of church leadership had been gravely affected by the removal of so many of its finest figures during the previous few years, this alone did not guarantee the death of religion. Metropolitan Sergius was arrested on 26th December 1926, an episode which has received little publicity and is of course passed over in silence in all his official biographies. He was in prison for under three months, but during this time seems to have undergone experiences which persuaded him to show an unexpectedly sycophantic loyalty towards the régime.

In a declaration dated 29th June 1927 Sergius stated: 'Let us publicly express our gratitude to the Soviet Government for the interest it is showing in all the religious needs of the Orthodox, and at the same time let us assure the Government that we will not abuse the confidence it has shown towards us. . . . We want to be Orthodox and at the same time to recognize the Soviet Union as our fatherland, whose joys and successes are our joys and successes and whose setbacks are our setbacks. Every attack directed against the U.S.S.R. . . . is resented as being directed against ourselves.'[1]

Fr. Alagiagian quotes the reaction of a priest whom he met in Moscow to Sergius's declaration: ' "I am ashamed of being a Russian and an Orthodox priest. We were taught from infancy to hate the Pope . . . but he greatly appreciates the resistance we offer to the Militant Atheists, and he has now raised his powerful voice in our support by protesting against the persecution of the bishops, priests and faithful; and on the other hand here in Moscow, our own Patriarch,[2] Sergius, declares with the utmost hypocrisy that there is no religious persecution. He has closed his eyes lest he might see the blood shed so generously by our heroic priests and people. He has sunk to such a depth of depravity that he regards all who have suffered martyrdom or exile for the faith as a band of criminals who well merited the punishment that they received." '[3]

Sergius's words caused a new schism in the Church. A faction, led by Metropolitan Joseph Petrovykh of Leningrad and consisting of important leaders in seven other dioceses, broke off relations with the main body of the Church and the division was healed only by the martyrdom or exile of its instigators. The exact fate of some is still not known, but Metropolitan Joseph was shot in 1938.

The new wave of persecution in the late 'twenties was more systematic than anything which had preceded it. According to the first Five-Year Plan (1929–34), education was to be the main instrument used in converting the people to atheism. Every factory, workshop and communal house had to have its compulsory course of instruction. Besides this, Stalin issued a decree on 8th April 1929 which formally restricted the Church's activities to the conduct of divine worship (though this merely legalized a state of affairs which already existed). The decree stated: 'Religious unions are forbidden . . . to give material aid to their members; they may not organize prayer groups or any other special meetings for children, young people or

---

[1] Given in full in Struve, op. cit., pp. 305–9.
[2] Alagiagian is mistaken here. Sergius did not become Patriarch until sixteen years after this declaration.
[3] *Pagan Missions*, Spring 1961, p. 13.

women. General meetings for any purpose whatsoever are forbidden.
... Religious associations may not organize excursions and children's
playgrounds, open libraries and reading rooms, or maintain sanatoria
and give medical aid. Only such books as are necessary for the
performance of services are permitted in church buildings and houses
of prayer.'

This illustrates three points. Firstly, religion had not folded up in
the way that the first atheists had expected it to, so that practical
administrative measures had to be introduced for the interim period
until it did disappear. Secondly, parochial activity, which in the West
is considered normal, in Russia is heavily restricted by law. Thirdly,
the Communists completely failed to understand the true nature of
religion. They simply did not see that to allow Christians to continue
celebrating the liturgy together was to spare their lifeline.

Most country parishes suffered acutely in 1929–30, the years of the
forced collectivization of agriculture. The seminaries had already
been closed, thus cutting off the supply of young priests to replace the
old. At the same time as they seized colossal numbers of churches,
the authorities claimed that as there were now so few parishes that
more priests would not be needed. Severe penalties awaited the priests
who objected to this sequestration of their churches; many were
arrested and sent to Siberia, while others were shot. Those who
acquiesced were totally deprived of their civil rights and it was difficult for them to get permission to earn their living by manual labour.
Those who renounced their faith altogether, which under such pressure happened not infrequently, had to prove themselves by five years
of hard work before they could be reinstated as citizens.

Apart from the fact that persecution tended to come in alternating
waves of greater and lesser intensity during the 'thirties, the picture
of the Church during these years is one of almost unrelieved gloom.
Perhaps the one heartening feature was that many of the priests who
were sent to the far north and east succeeded not only in keeping
their faith alive, but also in making some converts among the desperate ranks of political prisoners and even, in some instances, among
the sparse local population. In these parts there were some pagan
tribes who had never been converted to Christianity.

A few years of comparative respite in the early 'thirties, during
which there were almost no events of note as far as the churches were
concerned, were followed by the worst time of all, the 'Great Purge'
of 1937–8. During this time there was not a citizen in the Soviet

Union, no matter what his allegiance, who did not fear nightly the coming of the N.K.V.D. (People's Commissariat for Home Affairs, a euphemistic title for the secret police). Several fascist plots were 'discovered' among the clergy, and the executioner's blade hovered above the heads of all Orthodox clerics.

One salutary shock was administered to the Government which showed them that all was still not going according to plan in extirpating religion. A census was taken in January 1937, in which there was a question about religious adherence. The results were never published, but it is believed that some fifty million answered the question about religious adherence in the affirmative.[1] This so shocked the authorities that they refused to accept the returns. Many of the officers conducting the census were arrested, as were the leaders of the League of Militant Atheists. The latter organization broke down and many of its members were sent to join their victims in the labour camps.

PATRIOTIC ENDEAVOUR

By the time Hitler's guns were threatening Europe the Church in Russia presented a sorry spectacle. Of the 54,174 churches that had existed at the time of the Revolution probably not more than a hundred were open in 1939. There had been almost as many parochial clergy as churches: now there were a few hundred. There had been 163 bishops: now there were seven occupying their sees. Every monastery and convent, over a thousand in all, had been closed down and their hundred thousand inmates and dependants scattered. Of seminaries, church schools and hospitals, parochial libraries not a single one was left.[2]

It is strange that it took the threat of war to make any material improvement in the situation of the Russian Orthodox Church. The first encouragement of any kind that it had received for many years came when the Soviet Union annexed the Baltic States, Bessarabia and the eastern half of Poland in 1939-40. This brought several million Orthodox, members of well-organized parishes, under Soviet power; it also had the effect of making the Roman Catholic Church the third largest religious group in the Soviet Union, surpassed only by Orthodoxy and Islam. Some administrative measures were taken

[1] See Walter Kolarz, *Religion in the Soviet Union*, p. 12.
[2] See the statistical table on p. 234.

against the U.S.S.R.'s newly acquired Christian citizens, but before the repression could take its full effect the Government found itself immersed in full-scale war.

On the very day that German troops crossed the Soviet frontier, 21st June 1941, the Russian Church unconditionally threw in its lot with the patriotic cause. Metropolitan Sergius acted here with much more vigour and speed than might have been expected from the servile position he had adopted. He can have received no official directives relating to the course of action he was to take, for the nation was in a state of extreme shock. Rumours were flying in all directions and no one knew what was really happening on the frontier. Yet on the same day that the news of the invasion arrived Sergius sent out a pastoral letter to all Orthodox Christians of Russia, begging them to show themselves true patriots in their country's hour of greatest need. He made no mention of the Communist Government, but the letter was filled with a deep spirituality.[1] Perhaps this was Sergius's noblest moment.

The Government does not seem to have hesitated in accepting this aid. Sergius turned his words into deeds, calling on the faithful to make direct financial contributions to the war. Among other projects, they provided enough money for a fighter squadron called after Alexander Nevsky and a tank division called after Dmitry Donskoi, the Christian warrior-heroes of Old Russia.

A sign of the improved status of the Church during the early years of the 'Great Patriotic War', as the Russians call it, was the publication of a book entitled *The Truth about Religion in Russia*.[2] It was a sumptuous, illustrated production in an expensive light-blue cover, which broke on a world of near-starvation. Its main purpose was to assure its readers that they were right in supporting the war effort because the Soviet Government had always looked benignly on religion. The article which most sharply denied that there had ever been any persecution of Christians was unsigned.

At Easter 1942 the Soviet gun emplacements stopped their covering fire in Moscow, despite the danger of an aerial attack, so that the faithful could go to their midnight services.

The date which inaugurated a dramatic change in the relations between Church and State was 4th September 1943. Stalin summoned the three Metropolitans, Sergius, Nikolai Yarushevich and Alexis

[1] The full text is printed in Struve, op. cit., pp. 309–10.
[2] *Pravda o religii v Rossii*, Moscow, 1942.

Simansky, to the Kremlin to inform them that he was prepared to give the Church official recognition for its services. Four days later a Council met to elect a new patriarch. The bishops and archbishops who assembled totalled nineteen, and this meagre number of senior representatives must have been a grave reminder to those who were gathered there of the plight of their Church. Sergius was chosen unanimously, which set the seal of the Church's approval on his work over the past seventeen years, during which he had in fact been head of the Church.

Patriarch Sergius was now able to approach with dedication his task of reconstructing the Church from the ruins. Metropolitan Nikolai's sycophantic report on the meeting with Stalin must have eased his task. Nikolai wrote: 'We, who shared in the reception granted us by Joseph Vissarionovich, live and shall live under the charm of those impressions that overwhelmed us at the time of the meeting. . . . Our people see in him the incarnation of everything that is best and brightest; everything which represents the holiest heritage of our Russian nation bequeathed to us by our ancestors.'[1]

Although he had laid the foundations for it, Sergius never saw the fruition of his efforts for reconstruction. He died suddenly of a cerebral hæmorrhage on 15th May 1944, just eight months after his election. The work was carried on by his successor, Alexis, with such success that by 1947 the number of bishops had increased to seventy-four, the clergy to about thirty thousand, monasteries and convents to sixty-seven and open churches to about ten thousand. Most significant of all, eight seminaries for the training of priests were reopened, two of them incorporating academies where advanced theological studies could be undertaken.[2] This was the first time since the Revolution that the Soviet Government had in any way conceded that the Church might have a future, and it is true to say that while even one of these remains open the situation cannot again be as bad as it was in 1939.

The unity of the Church was formally re-established at the same time, for nearly all of the few remaining bishops belonging to the Living Church gave their allegiance to the Moscow Patriarchate.

It was not only the Christians who had remained under Soviet domination who gained from the war. A remarkable revival of religious life had followed everywhere in the wake of the German armies

[1] *Journal of the Moscow Patriarchate*, No. 1, Jan. 1944.
[2] See p. 92.

as they advanced on and occupied Soviet soil. And if this revival was short-lived, it was, while it lasted, extraordinarily intense. The Germans forbade most kinds of freedom except that of religion and this quickly fanned the flames of evangelism. The Metropolitan of the Baltic States, for instance, Sergius Voskresensky, organized a mission[1] around the Pskov-Novgorod area where before the war there had not been a single parish functioning. In fact in 1939 there were only five in the whole area of Russia west of Leningrad, yet by 1943 there were eighty-five priests to serve just over two hundred parishes. Every celebration of the liturgy was attended by throngs of people who often could not be accommodated in the churches, even though they were packed in shoulder to shoulder. Within a month or two, after the Red Army had reoccupied these territories, the situation had returned almost to 'normal'; but to this day one finds more churches open per head of population in those areas which the Nazis conquered than in any place which has been continuously under Soviet control since 1917.

This is an enlightening corroboration of the fact that where Christian activity appears to have ceased it does not mean that faith is dead. Given the chance to express itself openly, it can do so with remarkable energy—which makes it all the more sad that the Moscow Patriarchate has never been able to acknowledge these successes and that they have remained taboo in all its publications.

THE CHURCH FINDS A VOICE

In recounting the improvements in the religious situation in the U.S.S.R. as a result of the war, I do not wish to imply that the lot of the ordinary believer suddenly became easy. In the years of reconstruction which followed Nazi devastation the Government had too many problems on its hands to concentrate a great deal of attention on the Church. Its ultimate aim of eradicating all forms of religious belief remained, but its tactics changed.

The situation in Europe in 1945 was very different from what it had been ten years earlier and the Soviets saw that they could use the Church as a very helpful instrument of foreign policy. From this date, then, one has to keep two balancing considerations constantly in mind in order to assess what was really happening to Russian Christianity. The first is to see what was happening to the ordinary

[1] For a striking account of its work see Struve, op. cit., pp. 59–63.

Christian inside the U.S.S.R.; the second to follow the external relations of the Church with other countries, which during these years have been gradually extended to cover an ever wider field.

The internal situation of the Church from 1945 to 1959 need not detain us long. This was a period of relative stability during which the Church attempted to consolidate the concessions which it had been granted in 1943. It must have been encouraging to see churches flourishing which had been shut down for twenty years.

In 1943 a Government department was created with the object of controlling religious affairs and keeping the Party in touch with developments. It was called the 'Council for the Affairs of the Russian Orthodox Church' and has always been closely in touch with the secret police. In fact its first head, G. G. Karpov, had been a police official with responsibility for religious affairs before his appointment.[1] The office bears a remarkable resemblance to that of Procurator of the Holy Synod in Tsarist days. Its status is less exalted, but its powers probably about the same. The minister soon acquired the nickname of *Narkomopium*—an abbreviation for 'people's commissar for opium'.

The new Patriarch, Alexis, was elected and enthroned in February 1945. He had won the highest respect of Russian Christians during the war, when, as Metropolitan of Leningrad, he had remained in the city with his people during the terrible sufferings of the siege. He has now been in office nearly twenty years, during which time he has never been the subject of such controversies as was his predecessor.

The death of Stalin in March 1953 affected the Church less than it did most other sections of Soviet society. The years from 1954 to 1958 did not see a massive return to the faith or the reopening of a large number of churches, and perhaps an opportunity was lost for broadening the basis of Christian activity inside the country while the politicians were concerned principally with their own jockeying for position and had little time to worry about what to them were secondary matters.

Since 1959 the position has suddenly and radically changed for the worse. The Church has once again found itself engaged in a life or death struggle in which the Communist methods of the pre-war years have been taken up again, enhanced by an increased experience and subtlety in this type of campaign, but the consideration of recent developments must wait until the last chapter.

[1] See R. Magidoff, *The Kremlin and the People*, New York, 1953, p. 74.

The external relations of the Russian Orthodox Church between 1943 and 1958 present a much more diversified picture, though their pattern follows closely the general line of the foreign policy of the Soviet Government during these years.

There was a wave of pro-Russian feeling among the Allied nations after the victorious part the Soviet Union had played in the Second World War. This seemed an appropriate time for the Communist country to impress upon mankind that it had arrived at last among the great civilized nations of the world. The Church's contribution to this endeavour—and the event was certainly one of great significance for Christians in Russia as well—was to build a superstructure of great pomp around the enthronement of the new Patriarch, Alexis, on 4th February 1945. Church delegations were invited from all friendly countries, and Moscow provided a warm welcome for the Patriarchs of Antioch and Alexandria, representatives of the Patriarchs of Serbia, Rumania, Jerusalem and the Oecumenical Patriarch of Constantinople, as well as high-ranking delegations from many non-Orthodox Churches. The Anglican Communion was represented by the Archbishop of York, Dr. Cyril Garbett.

The Church's policy, with the Government's backing, or more probably at its instigation, followed two main lines during the next few years, which were so similar that they often intersected. The first was to help to reduce recalcitrant, particularly committed Christian, elements in the new Russian empire in Eastern Europe and the Balkans. The second was to reintroduce covertly the old ecclesiastical fiction of 'Moscow the Third Rome' and try this time to turn it into reality.

Patriarch Alexis followed up the new contacts made at his enthronement by visiting the Middle East, where he was everywhere received with such enthusiasm that it contributed to the reputation both of his Church and of his Government. Several delegations were exchanged with Bulgaria and Rumania with the same aim, and the Orthodox Churches in satellite countries seemed quite happy for Moscow to make a take-over bid. Especially interesting was what happened in Poland. The Polish Orthodox Church had about four million members at one time, and after the Russian Revolution had discussed the question of independence with the Oecumenical Patriarchate and been granted the right to become autocephalous. However, in 1945 it found that all its eastern dioceses (which had very high Orthodox populations) had been incorporated into the U.S.S.R.

and it could exercise no further control over them. With a typically Polish display of dogged independence, Metropolitan Denis of Warsaw kept control of the small part of his Church with which he could still maintain contact, but in 1948 he was denounced by the Patriarch of Moscow who broke off communion between the two Churches. Metropolitan Denis was then replaced by a Soviet bishop, Macarius of Lvov, who seemed intent only on playing the role of Moscow's pawn. The full story behind these intrigues has never been made known, but such episodes, to which there have been parallels in Czechoslovakia and Albania, should be borne in mind and their history carefully studied by any Western Churches entering into ecumenical negotiations with Churches from Eastern Europe. This is not a plea for the extension of the principles of the worst days of the cold war, but merely for an attempt to see the truth, on which alone sound foundations for better relations can be built.

Moscow's most flamboyant attempt at establishing herself as the centre of world Orthodoxy came in 1947–8. In the spring of 1947 Patriarch Alexis took upon himself the initiative of calling a pan-Orthodox conference on his home ground. He was only temporarily stymied in his intention by the Patriarch of Constantinople who curtly informed him that the right to such action lay with the Oecumenical Patriarchate alone. Alexis sidestepped this obstacle neatly by inviting all the same people to the thirtieth anniversary of the reestablishment of the Moscow Patriarchate (no mention of the fact that for only a third of this time had there been any incumbent of this office) and adding in passing that there would be a conference afterwards. After some hesitation the Patriarch of Jerusalem and Archbishop Makarios of Cyprus declined; the Oecumenical Patriarch and the Church of Greece decided to be represented at the jubilee celebrations only; while the Patriarchate of Alexandria said it would be represented by that of Antioch, which showed itself most eager to follow the lead given by Moscow and accepted by the numerous delegations from the Iron Curtain countries.

The conference lasted from 9th–17th July 1948. It condemned the Roman Catholic Church in bitter terms, the Ecumenical Movement, which was about to move into top gear with the approaching First General Assembly of the World Council of Churches at Amsterdam, hardly less outspokenly, and pronounced against the validity of Anglican orders. This work of devastation did not help to make Moscow the centre of world Orthodoxy. It brought Orthodox Christianity in the satellite countries more firmly under the hegemony of the Russian Church, but did nothing to the non-Communist world beyond antagonizing it. The one exception to this was the Patriarchate of Antioch. Already in 1945 it had shown itself subservient to Moscow; at the conference it joined enthusiastically in the chorus of condemnation and has ever since given to numerous observers throughout the world the impression of being in the fee of the Russians.

During these years if the Soviet Government blew hot or cold in any specific direction, the Church had to do the same. For instance when Tito defied Stalin by pursuing an independent Communist line in 1948, Alexis dutifully returned the decorations received from the Yugoslav Government and broke off ecclesiastical relations with the Serbian Orthodox Church.

After the death of Stalin the Church relinquished its bludgeoning ambitions for Orthodox hegemony in favour of a much more subtle role, totally in keeping with the general drift of Soviet diplomacy since that time.

In 1954 a crop of articles on the Ecumenical Movement appeared in the *Journal of the Moscow Patriarchate* (the only official source of information about the Church regularly published in Russia, which the Patriarchate acquired the right to print from September 1943). Still the tone was critical, but the basic objective of Christian unity was approved. In 1956 the Patriarch of the Serbian Orthodox Church visited Moscow, where he was received by Bulganin, and cordial relations were set up again between the Russian and Serbian Churches according to the pre-1948 pattern. Most unexpected of all was the Moscow Patriarchate's sudden recognition, in 1947, of the fact that the Finnish Orthodox Church belonged to the jurisdiction of Constantinople. Not only was communion with the Finnish Church re-established for the first time since 1923 but it was also thereby recognized that Constantinople could have jurisdiction beyond its own geographical limits (a tacit renunciation of Moscow's claim to supremacy in the Orthodox world).

In May 1958 Patriarch Alexis invited all the Orthodox leaders to Moscow again to celebrate the fourth centenary of the autocephaly of the Russian Church. At the solemn session which followed, Metropolitan Nikolai allowed the Oecumenical Patriarchate, on this occasion officially represented because of the signs of the 'thaw' which were now fully apparent in Moscow, to assume the position of having convened it and at the same time announced that the Russian Church was now able to prepare itself for taking a full part in the Ecumenical Movement.

The direct result of this change of face in Moscow was the pan-Orthodox conference on the isle of Rhodes, preceded by the Patriarch's visit to the Balkans and Middle East in December 1960. Although no official account of the conversation is available, it seems that when Alexis met the Oecumenical Patriarch he put several conditions for the coming meeting: that the Oecumenical Patriarch should recognize the Bulgarian Patriarchate and the independence of the Czech and Polish Orthodox Churches, and that he should abandon his claims on the branches of the Russian Orthodox Church in exile under his protection. A compromise was reached, in which Alexis gained his first three points, while the Oecumenical Patriarch stood firm on the last. There was probably, too, some discussion of the Albanian Orthodox Church, which was not invited to Rhodes. The conference took place under the chairmanship of the Patriarch of Constantinople. Its brief was not to deal in depth with theological or ecumenical matters, but merely to compile an agenda for a projected pan-Orthodox Synod.

The Russian Church's relations with the Vatican have eased in exact conformity with the changing attitude of the Soviet Government. The vehement attacks against the Pope and all his works which were such a feature of Stalin's era almost ceased after 1956, but even so the Orthodox Church originally decided against sending an observer to the Vatican Council. After Mr. Khrushchev's warm welcome for Pope John's message of 10th September 1961, it changed its tone, though still without committing itself on the question of whether or not to send an observer to the Council. The Oecumenical Patriarch felt that all the Orthodox Churches should act in accord on this point, but the Russian Church withheld its decision for so long (no announcement was made until the very day of the opening) that the other Churches withdrew. To the Oecumenical Patriarch's amazement, two Soviet priests then presented themselves in Rome, giving the impression to the world that the Russian Orthodox Church, which until recently had shown implacable hostility to everything the Vatican stood for, was now the only one prepared to enter into diplomatic relations with it. A fascinating account of this delicate piece of Patriarchal diplomacy is contained in Nikita Struve's recent book.[1]

[1] *Les Chrétiens en U.R.S.S.*, pp. 98–100.

The Prague Christian Peace Conference was established with full Soviet support in June 1958. Some people believed its aim was to provide an Eastern answer to the World Council of Churches, which was very largely orientated towards the West before the New Delhi Assembly. The Prague movement has gained little popularity with the Orthodox Churches of non-Communist countries (except, inevitably, with the Patriarchate of Antioch) and understandably the World Council of Churches has remained cool towards it. Its proclamations were at first as unswervingly in line with current Kremlin policy as anything the Russian Church ever said about germ-warfare in Korea or the American blockade of Cuba. However, the Assembly of 28th June–3rd July 1964 allowed much freer discussion than hitherto. It now seems unlikely that in future this movement will do much to serve the cause of Communism, and Eastern European Christians have found a valuable forum where they can openly discuss world problems with delegates from non-Communist countries.

All the other directions in which the activity of the Russian Church has been developing outside the territory of the Soviet Union pale beside the importance of the Russian entry into the World Council of Churches at New Delhi in November 1961, where the Third General Assembly was held. A consideration of this must be deferred,[1] however, because before we can appreciate its significance we must look more closely at the internal situation of the Soviet Union today.

[1] See Chapter VIII.

CHAPTER III

Orthodox Attitudes

THE PATRIARCHATE

Until recently it was difficult to form an unbiased picture of religious life in the Soviet Union from the published material available. Even in 1964 it is possible for a man of the highest intelligence and experience of life in many parts of the world, who conscientiously sets out to be objective in his reporting, to write of the contemporary scene: 'Three generations of Soviet indoctrination has destroyed almost all evidence of religion.'[1] Contrast this with the report of Dr. Serge Bolshakoff who, in 1960, paid his first visit to Russia since he left it in 1919: 'The majority of Soviet believers, as far as I could judge from my own experience, belong to the twenty-to-forty age-group. They were born and bred after the Revolution, yet their faith is as strong as in the ages of faith. It augurs well for the future.'[2] The article contains a series of comments on other topics which are just as strange.

Now, however, it has at last become possible to read about church life in the U.S.S.R. in books wholly devoted to the subject, whereas formerly one had to be content with gleaning odd chapters from more general works or following up journals dealing with Eastern European affairs. Some of these are both objective and well written.[3]

My aim is to present as fairly as possible my own impressions of various aspects of the life of the Orthodox Church as I saw them during my year's residence in Moscow, though my objectivity may at times have been affected by the moods which the daily round in the

[1] Laurens van der Post, *Journey into Russia*, Hogarth Press, London, 1964, p. 276.
[2] 'Russia Revisited', *Church Times*, 23rd September 1960.
[3] See Notes for Further Reading, pp. 240–3.

U.S.S.R. seems at times to impose on most foreigners. Most of the contradictions in my picture are, I believe, inherent in the subject itself, though some doubtless come from the situation in which I was placed. If I had been successful in realizing my original plan, which the World Council of Churches wished to back, of spending a year in a theological academy, my impressions would certainly have been different and more intimate. As it was, I was immured high up in the new university building on the Lenin Hills, seeming to survey the Church, represented by the domes of the Novodevichi Monastery visible below, from a remote ivory tower. Intellectually, too, the two worlds were far apart.

Yet my position held certain advantages. I was completely unencumbered by the official reception which is the inevitable accompaniment of ecclesiastical delegations and which gives their members a different perspective from mine. Their way leads along a red carpet through a series of open doors. My paths lay through the muddy and pitted lanes, which in Moscow pass for side-streets, ending often in a locked door which I could open only if I could improvise a key for myself. This led me sometimes to see a situation as it might appear to a young Russian outside the fold of the Church.

The one key which I hoped would be of great use was a letter of introduction from Dr. Michael Ramsey, then Archbishop of York, which he had sent to the Patriarchate of the Orthodox Church. Formerly the Embassy of Hitler's Germany, No. 5 Chisty Pereulok ('Clean Lane') is not the easiest of addresses to find in Moscow. The road itself, indistinguishable from a thousand other back-streets of the city, did not strongly confirm or belie its name—it was broader than a lane, but certainly less than clean. A huddle of old women were disputing supremacy with the winter's first snow, swishing their twig brooms busily, but they were losing the battle to the layer of coagulating brown slush.

I turned into the iron gateway of No. 5 and was accosted by a gruff old man in tattered working-clothes who came out of his little wooden box, just like those one reads about in Gogol, to bar my way and ask me what I wanted. When I explained my mission, I was admitted and he accompanied me down a long corridor past an assortment of babushki[1] and priests who were huddled on benches lining both sides

---

[1] The word babushka literally means 'grandmother', but is used to designate the old Russian women who put on black when they reach middle age and never take it off again.

of it. He knocked on a door at the end; I went in and was confronted by Mr. Buyevsky.

He is one of the numerous contingent of laymen who are in charge of the administration of the Russian Orthodox Church and is a well-known figure because he often looks after visiting delegations. I was not at all certain what sort of reception I would have. I had written to the Patriarch when I arrived in Moscow, asking whether he had received the Archbishop's letter, but I had never had an answer, though I waited over a month for one (being then very inexperienced in Russian ways). When I mentioned the Archbishop's letter and the one I had written, Mr. Buyevsky smiled, fished in a drawer and produced them both, saying he had been expecting me to call for some time.

From the way he talked, anxiously offering to help me in every way he could, I thought he would give me the master-key to all the inner-most doors of the Orthodox Church. He presented me with a book called *The Russian Orthodox Church, Organization, Situation, Activity* which, he said, would give me answers to all the questions I wanted to ask about the Church. 'If there are any points in it you want to discuss, you can ring me at any time to make an appointment and just come along here. I will give you a list of the most important churches which you ought to visit. If you want to be present when the Patriarch celebrates, telephone me and I will tell you where and when to go. When Metropolitan Nikolai returns to Moscow, which will be very soon, I will make an appointment for him to receive you.'

I told him that I was especially interested in theological education and wanted to learn as much as I could about the lives of students in seminaries, and he was most encouraging.

'How right you are to be interested in this—a most important aspect of the life of our Church. You must visit the seminary at Zagorsk, not as a tourist, but as a guest. Next time you can go there, let me know and I will ring the authorities to let them know you are coming. They will show you round and give you every possible help. Also if you plan to do any travelling, tell me the towns you intend to visit and I will contact church officials in each place. They will then receive you and give you an introduction to the life of their local church.'

This did indeed seem good fortune. I had been very depressed and homesick, and my meeting with Mr. Buyevsky injected a sense of purpose into the listless round of my everyday life. However, it was not long before I came to realize that many of the keys did not quite fit the locks. It turned out not to be at all simple to accomplish the projects I had in mind and to discover the inner workings of the Russian Orthodox Church.

I prefer not to believe that this was Mr. Buyevsky's fault. He may have been baulked by higher authority, by the bureaucratic frustrations endemic to all organizations of the Soviet Union, including the Church. It may well have been that there were persons senior to him who were anxious to keep me from the inner circles of the Church. It is difficult to tell.

There were times when it seemed that Mr. Buyevsky was the only person in the Orthodox Church with whom I could make fruitful contact. He was always charming and most obliging, and appeared genuinely pleased to see me. When I entered the room he would leap to his feet and pump my hand as if I were the first human being he had set eyes on for months. Behind his desk he looked like any other Russian official in his ill-cut blue suit with a fine white check, peering owl-like over the inevitable pair of steel-rimmed spectacles. When he smiled he showed a row of perfect steel teeth, which looked as if they had been fashioned out of the same lump of metal and by the same hand as the frames above. His hands moved constantly and the uninterrupted whine of his nasal tenor voice added to the impression of nervous bustle. His laugh was infectious and he exploited his sense of humour on a variety of topics. When a knock came to the door he would spring to his feet and reach it all in one movement. I have never seen a small man with such enormous strides and on the few occasions when I saw him walk in less confined spaces he seemed to roll up and down on each foot in turn, his head moving forward in a series of linked parabolas.

Every time I called, my personal health was the subject of prime concern, and Mr. Buyevsky seemed amazed and delighted that the rigours of minus 30° centigrade were not making me completely *hors de combat*. Then he would move on to the subject of the thesis on which I was working and ask me for an account of the work I had done on it since we last met. He seemed totally unable to understand that the present state of learning at the seminaries was of more interest to me than translating a piece of medieval Russian into modern, one of the tasks I was officially engaged on at the time.

Mr. Buyevsky, of course, represented the official voice of the Church, but it is to be heard most distinctly in the various publications which the Church has put out since 1943. *The Russian Orthodox Church, Organization, Situation, Activity* has appeared in several languages and the English version was on sale in some bookshops in England and America after its publication in 1958. It was compiled to mark the fortieth anniversary of the re-establishment of the Patriarchate in 1917.

I will not summarize its contents here, firstly because it is available in Western European languages and secondly because the historical section is as nauseating and unenlightening as most other Soviet works of history. It is not so much that it is guilty of patent untruths, but that the compressed account of forty years of Soviet rule is completely falsified by the omission of a whole series of important episodes; and of course there is no reference at all to the hundreds of thousands of loyal laymen, priests and bishops who gave their lives or their freedom for what they believed. There is no mention, for example, of Patriarch Tikhon's imprisonment and recantation, nor of the reason why the Patriarchal Throne fell vacant after his death, even though Sergius continued 'consolidating the relations between Church and State'.[1]

Anyone who reads this book knowing nothing about Russia would gain the impression that the situation of the Orthodox Church in the Soviet Union is utopian, indeed that it is the only Church in Christendom with enough places of worship, enough priests and seminaries, and that its members are working their way to salvation under the benign care of a sympathetic government.

Do we conclude from this that the Russian Church is so restricted that it has no voice of its own? I do not think so. Here is an extract from the *Journal of the Moscow Patriarchate*,[2] published while I was living in Moscow, which reports a resolution of the Patriarch and the Holy Synod:

'To regard as expelled from Holy Orders and deprived of all churchly intercourse the former Protopriest and former Professor of the Leningrad Theological Academy, Alexander Osipov,[3] the former Protopriest Paul Darmansky and the other servants of the Church, for having publicly blasphemed the name of God. "They went out from us but they were not of us" (1 John 2.19).

---

[1] English edition, p. 10.
[2] No. 2, 1960, p. 27.
[3] His case is discussed fully in the next chapter. He was on the teaching staff of the Leningrad Theological Academy before his dramatic act of apostasy. No other renegade priest has caused such a furore by his *volte-face*.

'To expel from the Church Yevgraf Duluman and the other former Orthodox laymen for having publicly blasphemed the name of God.'

The public excommunication of these renegade priests and laymen by what has been sometimes called the 'Church of Silence' may be one of the most significant events of recent years. Some people believe that Metropolitan Nikolai's influence lay behind this stand. It could conceivably have been one of the contributory factors to the renewed persecution of the Church which started around that time.

There is thus a positive official voice of the Russian Church which makes pronouncements on topics other than world peace, however intermittently it is heard. But the true quality of Orthodoxy in the U.S.S.R. today is to be found in the life of the believer, not in what the Church says.

THE PRIEST

I did not meet as many priests as I had intended, because they seem to be the most elusive individuals in the Soviet Union. I often used to stay behind at the end of a service, hoping to detain the celebrant on his way home, only to find that he had slipped out of a door behind the iconostasis. The chances of meeting a priest anywhere else were slender, and I sometimes wondered where they hid themselves once their official duties inside their church had ended. As a class, the priesthood seemed to have disappeared from the public scene entirely. I only once saw a priest in the street and rarely a figure who, from his flowing beard and mane of hair at the back of his neck, might have been one in mufti. Complete withdrawal from everyday life may be a tradition of Russian monastic clergy, but this tendency has certainly been aggravated by the persecution and anti-religious propaganda which have sealed their dreadful isolation.

Russia does indeed need men who are willing to give up everything in the world and dedicate themselves to a life of prayer. She also needs priests who can move freely among young people to show them that members of the clergy are not freaks—this is how students often thought of me when I alluded to my vocation—but are identified with their people in all aspects of their lives, cultural, political and material, as well as spiritual. In the present situation no such possibility exists. The State encourages the Church to appear as though it were living in the fifth century A.D.; it restricts the Church's concern to its own internal affairs and uses every available means of preventing the clergy from infiltrating into society.

Only very occasionally did I have any informative conversations with priests. When I did succeed in meeting one in his church, his part in the conversation ranged from the cold and distant or the frightened and monosyllabic (frequently) to the warm and curious (rarely). I was never invited to an Orthodox priest's home, nor did I come to know many well enough to be on familiar terms with them. At one stage I felt I was meeting so few priests that I complained to Mr. Buyevsky about it. He replied that it was due to my own lack of assiduity, but arranged for me to meet Father Mikhail Zernov (now Archbishop Kiprian, Patriarchal Exarch of Central Europe, living in East Berlin), whose church, dedicated to the Virgin Mary, 'the Consolation of All Sufferers', is one of the most important in Moscow. Situated behind the British Embassy in Bolshaya Ordynka Street, it is easy to find, though tourists who come to this area rarely go beyond the Tretyakov Gallery close by. This is a pity, because the choir is one of the finest in Moscow.

I had fixed a day carefully for my meeting with Father Mikhail—in the week preceding Holy Week, so that I could hear the Liturgy of St. John Chrysostom before our conversation. We talked for over an hour, and I have recorded only the most important points.

I asked him what his parish work consisted of, apart from the services in church. 'We do almost nothing outside the church building. We don't need to because, you see, for the Orthodox Christian, liturgy is life.'

'You pay no calls on your parishioners?'

'I personally go very rarely to visit a parishioner. A few calls are made, but these are by invitation only and I send my junior clergy to make them. My time, apart from when I am taking services, is taken up wholly by office work.'

'Where do you live, then?'

'I have a flat not far from the church, but most of the time I live out of town in my *dacha* [country house]. I can get there and back easily enough because I am very lucky in having a car.'

'You must be very well off. I don't know a single person in Russia who wouldn't envy you your car and your *dacha*—except my history tutor. He's a member of the Academy of Sciences and has both.'

'You must remember that your friends are young. When they have worked for a few years they, too, will be able to have these things. My stipend of seven hundred roubles[1] a month is a reward for a senior post.'

I was living very comfortably indeed on 150 new roubles a month, being able to save enough out of this for as many books and almost as much travelling as I wanted. A doctor or a schoolteacher begins by earning not much more than half this sum, a manual worker a third. It is not all that surprising that Father Mikhail voluntarily mentioned his stipend. One's income is a universal conversational topic in the U.S.S.R., and I have never known anyone have inhibitions about discussing it.

I asked Father Mikhail for his views about other Churches and found out that his experience was not confined to the Soviet Union. He had spent eighteen months in Jerusalem at the Russian Orthodox Mission (established there in 1847) and had also been in East Berlin for six months. 'You can see', he went on, 'that I have had some experience of Christian life in other countries.'

'Yes, that gives weight to your opinions on ecumenical matters.'

'I would feel better qualified to talk if I had been to your country and to America. Couldn't you manage to persuade someone in your Church to invite me to England?'

'I will do anything I can. . . . Do please tell me your opinions of other Churches.'

'Our relations with other Churches in the Soviet Union are quite normal, except with the Baptists. Saving your presence—and I know that your Church is in a middle position—I have always considered Protestantism the first step towards atheism.'

'Why do you pick out the Baptists? They seem to be doing good work among young people here.'

'I can say only that this is most unfortunate.' Showing surprising ignorance of the doctrine and practice of the Baptist Church, he went on: 'Re-baptism is a heresy, and because these people are so unfaithful to the ideals of the New Testament they are the only so-called Christians towards whom I feel mistrust. Roman Catholics tend to speak intransigently, but think much more tolerantly. We get on best with other Eastern Churches, especially the Georgian Orthodox and the Armenian. Our relations with these are of the essence of cordiality.'

'You know that your Church is considering applying for member-

---

[1] At the time the old rouble was still in use. It was worth one-tenth of the new heavy rouble which came into operation in January 1961. All the figures in this book are given in new roubles, the official exchange rate being £1 = 2·52 roubles.

ship of the World Council of Churches. Have you any experience of the work of this body, and what do you think of this possible move?'

'This is a purely personal opinion, but I feel that the World Council of Churches is rather wasting its time. You see, in the present situation with the world sharply divided into different camps, there can be no effective reunion of Christendom. There was a time when I felt that the World Council was merely trying to gang up the Churches of the West against the forces of Communism. Now I think they have relinquished this as hopeless and are turning to new tactics. I say this half in jest (*polushutya*), but I consider that with the world triumph of Communism, a united Christian Church will automatically come into being. There will be no more national barriers dividing people from people. Everyone will be able to travel where he likes, he will see how others live and worship, and so will very soon come to understand their traditions. Unity will come from below—it will not be imposed from above, as the World Council of Churches seeks to do. Also, under universal Communism men will have to work no more than four or five hours a day, so they will have time to reflect on eternal truths.'

Father Mikhail went on to admit that the honeymoon of which he spoke was a future probability rather than a present reality, for the marriage of Christianity and Communism had not yet taken place. 'Any courtship can be both stormy and passionate, but there are signs of an imminent betrothal.'

'I should have thought that hate had predominated over love in the relationship so far,' I chipped in.

'Oh no, you are losing your sense of proportion and have been listening to too much American propaganda. It's true that there have been difficulties. I myself studied at a time when there was a break in the instruction of the seminaries, so I was affiliated to a priest to learn my theology and church ritual. But at the same time the State has had a most beneficial effect on the existing organization of the Church. For instance, monasticism is clearly an outdated concept in the twentieth century. Before the Revolution it was sucking the life blood out of the country. Now all that has been changed, and we are very much the better off for it. Previously the monks tried, most unsuccessfully, to spread Christian morality throughout the country. They failed because they were themselves so infected by worldly standards. Now the Communist Party does what they were quite unable to do. It does it more efficiently because its coverage of the

76

country is so much more complete. It does it more effectively, too, because the sincerity of its members is obvious to everyone. No one can doubt that they have the very best interests of the people at heart, while the monks were notorious for their self-seeking and loose living. Even if most of the monasteries had not been closed down and their lands put to better use, they would now be dying a natural death.'

Father Mikhail bade me good-bye most cordially, presenting me with a signed photograph of himself in full regalia taken in Berlin. He also gave me an inch-square paper icon in a metal frame, one of the type sold to the faithful at exorbitant prices.

Already in 1948 one could find this same priest inviting all Christians to give their full support to the Party, for in no country does the Church 'enjoy such favourable conditions of existence as in the U.S.S.R.'.[1] His voice is now as loud as any of those in the Patriarchate who are saying in chorus that there is complete religious freedom in the Soviet Union.

A quite different sort of conversation was the one I had with Bishop Sergius Golubtsev of Novgorod. He has been banished from his ancient and magnificent cathedral in the Novgorod Kremlin to the other side of the River Volkhov, the *Torgovaya Storona* or 'Commercial Side'. I went to his church (*Nikola na Dvorishche*)[2] to attend the Saturday evening service; and when I found out that the celebrant was Bishop Sergius himself I decided to wait behind afterwards. I was delighted to have the opportunity of speaking to him. He was obviously pleased to meet a foreigner and talked to me in a much more relaxed way than any priest I had met in Moscow. This was one of the many indications of the difference in atmosphere between the capital and the provinces.

Bishop Sergius told me that he had been born in 1906 and so had been in the middle of his schooling at the Revolution. He had spent most of his early years at Zagorsk, where his father had been Professor of Ecclesiastical History at the Moscow Theological Academy. These surroundings had inspired him with a deep love of Christian art and architecture, so he qualified to become a restorer of old churches. After serving in the Red Army in the war he offered himself for ordination, returned to Zagorsk for his theological studies and remained there on the teaching staff until his consecration as Bishop of Novgorod in 1955. With such a large number of ancient churches

[1] *Journal of the Moscow Patriarchate*, No. 8, 1948, pp. 66–7.
[2] Now also closed as a place of worship.

in his see, many of which were damaged by the Germans during the war, his appointment was obviously a most appropriate one. It is gratifying to note, too, that he has kept it, despite the present policy of the Soviet Government of switching bishops from one diocese to another almost annually, so that they never have an opportunity to become popular with their people.

Bishop Sergius told me that he had met the Archbishop of York with his Anglican delegation when he came to Russia in 1956. 'I travelled to Leningrad to meet the party and to take part in the theological discussions. I was most impressed by their friendliness and their sympathy towards our Church.'

He asked me several questions about my interests and what I was doing in the U.S.S.R. I asked him about the situation in Novgorod, and he told me that they had four priests for the one church. We could do with more open churches, of course, but the Germans destroyed so much!' He went on to tell me that he had altogether forty churches operative in his diocese.

There was not a word in what he said which had a marked political slant. I did not press him with awkward questions because he was chatting to me in an extremely friendly way, leaning with one hand on the rail in front of the iconostasis and inclining his head towards me confidentially, and I did not want to do anything to cloud the atmosphere.

He soon warmed to his favourite topic, telling me that he did not claim to be a scholar at all, except in his own sphere of art history. He gave me a fascinating account of the Novgorod school of painting, its origins and its achievements, which could be studied only here in Novgorod and, to a lesser extent, at the Tretyakov Gallery in Moscow. He ended by telling me why he thought Theofan the Greek and Andrei Rublyov should be considered among the great Old Masters of painting and saying that it was a shame that so little attention should be paid to them by art historians outside the Soviet Union.

If I had been able to meet the Archbishop of Simferopol and the Crimea, Luke Voino-Yasenetsky, or the Metropolitan of Kuibyshev, Manuel Lemeshevsky, I would undoubtedly have received an even more positive impression of the senior Russian clergy. Archbishop Luke died in June 1961 at the age of eighty-one.[1] He was a remarkable man who in 1921 gave up the prospect of a brilliant career as a

[1] An account of his career is given in Struve, *Les Chrétiens en U.R.S.S.*, pp. 131–4.

surgeon to become ordained. He kept up his medical writing, and some of his books have become standard works on the subject. Although deported to Yeniseisk in the 'twenties, he continued to work as an evangelist, was appointed head of the Krasnoyarsk Military Hospital in 1941 and was later allowed to become Archbishop of the same place. In 1946 he received the Stalin Prize for his services to surgery, an unparalleled recognition in Soviet Russia of a churchman's secular activity.

Metropolitan Manuel is not a figure who plays a large part in the Russian Church's ecumenical endeavour. He was born in 1885,[1] studied theology in Leningrad and was deported to the Solovki Isles, the notorious monastery turned into a concentration camp, in February 1923, less than six months after his consecration as bishop. Of his last forty-one years about twenty-two have been spent in camps in four different spells. Each time he has returned to continue his witness to the faith in some way. Now an old but far from broken man, he has been at liberty for the last nine years, holding a position of responsibility commensurate with his sufferings for the Gospel. One hopes his safety will not be imperilled in the new wave of persecutions sweeping the Soviet Union. He is the type of man one would like ecumenical delegations to be able to meet.

Although I was not fortunate enough to have an audience with the Patriarch, Metropolitan Nikolai received me in April 1960—more than eight months after the arrival of the letter about me from the Archbishop of York. It was ironical that he who was normally at home to every visiting delegation, however short its stay, should have remained inaccessible to me for so long. It often seemed to me that the shorter one's stay in Russia, the easier it was to make valuable contacts—and not only in the ecclesiastical sphere. My theory is supported by the experience of an old friend of mine who came to Moscow on a teachers' exchange for three weeks over Christmas. I gave him the address of the Patriarchate so that he could find out more about the Russian Church. Next day he came back to my room with the news that Mr. Buyevsky had received him cordially and taken him straight to see the Metropolitan. He had achieved in a day what I had been unable to manage in four months. As a result of the long delay, when I at last received the invitation I looked forward to the interview as a grand climax of my stay. I thought of the Metropolitan as an enigma, and wished to try to resolve it.

[1] Struve, op. cit., pp. 136–8.

Metropolitan Nikolai had for many years been the most ambiguous figure in the Russian Church. He had been born Boris Yarushevich in 1892, studied theology in Petrograd and became a monk in 1914. He became Bishop of Peterhof at the age of thirty in 1922, but was soon exiled to Ust-Sysolsk for four years, before returning to his former diocese, where he remained until the outbreak of war. After it he embarked on a career as the main spokesman of the Church's peace campaign, supporting the Government in all its pronouncements on the subject for nearly twenty years.[1] Nevertheless, he was a great preacher, too, and in his sermons[2] there was almost nothing of the militant political tone he adopted elsewhere. The people I have met who heard him preach spoke universally of his deep humility and goodness. One old man told me that in a difficult age Nikolai had been one of the very few of the hierarchy to keep his faith untainted.

I prepared a whole list of questions to put to the Metropolitan, many of which I had been turning over in my mind for the last few months without being able to find an answer. This, I thought, was my final and best chance for enlightenment, though I should have already learnt that information of real value is picked up on the street corner, overheard by chance in a crowd, or comes in a casual conversation when least expected.

The list of questions I had prepared in my mind included such vital issues as religion among the young, evangelism and literature, finance, ecumenical relations (with especial reference to the Orthodox Church's attitude to other Christian denominations of the U.S.S.R.). He was undoubtedly a busy man at the time, but even so I had not expected that my reception would be so extremely brief. He treated me as if I were an official delegation from the Anglican Church, asking me about the state of health of some of its most prominent members, inquiring whether Dr. Hewlett Johnson were still alive, whether the Archbishop of Canterbury intended to retire and who was the Bishop of London. He went on to ask me a few personal questions about what I was doing in Russia, what my plans were for the future and whether I was married. When I told him I was to be ordained later in the year and that I was engaged to be married, he spent the rest of the time asking about my fiancée and requesting me to pass on his best wishes to her. All this was very pleasant, but of no practical use

---

[1] Kolarz, *Religion in the Soviet Union*, pp. 63–4.
[2] *Slova, Rechi, Poslaniya* (Sermons, Speeches, Pastoral Letters), four vols., Moscow, 1948–58.

An old woman brings greenery to church for Trinity

to me at all. In fact during the whole of the five minutes which I spent in his company, he did not give me the chance to ask a single question; when I thought he had finished the introductory part of the interview and was wondering which question to ask him first, he stood up to signify that the end of my time had come.

I was especially disappointed at not finding out from him anything of his Church's attitude to the World Council of Churches.[1] In December 1959 the General Secretary had led a high-powered delegation to Moscow which was cordially received by the Russian Church. I had guessed that this might be an important step towards the Church's joining and very much wanted to know what the outcome had been.

Six months after this interview Metropolitan Nikolai fell from grace, was put first under close supervision in his house, then in a hospital. He died mysteriously on 13th December 1961. Nikita Struve[2] has reconstructed the story of his last days and gives circumstantial evidence that he was murdered. Certainly many of the faithful believed he had been and raised a howl of protest during Rector Ruzhitsky's funeral oration at Zagorsk when he said the Metropolitan had died of overwork. His face in the repose of death gives away no secrets[3] and it is unlikely that the full story of his end will ever be told.

Many of my attempts to talk to priests were baulked by fear on their part. It was almost impossible to engage monks in conversation. Once, at the Monastery of the Caves in Kiev, just before the last monks were moved out, I saw a bent, bearded figure hurrying across one of the courtyards and set off after him. I caught up with him and tried to start a conversation. 'I am not allowed to speak to you,' he said in an agitated undertone, and scuttled off through a doorway.

Almost the same thing happened at Zagorsk on a subsequent visit I made to the Soviet Union. Not having any official introduction to the Theological Academy, I went to its grounds and stood outside the iron railing which fences them off from the rest of the monastery. Through the trees in the garden I saw a monk walking about twenty-five yards away. I called to him, he came over to me and stood in complete silence. At a loss to know what to say, I introduced myself by saying that I was a clergyman from England. He turned abruptly

---

[1] See Chapter VIII.
[2] *Les Chrétiens en U.R.S.S.*, pp. 271–4.
[3] Photograph facing p. 192.

on his heels and walked away without a word. Again I reflected on the difference between such an incident and the official receptions of churchmen who visit Russia as members of delegations.

THE CHRISTIAN IN THE PARISH

I first met Olga Sergeyevna on 7th November 1959, the forty-second anniversary of the October Revolution.[1] I had been in the Soviet Union just two months and felt extremely lonely during the general festivities celebrating an event for which I felt no particular gratitude.

To escape the elated crowds milling around in the centre of Moscow, I set out by tram for Kolomenskoye, a village in the outer suburbs to the south-east of the city. Here Tsar Alexei had built a magnificent wooden palace at the end of the seventeenth century. It has since disappeared, but there remains a fine park with a group of old churches overlooking the Moskva River. I walked the last part of the way which lay beyond the tram terminus. The unpaved roads at that time of the year were in a dreadful mess and by the time I arrived the mud had seeped in at the tops of my over-shoes because I had several times plunged ankle-deep into the morass.

Olga Sergeyevna was sitting on a seat in the park, a huddled and bent old woman of about sixty-five, a typical *babushka* enveloped in black from neck to foot. Her padded over-jacket filled her out into a shapeless huddle, while the only touch of colour about her whole person was the fawn shawl wrapped tightly over her head to protect all except her eyes and pale cheeks. She and a friend next to her, identically dressed, were deep in conversation as I came past, but she looked up and called to me with that spontaneous friendliness which is typical of the old peasant classes, but rapidly disappearing in the towns. She asked me to explain how I had got myself into such a mess. Then, without another word, she seized my hand and took me to a pool of melted snow close by. She stood me right in the middle of it, pulled up a clump of grass, went down on her knees, and started to scrub off the mud with her crude tool. I protested in embarrassment, but might have saved my breath. She answered not a word, while her friend looked on also in silence. After five minutes of this she asked me to step out of the pool, produced a clean

---

[1] The discrepancy in the dates is explained by the adoption of the New Style calendar in February 1918.

handkerchief from her pocket and wiped the over-shoes as dry as she could.

In the time I had so far spent in the Soviet Union I had met little in the way of kindness and consideration, except on the part of one or two isolated individuals at the University who wanted to be friendly. Nowhere had I experienced anything like this before. I was reminded, inevitably, of Christ when he washed the feet of his disciples and felt as utterly unworthy as they must have done. I did not know what to do to express my gratitude. Then I remembered the passion that all Soviet children have for foreign stamps, asked her if she had any grandchildren and produced some English stamps from my wallet. She said no, she was a widow and had had no children, but would love to have some stamps for her nephew. I gave a few to her and the rest to her friend. It was as if I had given them something for which they had been longing the whole of their lives.

We talked for a long time. They showed me first around the park and then over the churches, asking me finally if I would stay for the evening service in the one which was open for worship. This I readily agreed to do. I stood beside them for three-quarters of an hour before it started and for the further two hours and ten minutes of its length. I was amazed by their total absorption in the service; they were completely oblivious of me and of each other until the end. Afterwards I was preparing to say good-bye to them when Olga Sergeyevna invited me to come back to her home for supper. I accepted with delight, for it was the first time I had received an invitation into a Russian home.

After saying good-bye to her friend we walked for about two miles through a dark country lane to a modern suburb, where we turned into one of those huge, square, featureless blocks of flats which have sprung up in a broad belt the whole way round the city. We climbed to the fifth floor, walked along a broad, barren corridor, pervaded, like all Russian living-quarters, by the mingled smell of stale cabbage and cooking-fat, and turned off to her apartment. It consisted of a single room, just large enough for a high bed with an iron frame, draped with antique lace, a table and five upright chairs. The walls were totally bare, except for a mirror, a paper icon in one corner, and two dresses hanging on a rail. There was no cupboard space at all and she kept her crockery, pots and pans in a box under the bed, as I was soon to see. The only adornment was a green rubber-plant by the window, the indispensable adjunct of every Russian home.

She talked incessantly of how happy she was to have an unexpected guest. All the food she had she pressed me to eat, producing uncooked salted fish and milk from the space between the double glazing of the window, which I consumed with a hunk of dry bread. We had a glass, a mug, two knives, one plate and one teaspoon between us—all the utensils she possessed. It was the most overwhelming hospitality I had ever known. She punctuated every sentence of conversation with a further exhortation to eat and drink still more.

Olga Sergeyevna told me of herself and her circumstances. She considered herself well-off now, having three years before acquired a room of her own for the first time in her life. She had lost her husband in the war and since retiring from work because of ill-health a few years before, she had been on a pension of thirty-five roubles a month,[1] out of which she had to pay three for her accommodation. She said that it was difficult to exist on less than one rouble per day for food, but she tried to do so in order to have nine or ten roubles left over for church collections. Where could she find anything at all for clothes, which are such an appalling price?

The Church was her life. How delighted she was, she said, that since finishing her job she had been able to find so much more time for it. She could now devote her old age to sweeping, scrubbing and polishing the building which had been her only stay and support during all the difficult days she had lived through. Now she often spent as much as ten hours a day working there without even a break for a midday meal; and after her work she always stayed on for the evening service.

This told me more about the quality of Russian devotion than anything else I ever learnt. How could anyone stand[2] for two hours or more during worship at the end of a back-breaking day, completely oblivious of exhaustion and hunger, and then return home to a meal of dry bread and uncooked fish? For the first time I realized how spiritual food could satisfy physical hunger.

I met Olga Sergeyevna many times. She was always the same, treating me as if I was the only guest she had ever had in her life and bursting into tears of gratitude at any little gift I could find to bring her. Whenever I became too depressed at the prevalence of superstitious elements in popular Orthodox Christianity, I thought of her

---

[1] £14 approximately at the official exchange rate.
[2] There are never any seats in an Orthodox church.

and the tremendous fund of spiritual strength in modern Russia which she represents.

I have described her in detail rather than make generalizations about the class of older Christian which she typifies, but every time I witnessed the exaltation of a great festival service I thought to myself that this was the devotion of Olga Sergeyevna multiplied by five thousand.

It is a moving experience to attend the liturgy on any Sunday morning in a Moscow church, but when one is present in the depth of night for the first celebration of Christmas or Easter one realizes that a profounder devotion is still to be found in Russia than perhaps in any other country in the world.

Orthodox and Western Easters do not often coincide, but happily they did in 1960. In the middle of April winter had still not relaxed its icy grip. Never can Easter in Russia be taken as a symbol of the rebirth of nature, as it often is in England, for the spring comes too late.

My observance of Good Friday began with the long, rattling bus journey down from the University to the British Embassy. The Bishop of Fulham, who has charge of the Anglican chaplaincies in Northern and Central Europe, had flown to Moscow for the week-end and conducted a solemn, impressive meditation. After this I walked along the embankment and over the bridge to Red Square. The jostling crowd outside *GUM*, the huge department store which flanks one side of it, reminded me sharply that the State's timetable would take no notice of the great religious festival and that ordinary Muscovites had to be about their business. On the opposite side of Red Square straggled Russia's atheists in a long line, waiting to enter the Mausoleum and pay their respects to the embalmed bodies of Lenin and Stalin (still at that time in his place of honour).

'Is it nothing to you, all ye that pass by? Behold and see if there be any sorrow like unto my sorrow.' The words from *Lamentations* on which the Bishop had based his meditation were running through my mind. The people here seemed just as heedless, I mused, as the happy crowds at home who rush out to the football stadium or to the local beauty spots long before the dispersal of the darkness at the ninth hour. This year, however, I felt there could be no spring, no Resurrection.

But there was. Late the next evening a young Russian journalist took me to the Novodevichi Monastery. The scene there was unforgettable. Those fortress-like walls enclosed a seething mass of people, all trying, in the darkness, to push towards the one church where a service was to be held. There must have been twelve thousand there who could find no room inside. How many were old like Olga Sergeyevna? How many young? Who had come to worship, who just to observe what was going on? There was no time for such questions in this throng, nor even for accusations against the Soviet Government who had allowed so few places of worship to be open in this area of Moscow.

The long procession of priests, deacons and acolytes came outside, making its way with difficulty right round the church. Symbolically they were searching for the body of Christ in the tomb.

My friend somehow pushed us through the crowd to a side door through which foreigners and special visitors were admitted. I never much liked taking advantage of this privilege, but on this occasion I was particularly anxious not to miss what was going to happen inside. We reached the reserved space beside the iconostasis just before the procession regained the gloomy interior of the church. Not finding the body of Christ, the celebrant looked round him once more, and then proclaimed in a thundering voice, '*Khristos voskresi*' ('Christ is risen'). His assistant took up the cry, followed by the deacons, then one or two of the congregation, tentatively, as if hardly daring to believe the good news, then all at once a swelling chorus. Suddenly one or two people in front of us lit their candles and their faces were illuminated so that they stood out from the animated darkness like that of Christ on the Mount of Transfiguration. They passed the flame on to their neighbours before holding it motionless in front of themselves. Within a minute the whole church was ablaze with light, the place still resounded with the shout of joy. It was not the noise but the radiance on every one of five thousand faces which affected me so deeply. Seeing I had no candle, an old lady standing by the door through which I had entered came up to me, pressed one into my hand and said, '*Khristos voskresi*'.

'*Khristos voistinu voskresi*' ('Christ has risen indeed'), I replied in the correct conventional phrase—but there was nothing conventional about Easter that year. For the first time in the Soviet Union I felt sorry for Christians in England, whose Easter joy so often seems a pale counterfeit of the abundant spring around them.

The visitor who is in Russia for a short time only may not be fortunate enough to see the continuing vitality of the Orthodox

Church as it is exhibited at a major festival. However, to attend any 'working' church (as the Russians call those open for worship) for a whole Sunday morning will do more than prove the point. The church is always packed to the doors for the liturgy, which may be punctuated by as many as three sermons. The congregation takes a full and active part in the service. Often they do not have room to prostrate themselves properly so that their foreheads touch the ground in front of them, but they cross themselves ceaselessly and join in singing the Lord's Prayer, the Creed and other parts of the service, though they do not have any books to follow with. It can take nearly an hour at the end of the service for everyone to communicate. After the liturgy the church does not empty, but remains a hive of activity for most of the rest of the day. A number of priests remain on duty for baptisms, marriages and funerals, these ceremonies often going on at different altars simultaneously.

Just as in England, young couples who may not be practising Christians come to have their children baptized, possibly to placate grandparents, possibly from a lingering superstitious fear of the consequences if they don't. But many still come out of full conviction. This book does not deal to any great extent with statistics, but Nikita Struve estimates[1] that of the 160 million people in the Soviet Union whose roots go back to Orthodoxy, perhaps a hundred million have been baptized.

With marriages, the Government has tried to rival the emotional appeal of the church service by opening civil 'palaces' for this purpose in the main towns. Many young couples still refuse to be swayed and I know of several atheists who said they would not be married anywhere but in church, 'for the sake of my fiancée's parents'.

Most old people request a church funeral. On almost any Sunday you can see an open coffin lying in one corner of the church, with a pale waxen face surrounded by a cloud of expensive flowers. I have seen a procession following a bier coming out of church in which there was hardly a person over forty. The church's ministrations are still in full demand where they are available.

A direct result of the limitation of parochial activity[2] is the revival of Orthodox preaching. Before the Revolution this was hardly a feature of church life at all. Now sermons can be heard regularly in all churches. Many are devoted to the lives of saints (from which

[1] *Les Chrétiens en U.R.S.S.*, p. 154.
[2] See the law as stated on pp. 56–7. It is still rigorously applied.

practical conclusions about conduct today can be inferred, though they are usually left unexpressed). Others make frequent mention of the great Ecumenical Councils of the Church and state how closely Orthodox worship and life fulfil their decrees. Some expound the benefits to be drawn from the veneration of icons, and at least two of the sermons I heard on these lines were sharply and explicitly anti-Protestant. Not many explain the scriptures, and those which do tend to do so in a literalistic and (in view of the nature of current anti-religious propaganda) unhelpful way. More interesting, undoubtedly, are the informal 'conversations' which often take place at the back of the church after service on Saturday evenings. The name, however, is misleading. They are in no sense a dialogue between the priest and his people, but the parishioners send in written questions which the priest formally answers. Whether the questions sent in deal with any topics of burning concern one cannot tell, but certainly the preacher chooses only topics which would not place him in a difficult situation with the Communist authorities.

Lest anyone should still be tempted to underestimate the hold that Orthodox Christianity has over Russia, even over those who claim to have lost their faith, let me quote from *Men of our Division*, a book of military memoirs by A. L. Bankwitzer, printed by the publishing house of the Ministry of Defence in Moscow, 1962. The writer is describing his feelings in Novgorod Cathedral, as he and his fellow-soldiers prepare for a last-ditch defence of the city against the Germans:

'Stone steps and dark winding passages led up to the church above. I glanced at my watch; it was just twelve o'clock.

'The gold of the icons shed a strange feeling of spiritual peace in the half-light. The air still seemed to be filled with the pungent scent of incense and the perfume of wax candles. Will they not burn again, and also the oil-lamps in front of the icons? Will not the holy door leading to the innermost sanctuary open and a tall bearded priest call in Slavonic, "O Lord, we listen to Thee"?

'Outside the church walls death rages. Here in the semi-darkness is colour and life. High up in the vaulted dome the gentle face of the God-man looks down on us. His eyes seem to speak as if they were alive, expressing sorrow and anger, reproach and questioning, shame and unutterable suffering.

'I moved aside, but the eyes still followed me. I moved again—but they were still fixed upon me.

'What power lies in the art which painted those colours, that face, those eyes.

'Suddenly a bright light streamed into the church through two of the upper windows, but without piercing the darkness between the stone pillars and the low arches. All the gold in the holy pictures seemed to come alive and shone with a mysterious inner light, like myriads of burning candles. The walls tottered, there was a crash like thunder, and something fell from the roof.

'I stooped and picked up a piece of the priceless fresco which had broken away through the impact of a bomb. How its colours gleamed —painted nine centuries ago by a great genius.

'We left the cathedral meditatively—never to return.'[1]

FINANCE

The financial situation of the Russian Orthodox Church is a most intriguing problem and not enough data are available to elucidate it.

I was constantly amazed at the sacrificial generosity of all church-goers. Two or three times during the liturgy open baskets are passed round the church; each time they are returned brimming over with both coins and bank-notes. I have seen an old woman dressed in rags put in a three-rouble note and still find some kopecks to add when the basket was presented to her again later in the service. I calculated that, including the money they spend on candles, many of these women must give as much as a quarter, some perhaps even more, of their total incomes to the Church. Taken over the whole country, this represents a vast source of income for the Church and explains why until recently priests were so rich. I quote a perspicacious summary of the situation made by Francis House, an Anglican priest who has visited the Soviet Union several times:

'I once asked a Russion bishop what was his greatest problem. He replied unexpectedly: "We have too much money". Under the Soviet Law the money received in collections and from the sale of candles can be spent on only two things: the maintenance of church buildings and the requirements of the liturgy, and the salaries of the clergy. It may not be spent on any form of charitable work, on education (except for theological seminaries) or on publications (except for very limited editions of Bibles and service books). Consequently, the

---

[1] Translation taken from *Current Developments in the Eastern European Churches*, No. 1 (18), February 1963, pp. 27–8.

priests of a city church may be paid four hundred to six hundred roubles a month,[1] earnings equivalent to those of university lecturers and Stakhanovite workers. . . . People are beginning to say: the clergy live on the fat of the land! Many suspect that the motives for allowing the Church to accumulate so much money may well be Machiavellian. Certainly we can see that the present financial position of the Church creates many pastoral problems and temptations.'[2]

This article had a most interesting sequel. It was quoted (in a totally misleading way, leaving out the author's criticism of the Government for not allowing the Church to use its money as it thinks best) in the atheist periodical, *Nauka i Religia* (Science and Religion).[3] The author commented:

'Mr. House has divulged a "secret" which Russian bishops only tell foreigners and never disclose to their own church members: the Church has such a surplus of money that it doesn't know what to do with it. And, as the Church itself teaches, where there is a lot of money, the devil is always at work. It is a temptation to the "Holy Fathers" to commit all kinds of sins; in other words, the over-generous gifts of the church members may be pleasing to God, but it is really the devil who uses them. That is the only construction that can be put on the facts divulged by the Orthodox Bishop to the English clergyman.'

The article goes on to make further comments about the Church's desire to grab as much money as it can. It alleges that the fees for baptisms and weddings are too high and quotes a letter from a church-goer:

'. . . A short service of thanksgiving or intercession in the cemetery costs two and a half roubles, but if the priest has to walk twenty-five steps to the grave he receives five roubles. In other words, he receives ten kopecks for every step he takes. If the fee is too high, the church-goer has only two choices: either to refuse or to pay. But if he refuses he is committing a sin, so he has to pay.'

It is obvious to any observer that the Church nets vast profits from the sale of candles. Most of the ones I saw on sale were priced at about fifty kopecks (just under four shillings) each, though the amount varies according to the size of the candle. The article alleges that:

'The cost of producing a candle which is sold for between thirty

---

[1] Or more—cf., p. 75.
[2] 'The Witness of the Russian Church', *Theology*, June 1960, pp. 221–6.
[3] September 1960.

kopecks and a rouble is only from 0.6 to 2.8 kopecks. In the little town of Roslavl last year candles for which the Church had paid less than five hundred roubles were sold for the total amount of thirteen thousand roubles.'[1]

The article ends with various accusations about the moral laxity of the clergy and their profiteering motives, but a valid point has, I believe, been made. The figures in the article may not seem so exaggerated when one considers that every worshipper buys a candle for a festival or a saint's day and that they are purchased on many other occasions, too. Often there is no room to burn the candle before an icon, as all the holders in the stand have already been filled. In this case the candle is usually given back and resold. It is a pity that the Church allows practices like this to continue. Francis House is possibly right when he says that the State may have had a great interest in allowing the Church to accumulate so much money, but the policy since 1960 has again been to attempt to tax the Church out of existence.

I have made many inquiries about the fees the Church charges for baptisms, weddings and funerals. The answers I have received vary considerably, but the discrepancies may be partially explained by the fact that for any of these ceremonies it is obligatory to buy candles and the number of these may vary from church to church. Baptisms (free in England) cost, according to my sources, between twenty kopecks and two and a half roubles. Marriages are sixteen or seventeen roubles (most church weddings with music in England cost more), while funerals cost from ten to twenty roubles. I have been told that for the latter there can be a considerable reduction for the poor.

It is undeniable that the possibility of gain presents a temptation to the clergy. There could be no other reason for a statement in a type-written textbook on preaching by Archpriest Alexander Vetelev which is used at the Leningrad Theological Academy:

'A negative quality often found in the preacher is a desire for gain, which takes the spirit prisoner and damages it. It is very depressing and serious to hear a priest say in the church: "This is not enough; you must pay something more". A family in mourning is full of sorrow and thinks, of course, that the priest feels deep sorrow too. Then they hear, "This is not enough". So, at the graveside, they bury

[1] A summary of this article is found in *Current Developments in the Eastern European Churches*, No. 4 (8), November 1960, pp. 19–22.

not only the dead in the grave, but also their belief in the priest, in the Church and in God.'[1]

Students of Moscow University with whom I discussed this subject were very bitter because ordinands in the theological seminaries at that time received a higher grant than even postgraduates in secular institutions—one hundred roubles a month during their first year at the seminary and increasing annually, compared with twenty-seven for first-year students at Moscow University, with annual increments up to eighty for a postgraduate. Whether this tempted anyone into the ranks of the clergy for wholly the wrong reasons, or even to study in affluence for a few years at a seminary without any intention of becoming ordained, is an impossible question to answer, but that it could be asked at all shows the danger of the situation as it was. Now all this has changed. In the new wave of persecution heavy taxes have been imposed on all clerical incomes and there are rumours that priests are again in penury. In the seminaries the stipend has dropped to twenty roubles per month for first-year students, rising to twenty-six for those in the academies. Though this is a very sharp drop indeed, it is not an impossible sum to live on (provided the students do not have to buy clothes for themselves while they are seminarists), because in addition full board is provided free of charge.

THEOLOGICAL TRAINING

Between 1923 and 1944 there was no formal theological education in the Soviet Union at all, and bishops were forced to ordain untrained men—if any could be found who were willing—to fill the gaps in the parishes where men had died or been forcibly removed. As a result of Patriarch Sergius's concordat with Stalin, theological education was put on its feet again and eight seminaries were opened:[2] at Zagorsk (near Moscow), Leningrad, Kiev, Odessa, Saratov, Stavropol, Lutsk (in the former Polish province of Volhynia) and Zhirovitsy (called the Minsk Seminary). The first two of these contain theological academies in the same building.

Figures for the total number of students under training have never been made available. If there were ever enough to provide with

---

[1] A. Johansen, *Theological Study in the Russian and Bulgarian Orthodox Churches under Communist Rule*, Faith Press, London, 1963, p. 27 (the author is here summarizing, not quoting, his source).
[2] *The Russian Orthodox Church, Organization, Situation, Activity*, English ed., pp. 103–18.

priests all the areas which had been deprived of them by the beginning of the Second World War, now there are certainly not enough men qualifying each year to make good the gaps which occur in the parishes. The seminaries at Kiev, Saratov, Stavropol and Zhirovitsy have been forcibly closed down by the Soviet Government since 1960, while that at Lutsk has had no intake of students for the last two years, which certainly means it will close when the last students now resident have received their diplomas. The seminary at Odessa seems to have escaped a similar fate by promptly removing itself into the suburbs when its centrally situated buildings were requisitioned. One even fears for the safety of the Moscow Theological Academy because so few foreign visitors have been able to visit it recently.

The whole course of study at a seminary takes five years and includes a very thorough basic theological training, with compulsory subjects ranging from the Bible (text and history), moral and dogmatic theology, comparative religion, to pastoralia, homiletics, church order, liturgy, church history, Soviet constitution, singing, Old Church Slavonic, Greek, Latin and one modern language.

Students who attain a sufficient standard at the seminary may enrol for a further four years at one of the academies. Here an even wider range of subjects is embraced and the fourth year is spent on a thesis, which, if accepted, confers the degree of *Kandidat*. This gives one the right to submit a thesis for the 'Master of Theology' degree.

I was very anxious to find out what it was like inside the seminaries and to get to know some of the students, but I was never given permission to attend any of the lectures and I had to make all my own contacts.

I made my first visit to the Moscow Theological Academy at Zagorsk early in October 1959, before I had been to the Patriarchate, because I did not want any special plans laid on for my reception.

Although Zagorsk is outside the forty-kilometre radius, it is very easy to get to from the capital. There is a frequent suburban train service to it from the Kazansky station and the cost of a return ticket is only one rouble.

To travel in local trains and buses is one of the best ways to get to know Russia, as most other countries, and one often finds the people friendly and eager to talk in order to pass the time. The different classes on trains in this classless society are pithily distinguished from each other by the terms 'hard', 'soft' and 'international'; the suburban trains are strictly proletarian and very hard indeed. Most of the peasant women who had bundled into this one looked as if they were on their way home after taking their livestock to market. Others, with oddly shaped bundles of objects tied together in sacks, were probably pilgrims bringing a few of their scanty worldly possessions with them on a journey to the holy shrine. As the train started many of the people in my carriage crossed themselves, which always used to be the custom at the beginning of a journey. The coach was not divided into compartments and the double glazing of the windows soon made the atmosphere thicken into a desperate stuffiness.

This was the first time since my arrival that I had been outside the city. The suburban landscape gave the impression of a civilization arising from the primeval slime. Everywhere were vast new blocks of flats in various stages of completion, all the same in their buff colour and box-like design. They looked like volcanic islands in a sea of mud.

Soon, however, this gave way to a more pleasant prospect of country villages, which, as in the surrounds of any other great city, are rapidly being devoured by the expanding urban development. These were the first individual houses I had seen, full of character compared with the uniformity of the new buildings. They appeared in clusters against the soft background of the silver birch trees. They had once been painted a variety of bright colours and enough paint still clung to them to make them stand out like a patchwork relief. The ones in the foreground revealed wood carving of intricate design around the doors and windows, a relic of the craftsmanship of former days. 'They are pleasanter to look at than to live in,' a young Russian told me and he was undoubtedly right, but one can't help feeling some regret at the passing of the old way of life.

After a few miles of alternating forest and village, I caught my first unforgettable glimpse of the monastery: a multi-coloured constellation of towers and domes that seemed chiselled out of air and suspended above the tree-tops. The baroque pink bell-tower tapering elegantly towards the golden cross on top surmounted the group. Slightly below was a cluster of domes, swelling like sails in the wind. There were golden ones of different sizes and a group of huge blue ones spangled with gold stars. As we drew nearer, the fortified outer wall, broken by squat hexagonal towers, appeared and seemed to clasp the ensemble tightly within its embrace. If there is any truth in the old legend that this type of Russian architecture was evolved by late-medieval craftsmen to relieve the monotony of the rolling plain (of which European Russia consists), then there is no place which better illustrates the success of the enterprise than St. Sergius's Monastery at Zagorsk.

My meditation was sharply interrupted by the fierce jolt of the train against the buffers. I left the station, and wading through a mile-long river of ankle-deep mud, which may, in the height of summer or the depth of winter, have been a roadway, I reached the foot of the mound on which the monastery stands; at this point my path joined the asphalted highway from Moscow.

An old woman was feeding a flock of pigeons in the cobbled square outside the main entrance. Inside, the massive sixteenth-century Uspensky Cathedral with its huge blue, ungainly domes dominates the central area, dwarfing the infinitely finer craftsmanship of the Troitsky Cathedral, built 150 years earlier. A single helmet of gold surmounts this white and graceful building. Entering its sculptured portal, which tapers upwards to a delicate point, I was met by a blanket of darkness and the smell of incense. When my eyes grew accustomed to the lack of light, I could see figures sprawling on the seats which line the walls of the ante-chapel. Some of them were motionless and nearly prostrate, as if they had been hewn out of the stone itself. An old monk was selling candles at the door. Inside the church itself was a sight of subdued splendour. Beyond the huge gold candelabrum, in a corner to the right of the iconostasis, was the tomb of St. Sergius himself. Here from five o'clock in the morning until midnight, seven days a week, a continual chant is raised in honour of the saint. One monk replaces another to lead the litany which passes antiphonally from him to the huddle of old folk who surround him. One feels as if one were participating in a ritual which time has sanctified and crystallized into an immutable act, as if the course of Russian history had never been disturbed. But in 1921 the Saint's ashes were seized, the monks were evicted, the finest works of art confiscated for housing in State art galleries, and a museum of atheism opened in part of the premises, while the rest were taken over by squatters who rapidly turned the living-quarters into slums.

The bells pealed forth at Easter, 1946, for the first time in over twenty years to mark the new concessions which the Church had gained. A few monks reappeared (their number still seems to be very small); the relics of the Saint were returned to their traditional place of rest; the gap in the iconostasis where Rublyov's icon of the Trinity had been was filled by a copy of the original; the label 'of Atheism' was removed from the name of the museum, though many of the exhibits demonstrating the history of monasticism still bear an anti-religious bias. No one, even now, will say where the relics of the Saint were kept after they were confiscated.

So now the outward signs of this great persecution are dimmed and the casual visitor will be impressed by the freedom which has been accorded to the Russian Church in this place—which is just what the Government wishes. An attentive person, however, can still discern the marks of the past. In the museum the descriptive labels (not translated into any foreign language) still carry a tone of sharp aggression against the Church. The residential quarters are in a state of squalor, with families who have nothing to do with the monastery swarming in them. These buildings have not been touched by a lick of paint since the monks were evacuated from them after the Revolution.

The seminary occupies the whole of one side of the monastery, an attractive, long classical building with a garden in front. No one is allowed in without an introduction, except for evensong in the chapel. Luckily I already knew about this and when I went into the chapel I experienced for the first time the purely aesthetic pleasure which is undeniably an essential part of Orthodox worship. I have no doubt that a strong reason for the Government's failure to stamp out church attendance is that they have failed to provide an even remotely comparable ceremonial to take its place; and so the Church festivals continue to be eagerly awaited in lives of otherwise extreme drabness.

Two choirs sang antiphonally, separated by the width of the chapel. One consisted of monks and the other of students. The crisp attack and perfect balance of the two sides held one in a constant state of tension, as if praise was being offered to God now from one end of the earth, now from the other, and then from the whole of creation exploding in joy at its vision of the Divinity. Those who worshipped in St. Mark's, Venice, when the Gabrielis were in their heyday, must have experienced something like this. Not, of course, that the style of Orthodox chanting has anything in common with music of the Renaissance. Its melodies are earlier, though now, except in the churches of the Old Believers, they are used only in modified form to suit nineteenth-century harmonizations. These harmonizations, far from ruining the old melodies as so often happened with nineteenth-century treatment of folk tunes, seem to add to their depth and expressiveness, giving full freedom to the range and tone of the voices. These two choirs seemed to have almost the compass of an

Students at the Moscow Theological Academy (Zagorsk) are being taught to paint in the traditional style

organ. Their tone, too, was very like the tone of an organ in all registers, perhaps even surpassing it in the richness of the bass and certainly doing so in the wonderful balance between every part and in the exquisitely subtle phrasing and gradations of tone in each individual line. If anything, the students had slightly more flexibility than their seniors, and their singing conveyed an impression of indescribable freshness.

During the course of the service there was a short sermon by one of the students. He seemed rather unnerved by the occasion and spoke falteringly. His subject was whether or not there is literal truth in the biblical account of Elijah's calling down fire from heaven, and he concluded that it could as easily happen today as in the days of Ahab, if the belief of any individual were strong enough.

I stayed until the end of the service before returning by train to Moscow.

For my second visit to Zagorsk Mr. Buyevsky asked me to let him know in good time when I wanted to go, so that he could telephone the authorities there and let them know about my coming. I told him I would go on the next free day I had, a Saturday in mid-November. He promised to make the arrangements.

The day I had chosen was superb. Although the winter had already set in, the temperature was about minus 10° centigrade. This is the ideal for a Russian winter day—not warm enough to make the snow soft and unpleasant, nor cold enough to penetrate one's outer layer of protective clothing, even in a long spell out of doors. When I arrived at Zagorsk the sky was a brilliant sapphire blue, unbroken by a single wisp of cloud. There was no wind and underfoot six inches of clean snow crackled and compressed gently as my boots broke through its frozen upper crust.

The day had worked a transformation at the monastery. The scars of slum-dwelling seemed to have been healed; the snow had covered and frozen solid the oozing muddy pathways, and the rubbish tips and piles of broken masonry were concealed by a blanket of dazzling whiteness. The silhouettes of the gold and blue domes, now edged with frosty incrustations, added a touch of fairyland to the scene. As I entered the massive gateway, I felt something of the elation which Russian pilgrims must feel at their journey's end.

This mood did not persist, however. As there was no one at the office inside the main gate, I walked straight into the private garden of the Theological Academy and rang the bell at the door. There was no reply. I rang again and a man, poorly dressed in *valenki* (felt boots) and overalls, evidently a servant, came to the door. I told him what I wanted and that Mr. Buyevsky had sent me. He disappeared and returned after a few minutes with a monk at his side. The latter asked me who I was, so I gave him a detailed account of why I had come and of the arrangements which Mr. Buyevsky had promised to make.

'Nothing is known of you here, so we can do nothing to help you.'

'I shall be bitterly disappointed', I said, 'if my journey has been for nothing. I can't understand what has happened.'

'I do not have the authority to let you in. I suggest you go and see Father Bartholomew at the office first so that you can be shown round the churches. Then come back here in about an hour and ask whether anyone is free to see you.'

I assumed that this was a convenient way of gaining time during which to hold various consultations about the advisability of letting me in. They may even have wanted to check on me by ringing Mr. Buyevsky. I had no alternative but to agree to their suggestion.

When I returned to the Academy the *Inspector* (senior tutor) was waiting to greet me. He invited me in warmly and presented me with a fine collection of photographs illustrating the monastery buildings and the life of the students.[1] He took me to his study where he introduced me to a layman who, he said, would show me round. The *Inspector* asked me what I wanted to do and how long I would like to stay. I replied that I had the whole day at my disposal and would like to spend it seeing the various types of activity which are carried on in the Academy and meeting the students. If he was agreeable, I said, I would stay on to attend the evening service before returning to Moscow. 'I am glad to agree to all this,' he replied. I was delighted, and felt that at last I had the chance of obtaining some really valuable information about the Russian Church. The layman asked me to accompany him and we left the room together.

Another layman—both were on the teaching staff—joined us and they took me first to the museums of the Academy, which housed a magnificent collection of early Russian Christian art—icons, chased ritual vessels, embroidered vestments and various archaeological finds. They readily answered many questions which I put to them about the significance and history of these objects.

We moved into the assembly hall and I was shaken to see, in the

[1] See photograph facing p. 96.

most prominent position, framed by the arch which divides off the speaker's table from the body of the hall, a portrait of Lenin. The high priest of the atheists was casting the same glance of benign menace on this religious establishment as he was on countless thousands of secular assembly halls throughout the U.S.S.R. I had hoped, in this sanctuary at least, to be liberated from the omnipresent stare of those eyes which seem to hunt one down relentlessly wherever one goes. Later, when I had time to study the wad of photographs which I had been given, I noticed that in the one showing the assembly hall the place of honour was occupied by a different portrait. The features are indistinct, but the attire is clearly that of a Patriarch. I wondered whether there was any significance in the change.

Next I was taken to the chapel, quite empty of students, like all the other rooms I had been in. After looking round it I asked where the students were. 'They are all at lectures,' replied one of my guides. For all I had seen of them they might have been away on vacation.

'Could I go to a lecture to see what it is like?' I asked.

'Unfortunately this isn't possible. You would be disturbing the academic work of the institution.'

I wondered how they would fill my time between then (midday) and lunch, which I expected to be about the usual Russian time of three o'clock. I was not left in doubt for long. They led me down a corridor and opened a door. We were back in the cloakroom where I had left my coat and hat. One lecturer lifted them off the peg and handed them to me, while the other picked up my over-shoes. I thought at first that we were going to cross a courtyard to one of the other buildings, but they took me to the front door, opened it for me and said 'Good-bye'. This was the end of my visit, its conclusion marked in no uncertain way. I searched for some excuse which would permit me to remain longer inside the building. I asked if I could see the library, because I was very interested in theological books.

'Today you can't. It's half-day and it will be closed.'

With the day less than half gone I found myself outside alone in the snow. There was nothing more I could do. I went back to Moscow.

Next day I rang Mr. Buyevsky. He said he was sorry about what had happened and that next time I wanted to go he would ensure that the arrangements were properly made. By this time I had put in a written application to attend lectures at the seminary and decided to wait until it was granted. However, although I kept inquiring about it, I did not receive permission until I was on the point of leaving on a tour which was to occupy my last month in the Soviet Union. Thus I never discovered what lay beneath the magnificent façade of the Church's great show-place, nor was I able to see for myself whether there were in fact three hundred students there, as the Church authorities claimed. Most frustrating of all, I was not able to make any contact with the students themselves.

I had high hopes of making good this setback by visiting the seminaries in Leningrad and Odessa. Before I left Moscow for Leningrad, Mr. Buyevsky had promised to inform the Theological Academy of my visit and had given me the name of Professor Pariisky, the *Inspector*, together with his telephone number. I rang him on my first morning and explained who I was. He told me, somewhat abruptly, that he had never heard of me. I asked if I could come and see him, so that I could explain about myself in a little more detail. He said that I was on no account to come unless I had special business there. I went, nevertheless.

The Seminary is situated in the grounds of the former Alexander Nevsky Monastery, which is now completely derelict except for a small part occupied by the students of the Academy and the one large church reopened for worship in 1957. The Academy itself is housed in a most unprepossessing building beside a filthy stagnant canal and opposite a timber yard.

I knocked at the front door. A janitor answered it and asked me to wait in the hall while he went to look for Professor Pariisky. A short fat man with very wide baggy trousers appeared. He had grey hair and gold-rimmed spectacles (a sign of affluence), and he looked about sixty. He greeted me brusquely:

'I am Professor Pariisky, *Inspector* of this Academy. Who are you?'

'I am a British student studying in Moscow and I have been sent here by . . .'

'Let me see your identity documents.'

I showed him my passport[1] and university pass. His face warmed to a cold smile: 'This is an academic institution. We can't have anyone wandering in to disturb us unless he has official business.' It appeared that they had had absolutely no information about me from the Patriarchate, and without any form of introduction from Moscow, I could not make out a very convincing case for myself. I thought for

[1] All Soviet citizens have to carry an identity document, called a 'passport'. I was issued with a special one for foreigners and had to have it with me all the time.

a few moments that I would not be able to stay to look around and that the situation would be worse than it had been at Zagorsk.

'What do you want to see?' asked Professor Pariisky. 'We are just like any other place of learning.' I stood my ground and said (with something less than truth) that my main aim in visiting Russia was to find out about theological education. If I could not be admitted here, one of the two academies in Russia, I would be failing in my mission.

Gradually he softened and said that I could see around the buildings, though this was not before he had commented unfavourably on the Anglican Church, telling me how it was divided against itself, while his Church was one. I was put on my mettle by this, and my refutation of what he said seemed to please him and make him wish to continue talking to me.

Professor Pariisky asked about my work at Moscow University. When I told him that I was studying the conversion of Russia to Christianity and working on old texts, he called the lecturer on Byzantine studies, who took me to his room for a discussion. Professor Pariisky came too. I said that I was particularly interested in Metropolitan Ilarion's role in eleventh-century church history and his relations with the Greeks, and Professor Pariisky interrupted to tell me that there was no room for a thesis on the subject, as these questions had long ago been decided by Russian scholars. I replied that as there was almost no material on the subject in English, a thesis was from my point of view amply justified. The lecturer was far more pleasant and when we had discussed the subject for a little while, he told me that he, personally, would be very interested to read what I had to say.

Both of them then conducted me on a tour of the buildings. It took us a long time to look over the chapel because of the number of times my guides stopped to cross themselves before various icons. Then we saw the dining-hall, where I was told that the lives of the saints are read during meals. Finally we came to the library. Here repairs were going on and large sections of it were shrouded in dust covers. However, I found the section where foreign books are kept, and in this bookcase there was a shelf and a half of English publications. Like the German books below, they were mainly devoted to doctrine and church history, but I was impressed to see that they included some recent titles, such as Canon J. N. D. Kelly's *Early Christian Doctrines*, which had not been published more than eighteen months previously.

At the end of the shelf stood the *Oxford Dictionary of the Christian Church*. I looked inside and saw that it had been presented by the delegation of Anglican monks who had visited the U.S.S.R. in May 1958.

I was told that the number of students in the Seminary and Academy combined was now 180, not counting the external students who do a correspondence course. Professor Pariisky confirmed what I already knew—that the institution had been closed from 1919 to 1946. I asked him what he had been doing during those years, but all he said was, 'I was teaching elsewhere.'

By this time I had finished the tour and was now politely shown out. They said, as they had done at Zagorsk, that it would not be possible for me to disturb the academic programme by attending a lecture. Professor Pariisky called over two students who were standing near the entrance and asked them to show me the way back to the trolley. They seemed pleased to do this but our conversation was confined to the most general topics, and they answered all my questions in conventional phrases.

On a more recent visit to Leningrad I went to the Academy on two successive days. The first time I waited for hours outside by the canal, watching men sawing timber in the yard on the opposite side of it and waiting for a chance to talk to some of the students. Only one came out. He was in his first year, he told me, but when I said I was English he showed no further inclination to continue the conversation.

I went there again the next day and simply walked in. I hoped to mingle with the students without being observed. I engaged some of them in conversation, but they soon had to break it off because the bell sounded for chapel. They told me that now the number of students was about 160, including several from abroad. I stayed for the whole service, hoping to find others to talk to afterwards. However, the fifty or sixty students who had been present, all standing at the front to sing in the choir, had walked out in pairs straight to the dining-hall. Here they sang a grace and the doors were closed on them.

It was in Odessa that I made my best contacts with theological students. By June 1960 I had come to realize that it was quite useless trying to make official arrangements for a visit to a seminary. My tactics of simply going in unannounced paid far higher dividends than my former method of attempting to arrange to be received formally and taken to lectures.

I found the Odessa Seminary without difficulty and went straight inside to the chapel. It was very small and there were many *babushki* as well as a handful of students attending the service which was in progress. Some seminarists were singing in the choir at the front, while one or two were standing in the crowd near the back. I asked one of them a question about the service. As soon as he recognized me as a foreigner he invited me to go out for a walk with him.

From the first Oleg showed himself not only willing to talk about any subject I liked to mention, but avid to find out anything he could about the Church in other countries. We sauntered along talking in undertones for several hours. It was one of the most valuable and encouraging discussions I ever had about the Orthodox Church. We covered a wide variety of subjects, so I must summarize what seemed to me the most important.

Oleg was in his third year at the Seminary and came from a Christian family, though this was by no means the rule among the students there. He thought that the majority of his fellow-students were converts to the Christian faith from the ranks of the Komsomol (the Young Communist League, to which all secular students are virtually forced to belong). He said that he himself had frequently been in trouble with this organization and that they had brought great pressure to bear on him before they had finally acquiesced in his studying for ordination. After this the Komsomol had kept a specially close watch on his best friend who had been inseparable from him at school. On one occasion after the friend had been to church, three senior members of the local Komsomol branch accosted him in the street, beat him until he was down and then kicked him into the gutter. 'From that day my friend knew his vocation,' said Oleg. 'Now he is studying at the Lutsk Seminary.'

He seemed so willing to talk openly that I decided to broach the subject of Communism. He maintained quite categorically that no reconciliation is possible between Christianity and Marxism. I mentioned that I had met some priests whose Christianity was tainted by Communism. 'Oh, they must be absolutely the exception,' said Oleg. 'I don't know anyone myself who tries to equate Christianity with the practice of Communism in the Soviet Union. We often hear about your Hewlett Johnson, of course, but he's wrong, quite wrong. Marxist atheism is totally opposed to everything that Christianity stands for and Hewlett Johnson simply doesn't understand the real situation here.'

103

'Do you have lectures about the two systems of thought at the Seminary, then?' I asked.

'We have a complete grounding in the Christian faith, but we are all desperately short of material which sets out the Christian answer to Communism. Have you any books about it?'

'I have one, but I left it in Moscow. It's in English, so I don't suppose it would be any use to you.'

'Yes it would. I realize we shall never have anything in Russian about this, so I am working hard at my foreign languages. My English isn't good, but if you can send this book to me I shall work at it word by word in order to understand it. We have so little to combat materialism with that the slightest chance of improving our arguments is worth any amount of effort on our part. I may even write a translation and circulate it.'

I did not dare, however, to send such a book to him through the post.

I asked him whether he, as a theological student, was now subject to any direct pressure from the Communist State.

'Things haven't been easy recently,' said Oleg. 'Since Osipov deserted his students in Leningrad we have been too much in the limelight and pressure on students in all the seminaries to follow him has been increasing.'

'Do you know him personally?'

'No,' said Oleg, 'I haven't met him. I know, though, that he's a complete traitor and a vile turncoat. The Orthodox Church is cleaner without him, though, and for that we must be thankful.'

The vehemence of his manner startled me. He had spoken so softly up to this moment, but in expressing his feeling about Osipov he paled, his upper lip quivered and he raised his voice so high that passers-by turned to look at us. I nudged him to remind him to be cautious.

I took my leave of Oleg with great reluctance, wishing that I were studying in Odessa instead of Moscow so that I could keep up my friendship with him.

While there are people like him in training, there is great hope for the future of the Orthodox faith in the Soviet Union. Most of all I was impressed with the realistic way in which he looked ahead—a complete contrast to the naïve optimism prevalent in official circles. He knew that he had an immense struggle on his hands, that he would have to marshal all his strength to win it and that even then victory would be possible only with the help of God. Even without taking direct persecution into account, he will have to work hard to help people of his own age overcome grave intellectual difficulties, the first being a barrier of complete ignorance about all the essentials of the Christian faith. However, I did already know enough about young Russians to realize that the difficulties were not totally insurmountable. If Oleg were to reach through to only one individual, he would still have demonstrated the fallacy of materialism and done his part to perpetuate Christianity in the Soviet Union.

I left Odessa as optimistic about the future as I had been pessimistic when I left Zagorsk.

CHAPTER IV

Great Lenin, Our God

As my stay in the U.S.S.R. came well after the first years of active religious persecution and just as the new phase of it was beginning to show itself, I cannot present the conflict between Christianity and Communism as a consecutive narrative. I have outlined the history of the physical struggle of the Church in Chapter II and this will be continued in Chapter VIII. In between these two periods came the years of relative stability, during which the conflict was mainly ideological. Having set down some positive and negative impressions of the Orthodox Church itself as I saw it in 1959–60, I would now like to offset this with a consideration of various aspects of the Government's anti-religious campaign as I encountered it during the months I was there. This was a time when it was possible to make a relatively unemotional assessment of the situation, because things appeared to be quite calm and because I was not, at any rate at the beginning, aware of the sudden change for the worse which was about to occur.

This chapter, then, sets out the conflict between God and Lenin in its mildest form. It recounts ideas rather than atrocities, the pen and the exhibit rather than the chain and the prison cell. It does not recount the whole history of atheist propaganda, much of which is far too dull to consider in detail. Rather it picks out a few salient points of sufficient interest to merit consideration in depth.

THE ABOLITION OF GOD

The anti-religious propaganda prepared for the home market is often unbelievably naïve. Of the former anti-God museums, so many of which were set up between the wars, now only the one in Leningrad is left, though many other museums and exhibitions have a bias

106

towards this subject or an individual section devoted to it. Assuming that the remaining one is the best of the species, one can hardly be surprised that it has nearly suffered extinction.

The appearance of the Cathedral of Our Lady of Kazan in Leningrad, imperiously dominating the Nevsky Prospect, is incongruous with its present use as the Museum of the History of Religion and of Atheism. Not many Russian intellectuals take it seriously any more, though official figures claim that the number of visitors rose from 250,000 in 1956 to half a million in 1960. It is worth visiting for a view of the lighter side of religious persecution in the U.S.S.R. There is hardly an item which anyone with the remotest claim to scholarship would have dared include. Here are a few statements which caught my eye on the walls of the museum, each one either amply illustrated by diagrams or itself forming the caption to an exhibit.

'The ark Noah built could not have accommodated all the animals which then populated the earth, which disproves the legend of the flood. The biblical story about it served as a weapon against agitators and implanted an attitude of patience and submissiveness in the downtrodden masses.'

'A whale's mouth is so constructed that it could not have let Jonah in, even if he could have lived three days inside the creature.'

'Engels: "If in the Bible there is one single contradiction, then belief in the Bible as a whole is invalidated." ' The contradiction exploited for this purpose is the similarity between the law-codes of Moses and Hammurabi: if the Egyptian one was so similar to the Jewish, then the latter was borrowed, not given by God.

'About the Apostles, as about Christ himself, no reliable evidence at all has come down to us. . . . The authors of the Gospels did not know the history, nor the flora and fauna of Palestine.' The story of the Gadarene swine and the parable of the mustard seed are brought in to illustrate this point: if the breeding of pigs was in fact forbidden, the story must be fictitious; and since mustard seed does not produce a plant larger than a cabbage, how can the birds have roosted in its branches? Another panel is devoted to the Tammuz cult, with the object of proving that Christ can be explained purely in terms of an extension of the myth of a dying and rising god. 'In any case,' they add, 'the legend recounting how Christ suffered without a word of protest has done the world untold harm.'

The culminating section, which one reaches by descending a dark flight of stairs, is a chamber of horrors depicting the tortures of the

Spanish Inquisition; and it looks suspiciously as if the instruments were borrowed straight out of some local prison where they could have been in recent use. The whole exhibition is so near to farce that it looks almost like a parody of the anti-God movement.

On a recent visit I noticed that some of the more obvious crudities had been toned down. There was more emphasis on present abuses than on the darker corners of Christian history. The sectarians come in for especial criticism: the Baptist practice of total immersion is presented as a great hazard to health. One exhibit showing the death-certificate of a child says that some fanatics sacrifice their children to an implacable God. The Christian faith is presented as a negation of life.

One could laugh off the Museum of Atheism altogether if it were not for the fact that one often meets people who seriously put forward the same kind of arguments as the ones presented here. On a visit to the U.S.S.R. not long after Gagarin's orbital flight, I heard a man vehemently claiming that this exploit had finally disposed of God and heaven. 'He's been to see if God was there,' he protested, 'and found nothing.' I thought this was his own individual fantasy, but was later most surprised to find what may have been the source for his ideas, an article printed not long before in the atheistic journal, *Science and Religion*.[1] These words are by someone styled an Academician of the Estonian Soviet Republic: 'The beginning of the cosmic era in human history, marked by the sending up of artificial earth and sun satellites, delivers one further really crippling blow to the whole system of religious beliefs, to the very idea of God.'

I could produce better anti-religious arguments than that myself, and several times I thought of offering my services to atheist agitators for this purpose while I was living in the Soviet Union. If the verbal barrages of the Press consisted solely of such arguments and if this were the sum total of government pressure on the Church, then the Party would every day be striking resounding blows on behalf of Christianity! Unfortunately, this is the most harmless line of attack.

THE HIGH PRIEST OF COMMUNISM

Much more serious is the prominence which has been given to the recent defections of various Christians, some well known, others

[1] G. Naan, 'Man, God and the Cosmos', *Nauka i religia*, February 1961, pp. 5–14.

obscure, from the ranks of the faithful. Rather than discuss these generally, it would be more enlightening to present one dramatic instance in detail.

I first came across Osipov's name in *Pravda* on 6th December 1959, when an article entitled 'Rejection of religion—the only correct course' appeared on page four. It was signed at the bottom 'Alexander Osipov' and was in the form of a letter to the editor. My first reaction on reading it was to wonder whether it had been written by an agitator and dressed to look as though it had come from an apostate priest. I did not realize at the time that he was already well known to some Anglicans, because he had been a member of the group which had received the delegation of theologians led by Dr. Michael Ramsey in 1956.

In this letter to *Pravda* he wrote:[1] 'Yes, I, Professor of Old Testament and Classical Hebrew at the Leningrad Ecclesiastical Academy and Seminary, formerly *Inspector* there, Master of Theology and Archpriest, have broken with the Church and with religion. I have publicly professed my atheism, attained logically by study and scientific method after a considerable and protracted inward struggle and a complete reconsideration of my outlook on life.

'I have abandoned that world, which I now believe to be one of illusions, of retreat from reality, sometimes even of conscious deceit for the sake of financial gain. I walked out, carrying forty-eight years on my shoulders, and for almost twenty-five of these I had occupied positions of intermediate responsibility in the Orthodox Church. . . .

'But how did I come to this? Briefly: as the result of an honest historical and critical study of the Bible, of careful study of the history of religion, of following the development of the natural sciences, of a practical acquaintance with all the repulsiveness of the capitalist world and the pitiful, despicable role which religion plays there; as a result of studying Marxism-Leninism and its philosophy; and finally as a result of seeing our own Soviet reality which powerfully invites us to follow its unique path of truth.

'All this taken together made me profoundly convinced of the nonexistence both of God and of any spiritual "beyond" whatsoever. Religion is an illusory image in the human mind, a compensation for the secrets of nature which are not yet understood, a reflection of the

---

[1] In many places Osipov's style is pleonastic and he does not clearly express what he obviously means. To avoid boring the reader in such a long extract I have made some improvements.

laws of social relationships, of the psychological and physiological peculiarities of people themselves. Fostering reliance on the mercy of a non-existent God, of his saints and angels, religion by the same token deceives, leading man away from real life into a world of fantasy, substituting for a practical and useful activity the senselessly heroic goal of saving one's soul by fasting, prayer, performing rituals and almsgiving at church.

'A little about myself. I am not of the priestly caste. My mother worked as proof reader in one of the Tallinn[1] publishing houses. We lived poorly, but she did all she could to give me an education and I left high school with a distinction mark. Our family had an ordinary faith which went no deeper than going to church at festivals and carrying out the usual rites.'

Osipov goes on to recount how under the influence of friends he became interested in the Tallinn branch of the Franco-Russian Student Christian Movement, an *émigré* organization which began its activities there in 1928. 'I attended it with mistrust, but then became fascinated. I started studying questions of religion and it seemed interesting. . . . Soon I became a popular youth lecturer in the local movement, and then Archpriest I. Ya. Bogoyavlensky asked me to consider studying for the priesthood; he also promised me a scholarship.

'My mother said to me, "I don't want you to reproach me later with pushing you into anything. It's your life and work. You must decide." I thank her for this. I blame no one for my choice, for my complex destiny. I went of my own accord.

'How did I decide to do this? You see, earlier I had dreamt of being a geologist or a writer. . . . There were arguments for and against. More than anything else on earth I wanted to live a useful life. And they told us that a priest's life consists of doing good to everyone, comforting the unhappy and the afflicted, teaching good morals and an honest life.

'What was there against it? First—a prospect which I found highly embarrassing—there was the cassock! I confided this naïvely to the priest and he told me that one should respect traditions, that one should not drive away from the church simple souls who live more by their accustomed rituals than by reason.

'Secondly, I objected to the way Orthodox worship deceives by the wording of its prayers. As one who seriously believed in the philo-

[1] Capital of Estonia.

110

sophical premise of God's existence, in the reality of another spiritual world, who read with interest the arguments of theologians and church historians, I could not help feeling the deep contradiction between the philosophy and the practice of the Church. Indeed, if God is all-good, omnipresent, gracious, if he gave his son to save the world, why is it necessary to repeat hundreds of times the so-called "Jesus-prayer"? . . .' Here follows an indictment of Orthodox worship and a repetition of the argument that those who go to Church often live worse lives than those who do not.

'. . . How many times during those years did I hear people say that all the theatricality of their worship only distracted them from their prayers and that they preferred to go to church on working days, when all was simpler and less pretentious. . . .

'Such were my objections. But with them, too, I went to a confessor. About episcopal services he told me that he himself did not like them and to have them in church is an undesirable heritage from Byzantium. And about such services I heard again: "People have become accustomed to them, they have penetrated into their very bones. . . . They naïvely think that God needs them. One should not shake their faith. Humble yourself! Do not philosophize so cunningly!" And humble myself I did.

'Telling myself that apparently I had not yet grown to understand what troubled me, I said "Yes".'

Osipov then gives an account of some articles he published at this stage in his career and the course of wide reading he undertook.

'In January 1931 I became a student in the Orthodox department of the theological faculty at Tartu University. I took a room from the local deaconess in the clergy house. There I first of all became acquainted with the terrible milieu of the priestly caste, with all its squalor, the baseness of everyone's interests, the prevalence of uncontrolled petty passions. How did this not stifle my faith? . . .' He quotes Berdyaev's arguments about faith being stronger than the defects of the individuals who practise it, which seemed to him very weighty at the time. 'At the end of my university career I wrote a thesis and had the degree of Master of Theology conferred on me.'

Osipov left the Franco-Russian Student Christian Movement to which he had belonged when it started active anti-Soviet propaganda. 'My work at the university lasted a year and a half. During this period the foundation was laid for my gradual retreat from the faith.

In studying the Bible I kept coming up against the problem of the so-called divine inspiration of the scriptures. Students of the Leningrad Seminary and Academy will, I expect, remember how often I used to say in lectures and classes: "According to the teaching of the Orthodox Church" or "Orthodox theology considers . . ." I used to do this in every instance when I could not inwardly agree with the teaching which, as a professor of an Orthodox seminary, I was obliged to impart and elucidate to my pupils. At the same time, moreover, independent study of the problems of biblical theology, together with the arguments and discoveries of genuine scientific method, led me to discover that the Bible had been put together gradually, that it had developed century by century in the course of the historical life of the Jewish people, and that its individual books do not in any way belong to those authors to whom tradition ascribes them. I found that in the Bible (certainly necessary as a work of ancient literature for the scientific study of history) there are, closely interwoven, myths and tales of the ancient Orient, the legends of chronicle and folklore, ancient stories and poetry, and magic charms from the age of primitive man—in a word, it has nothing to do with the revelation of God on earth.

'The outbreak of nationalist feeling in Estonia in 1936 compelled me to leave the university. I was given a Russian parish in Tallinn. I taught on private Russian theological courses and continued writing and publishing. All this time a deep dissatisfaction brooded in my soul.'

The war, service in the army and work as a priest in Perm and Tallinn preceded his transfer to the reopened Leningrad Academy, where he was appointed *Inspector*. 'I hated the sloth, the narrowness and the dullness of the priestly caste and I wanted to educate the young church servants of the future thoroughly so that they should become mature preceptors, far removed from superstitious fanaticism, who would lead good, active lives of high moral quality. Under my jurisdiction students frequented theatres, regular film entertainments were held, the reading of secular literature was encouraged, there were lectures on political and general educational subjects and evenings of questions and answers.

'As a result, there was extreme unpleasantness. I was supposed to be following too Soviet a line and paying too little attention to fasts and vigils. . . . The students should have been living in strict accordance with the precepts of patristic literature and their cultural and

112

scientific development should have been on a level with that of the notorious "Church Fathers" in the first five centuries A.D. I retired from the position of *Inspector*.

'I have not recorded that on my return to Tallinn after its liberation from the Germans I did not find my family. Frightened by fascist propaganda and receiving false news of my death, my wife and two daughters had left for Germany. Later I learnt that she had divorced me, married again and taken my children overseas. In 1951 I married a second time. For this I had to suffer many reproaches from the fanatics. There were church leaders who had seriously said to me: "What do you want with marriage? Live with whom you like. You're not an old man. You will be forgiven, but everything must be done discreetly. Don't break canon law, that's all! . . ." But I wanted to be an honest man even in my private life. I did not want to join myself to those, so numerous in the priestly milieu, who have been the heroes of despicable romantic adventures. Apparently the Patriarch himself understood this. I put in an application to be removed from holy orders. But, alas, even this did not save me from the cassock. The Patriarch, not wanting to give others a bad example by removing someone from holy orders, preferred to leave me in the Academy as a professor, under perpetual ban from serving as a priest, but still wearing a cassock. At lectures I was obliged to continue wearing this yoke of backwardness and degeneracy.'

From 1948–50 Osipov gave a course in the history of religions and in his reading for this went far beyond the accepted Orthodox view. 'A more profound and genuinely scientific study of religion in the context of history supplied my atheism, which had been developing over a period of years, with one last link which had been lacking. Everything fell into place for me. I realized that the history of religion up to the present day was a single process in the development of false ideas and superstitions, a projection of human relationships in the empty heavens.

'The roots of the "participation in sacred mysteries" stretched back to the wild and bloody rites of a succession of primitive peoples; priests and bishops were brothers of the *shamans*;[1] the holy scriptures became once and for all a textbook for and a propagator of a slave-owning morality; God, by his relationship with the faithful, became a heavenly reflection of some universal, feudal ideal, to which all men are for evermore slaves, most often bad ones. Even Satan himself

[1] Sorcerer-priests of pagan Russia.

turned out to be not God's enemy, but merely his functionary in especially delicate punitive undertakings.

'In 1955–6 I was persuaded to work as academic adviser on a new edition of the Bible (in particular, of the New Testament and the Psalter). Work on the Bible attracted me, but I was depressed by the knowledge that the edition would be used not in objective historical or critical work, but as a tool of religious propaganda and for stultifying human souls.

'At the same period I had a series of articles printed in the *Journal of the Moscow Patriarchate*; they defended peace, always my personal favourite subject. However, I was soon obliged to cut short this undertaking, for the editors demanded from me as much oiliness as possible,[1] and for this I have less aptitude.

'My decision to break with religion was growing stronger all the time and becoming more clearly formulated. Why did I not leave the Academy several years earlier? The gradual evolution of my outlook progressed by stages. I did not all at once overcome the submission to a non-existent (*sic*) abstract moral code which religion preaches. Then for a long time I thought that I could be of some benefit to people, trying, since the Church exists anyway and the faithful attend it, to use my influence in educating pastors who, though they might still talk of the faith, would at least not preach the coarse superstitions of fanaticism.

'However, with each year I became more and more convinced that my decision was wrong.' His endeavour to become a beacon of light seemed to be meeting with little success. 'It made me cringe when the "academic council" of the institution met to appraise degree theses (supposed to be "work") devoted to the subject of "Evil Spirits", where, for example, it was said that Satan still—in this day and age— appears amongst us. He is not now seen with horns and hooves, but in the guise of a beautiful naked man with bronzed face and body.

'I was coming to realize more and more clearly that only a complete break with religion could reconcile me with my conscience and give me the right to call myself an honest man. With this I thought: "Have you not been teaching publicly? Have you not been preaching to all? And you'll quit, you'll creep away like a snake. That's dishonest. You should be brave enough to announce your decision as openly and publicly as you have been preaching what you now admit

[1] An interesting comment on the nature of the Orthodox Church's peace-propaganda.

to be false and deceitful. You knew how to teach: you must now learn how to expose the falseness of what you have taught."

'One seemingly trivial experience forced me to pause and reflect. It was the morning of 7th September. I arrived at the Academy to invigilate examinations. I went into the conference hall. A very nice person of naïve childish faith, *Dotsent*[1] Mirolyubov, was discussing with one of the tutors articles on religion in the newspapers. The *Inspector* of the Academy, Professor Pariisky, came up to them. Mirolyubov asked him: "Should one discuss such articles with the students?" Pariisky answered abruptly, raising his voice: "Under no circumstances. I have given instructions to the library that newspapers and journals in which any such articles appear should not be displayed there. There's nothing for us to say about such stuff. We should ignore them, as if they didn't exist." Mirolyubov: "But if they ask? The articles include purely scientific matters you know." Pariisky: "They contain no science at all."

'The Rector, *Dotsent* Archpriest Speransky, came up and said: "But all of them are not purely controversial. Some are very serious articles with a scientific basis." Pariisky literally exploded: "They're unscientific!" Everyone fell silent. The Rector moved away. I felt unbearably heavy at heart. I was physically oppressed in this world of scholasticism, where science amounts to no more than ossified dogmatic formulæ and teaching about obligatory censing and genuflections.

'I started to look for a concrete way out of the impasse. On 2nd December I officially sent in my resignation from teaching to the Rector of the Academy and included a letter in which I clearly set out my reasons for leaving the ecclesiastical department, asking him to read it out to my former colleagues and to the pupils who had studied under me.'

ALEXANDER OSIPOV

Obviously Osipov's defection and his public account of it represent a triumph for Communist atheism in its fight against Christian commitment, and as such, maximum use is being made of it. By such acts of apostasy and the publicity accorded them, the strength and confidence of the faithful could be sapped. The strongest will not be touched, but there may well be some who will ask: 'If I cannot rely on my spiritual leaders to fight the battle for me, what can I do in my

[1] University lecturer.

weakness? Perhaps after all they are right, those who attack us in the Press and close down our churches. Maybe the survival of our faith is only a relic.' One can imagine the conflict such an article must arouse in a person whose experience of Christianity is perhaps incomplete and who has no source of information other than the Communist Press and the occasional sermon.

More important perhaps is the individual tragedy which this rather glib narrative has not brought out. Leaving aside the phrases which were obviously dictated by the demands of Soviet propaganda, we are left with the impression of a man who was, within the limitations of his own mental environment, fundamentally honest. I do not believe, as some people in the West apparently do, that Osipov was from the first a Communist agent.

Here is a person who admits he began his ministry as a venture of faith, having felt the call of God, but with many unsolved questions in his mind relating to the doctrines and practices of the Russian Orthodox Church, into which he had been born. He believed that God would strengthen his call after his response. When he disagreed with what he had to teach, he still attempted to put the official view fairly. He used his position of authority to try to bring some of the light of the outside world into the Russian Church. But consciously or unconsciously, he picked up too much from his predominantly Lutheran and Western surroundings during his student days in Tallinn, and from the first he fitted only uncomfortably into an Orthodox mould. His conduct at the Leningrad Academy does seem to have been basically scrupulous and honest, and some of the disputes he says he had with his Church (for instance, his refusal to imbue his 'peace' articles with an excess of oiliness) sound entirely authentic.

A young priest whom I met later at Kiev told me he had studied under Osipov at the Leningrad Academy and was there when he left. He had nothing but bitter words for his former teacher.

'I talked about him violently,' he said, 'because I used to think so very highly of him and feel that no one could have treated me worse in return. I couldn't believe the news of his defection when I first heard it, and in fact I went on refusing to believe it for days. I thought I was being tricked. It was not until he started to lecture on atheism at Leningrad University that I had first-hand evidence of it, and so had to accept it.'

'What did you think of him as a teacher while you were studying under him?' I asked.

'I always found him the best we had,' replied the priest. 'He was so inspiring and taught me so much more about the Old Testament than I could find in our textbooks. He was the only one who con- scientiously tried to keep up to date with recent discoveries in the Holy Land. Also he used to encourage us to go to the theatre and keep as well informed as we could about the outside world. They have clamped down on this since he left.'

'Do you believe he was a fully convinced Christian at the beginning of his ministry?' I asked.

'I'm sure he was,' came the answer, 'but his fundamental intellectual honesty never allowed him to accept anyone else's ideas on the Bible without first convincing himself personally of their truth. If he did doubt any of the fundamentals of the faith, he kept this to himself, even at the end of his time here.'

This is the tragedy—the tragedy of a Church which has no place in its ranks for such an admirable teacher. The real point of conflict between Osipov and the ecclesiastical authorities was not his teaching but his discipline. This may not appear to be a question of ultimate importance, yet in the circumstances it is a vital one, crucially affect- ing the way the Church faces the world. Osipov encouraged his students to equip themselves for life by understanding it and to understand it by entering fully into it. In taking this attitude, Osipov collided headlong, he tells us, with his superiors. They believed that the Church of the twentieth century could play its proper part only if it was spiritually and materially in the same condition as the Church of the fifth century.

On the resolution of this conflict may hang the future of the Russian Orthodox Church. By retreating into the cells of history and letting the stream of modern life pass over it, it is playing right into the hands of the atheist State. This is exactly how the Party wants the Church to appear—a withered relic of the past, using a dead lan- guage,[1] seeking to guard its former strongholds against a new and successful world-system, allowing into its ranks only those who will give up everything in honour of its own rigorous and misguided standards. Evangelism is not foreign to the Russian Orthodox Church, as the history of its missions in the Middle Ages and the nineteenth century shows, but I sometimes used to wonder whether

---

[1] Old Church Slavonic, the language of the Russian Orthodox liturgy, was crystallized in the earliest days after the conversion to Christianity. It is, however, much closer to modern Russian than Latin is to Italian.

its members were a little too ready to acquiesce in allowing it to be shown up as a medieval survival.

Osipov wanted to see a Church which was in touch with life and could thereby redeem the world through its understanding of and involvement in it. He wanted to see priests who were well educated by secular standards, who were equipped to share the cultural lives of the people they were called on to serve. I wonder if those who accused him of being too 'Soviet' in his approach and who reproved him for being contaminated by the world's standards realized at how profound a level he was trying to tackle this central problem which confronts the Russian Orthodox Church, even though he had not fully worked out his own ideas. Disillusionment following the bitter attack of his seniors may have turned him into a kind of Russian Judas, but his work is not dead. The priest who studied under him at the Leningrad Academy still respects the memory of his inspiring teaching, and his influence on him has perhaps been more radical than he himself realizes. Although the former admiration he had felt for Osipov has now turned to hate, he remembers the freedom he knew under his guidance and the way he broadened his outlook. Yet nowhere in the Soviet Union did I meet anyone more deeply critical of the régime than this young priest.

I do not wish to say as much about the other cause of Osipov's disillusionment—his second marriage. It is not for me to judge the rightness or wrongness of the course of action which he chose. That his re-marriage was a matter of contention is a fact. Whether his allegations against the other members of the clergy are also fact or mere propaganda of a familiar Soviet type I do not know. If the Russian Orthodox Church did offer to condone his living in sin as a preferable alternative to breaking canon law it was a despicable action which deserves to be exposed. The allegation does, however, stand in line with many similar charges of moral laxity against individuals or against the Church as a whole which appear from time to time in the Soviet Press. After great Church festivals, for example, reports often appear in the Press of 'the usual drunkenness and debauch' among the monks of Zagorsk.

Since the first days of the Revolution the most horrifying calumnies have, periodically, been brought against individual priests. The danger of being 'framed' is for them very considerable, and the consequences of a peccadillo are, therefore, likely to be much more serious for a Russian priest than for one of any other nationality. All I can

118

say is that in my limited experience, I never witnessed any mis-demeanours on the part of priests, nor had the slightest ground to suspect any. None of the many people I met who were hostile to the Church had had any first-hand experience of such ill-conduct, nor was it one of the most usual accusations made against the Church in conversation.

I had heard that Osipov's lectures tended to be lively. In a brief debate following one of them, someone had put the question: 'Judas received thirty pieces of silver. How much did you receive?'—which he brushed aside with an amused shrug, as if he had been expecting to be asked this. I was hoping to go to one should the opportunity ever arise, and I was pleased to see that he was due to lecture once during a visit I made to Leningrad in May 1960. The talk was prominently billed all over the University, under the title, *How I lost my faith in God.*

Despite the advance publicity, an audience of no more than two hundred filled about one-third of the hall. 'Those who frequent the temples of atheism are no more enthusiastic in their worship than those who come to the house of God,' I reflected. With slight appre-hension, I awaited the appearance of this man, wondering what form the manifestation of the Antichrist would take. How different he was from the figure which I had vaguely imagined!

The whole hall immediately fell under the spell of his presence. His penetrating blue eyes alone could hold an audience, as they flashed out from above his luxuriant brown beard, beginning to grey where it curled. This power was heightened by his rich, finely modulated voice, which he reinforced with dramatic gestures from his large expressive hands. He was a truly accomplished orator, and I have never seen a man who looked more like one's mental image of the incarnate Christ. I could well understand the influence he had over his pupils.

In the lecture he said substantially the same things as he had said in the article in *Pravda.* Time was set aside afterwards for questions, which had to be put in the usual Russian way—written down and passed forward so that selected ones could be taken from the pile in front of the lecturer. I had no difficulty in thinking of one myself and was determined to take this opportunity of tackling him. I printed it, hoping to disguise the foreign handwriting, folded it and passed it forward.

By this time the questions had started. The first one was: 'What kind of young people today go to the seminaries?' Osipov replied that 60 per cent of them are fanatics who are sincerely deluded through no fault of their own. Others who enter the seminaries as more stable characters become slightly deranged as a result of their experiences in such a closed community. The backgrounds of those admitted vary. A few are from collective farms and large towns; most are from small country towns, sons of poor workers in whose families the religious tradition is still strong. A high proportion come from the south-west, where, beyond the effective reach of party organs, the monastic influence is still strong.

'Can one extract any secular wisdom from the Bible?'—'It is possible, but this must be done with great caution. The Bible is a many-sided book and draws on the literary traditions of several lands, including Egyptian proverbs and law-codes and Babylonian mythology. The book of Psalms is great poetry by any standards. But it all has such a tendentious overlay that one must be extremely wary in sorting it out. It's better to use the Bible as a storehouse of literature than for any kind of practical guidance.'

My question was then read out. The weakest aspect of both lecture and article was that, for an archaeologist and historian, Osipov had paid scant attention to the historical element in Christianity. Indeed there had been no mention of Jesus Christ at all. Although I could sympathize with many of the practical difficulties which had confronted him, I could not understand the way in which he seemed to have turned his back completely on what ought to have been the foundation of his faith. My question was: 'In your *Pravda* letter and in your talk you did not mention the historical existence of Christ. How can a person who has studied the Bible as a historian completely ignore the fact on which the Christian faith is founded?'

'I did not mention this because it is impossible to discuss everything in one article or one lecture. There are two theories about the life of Christ: (1) that he existed; (2) that he did not. The latter theory has been virtually proved to be the true one since the discovery and decipherment of the Dead Sea Scrolls a year or two ago. The information they contain about the Teacher of Righteousness illustrates a variant form of a legend current about two thousand years ago—that of a dying and rising god—and common to several Near-Eastern mythologies. Christianity is merely the most successful formulation of the legend. Jesus Christ was invented by the early Christians to compensate for their deprivations at the hands of the Romans.'

I was appalled at the impossible logic of this answer and at its intellectual dishonesty. He quoted the documents as 'virtually proving' something on which they have only a marginal bearing, (as all but a few sensation-seeking writers in the West would agree). This would have been laughable if his Russian audience had any access to the texts of the Dead Sea Scrolls, but they had none then and have had none since. Such a remark would be quoted as coming from a reliable scholar and frequently repeated in anti-religious arguments. Inevitably, however, such methods can have only a temporary success in the struggle against religion, as the texts themselves cannot be withheld for ever. On a recent visit to Leningrad Academy I was begged for copies of them.

I left the lecture room with conflicting thoughts which I have not yet succeeded in resolving. The article in *Pravda* bears in places a certain stamp of honesty. It talks to us of genuine spiritual difficulties which many of us have experienced to a greater or lesser degree and which we know would assail us more powerfully if we happened to be living permanently in the Soviet Union; but how do we reconcile this with the unsatisfactory answer to my question? I would hazard the guess that Osipov became increasingly disillusioned with a Church which was quite unable to understand his problem and help him resolve his difficulties. This eventually led him to turn away from it, and once he had made the decision to desert the Church he had served for so long he started to out-Herod Herod, seeking every opportunity to denigrate the object of his former loyalty. Having broken with the Church which had, he believed, treated him very badly, he had to justify himself further by rejecting everything to do with the faith, despite the significant contribution he had himself made to the modern study of it in the U.S.S.R. It does not seem to me psychologically improbable that he should thus betray the fruits of his own scholarship. This makes much more sense than the argument, which I have occasionally heard put forward in the West, that Osipov, if not a crypto-Communist all the time, had never believed in God and thus offered an easy target for the attackers of religion. It would also explain his activities since 1959, during which time he has tirelessly lectured all over the Soviet Union, broadcast, appeared on television and written articles for many different journals. Although his arguments now seem stale and uninteresting through their stereotyped repetition, he seems to rejoice in the role which has been accorded him as the high-priest of atheism. It is certain that there are 'plants' in the Russian Orthodox ministry, placed there by the Party to give it a foothold in the opposite camp and to keep them informed, but I do not believe that Alexander Osipov was one of them.[1]

I have written in considerable detail about him because he personifies a dilemma which must exist in the minds of many who have been bred in traditional Orthodoxy, whose schooling has not shaken them into atheism, and yet who feel secretly unhappy about some of the practices they find in the Church of their allegiance. These problems are sharply defined in the light of Osipov's defection.

A NEW RELIGION?

Where Communism has already won the battle for men's minds, how near has it come to usurping that place in the human psyche which was formerly occupied by religion?

Some Western observers of the Soviet scene make elaborate attempts to depict Communism as a system which aims at replacing religion at all points. They say that Marx is God, while *Das Kapital* is his divine revelation, valid only as interpreted by Lenin, the great prophet; the cult is served by the new priesthood, those select few who become Party members. This can be expanded to form an interesting fantasy—but it is valid only in its general outline.

More than once I heard Russians talking of Marx and Lenin in terms of religious awe, though if questioned directly about it a Party member would hotly deny that he ever thinks of the founders of Communism in this way. However, a middle-aged and distinguished-looking man whom I met in a restaurant, slightly inebriated both with Georgian wine and the heady success of the latest space exploit, boasted to me: 'Great Lenin is our God, his spirit inspires and guides everything we undertake.'

The main point of interest is this: Communism does claim to replace religion as the dominant ruling power in the world and in so far as it is successful it has to fill, or find something else to fill, the void left in the place religion formerly occupied.

The deepest appeal of Christianity, which furnishes its main claim to be considered the unique religion of the world, lies in its personal aspect. It goes beyond the God who cares for each individual (a feature shared by Judaism and Islam) to the complete identification

[1] For a different view from mine, see Bishop John of San Francisco, 'L'Affaire Ossipov', *Messager Orthodoxe*, No. 10, 1960, pp. 14–18.

of the Godhead with a Man. Before the Revolution in Russia the popular faith of the country was a massive monument to this intensely personal aspect of the Christian religion. How could this possibly be replaced in a decade by a deeply felt commitment to the abstract philosophy of dialectical materialism? It is no wonder that Marxism has made such slow progress in ousting Christianity.

A man must have something personal to believe in. Even if not a Christian, he is much more likely to be inspired by the ideal of doing well for the sake of his family rather than the collective: of excelling himself for Lenin's sake rather than that of dialectical materialism. If the Soviet system is to hold people's allegiance, a personality cult of some sort is essential to it. This can make up for something of what is lost with the passing of Christianity.

This goes a long way towards explaining why Stalin's dethronement by Khrushchev caused such a great upheaval throughout the Communist world. It was not defaming the character of the national hero; it was defiling the most sacred temple of men's hearts. Stalin had been depicted in films and literature as winning the war almost single-handed; he had personally united lovers at the end of it; children who saw lights burning in the Kremlin late at night believed that this supreme being did not need sleep.[1] When this image was shattered, Khrushchev wisely decided that there was to be no more cult of living personalities. He himself undoubtedly shared in the latest manifestations of this phenomenon, but at least all official worship was directed towards the safely embalmed figure of Lenin. In one of Moscow's boarding schools I recently talked to a little orphan girl. She told me that if she could bring back three people to life she would choose 'Mummy, Lenin and Patrice Lumumba', but if she had to choose one of these three she would choose Lenin.

I paid my only visit to the Mausoleum in Red Square purely by accident. A friend and I wished to photograph the long queue of people waiting to enter. It stretched, as usual, from the Mausoleum half-way along the length of the square, down the dip to Revolution Square where it swung away out of sight on the left. As my friend was raising his camera the policeman guarding the head of the queue came up to us and instead of complaining about our taking photographs, as I expected him to, ushered us straight into the holy of holies.

One descends a deep flight of steps to well below street level, turns a corner, and there are (or were) the bodies of Lenin and Stalin lying

[1] cf., pp. 51–2.

on biers in glass cases. I saw the pair before Stalin's remains were removed, following a demonstration by students demanding this in October 1961. I had the curious feeling that they were both asleep and might wake at any moment. The Russians who came through had to keep circulating and were allowed only a few seconds inside the shrine. They removed their hats, gazed for a moment in hushed awe at the figures, almost as if they were saying a prayer, and then moved on. Prayer has sometimes been offered, for the former Yugoslav Vice-President, Milovan Djilas, writes: 'As we descended into the Mausoleum, I saw how simple women in shawls were crossing themselves as though approaching the reliquary of a saint.'[1]

If Lenin, Stalin and the personality cult have never been really satisfactory psychological substitutes for religion, some other features of Soviet life have shown more likelihood of becoming so. I believe that the arts have a better chance than a political philosophy of replacing religion as the spring of man's activity; and this would perhaps help explain the fantastic popularity of music, films and the theatre throughout the Soviet Union.

In a world where universal drabness is the rule, it is not surprising that the sumptuous productions of the Bolshoi and other theatres have an immense mass appeal of a sort which similar enterprises could not generate in the West. The great Hollywood spectaculars, if only they could be shown in the Soviet Union, would probably prove the biggest box-office draw of all time.

Yet the appeal goes beyond this. At first it seemed strange to me that of all non-Russian composers Bach should have the most devoted audience. I could understand the Russian response to the purity and gaiety of his orchestral suites or the Brandenburg Concerti, but I was amazed by the wild enthusiasm with which his organ music was invariably received. Despite the absence of church organs, there are two good instruments in the Tchaikovsky Hall and the Conservatory, and Czechoslovakian and East German organists were frequent and popular visitors. On one occasion I remember Hans Kästner included a number of chorale preludes in his recital. They were not named on the programme, but the whole audience sat, enraptured, in an atmosphere of quiet reverence.

Anti-religious propaganda has failed in raising a totally atheistic generation firstly because it has never found anything satisfactory to substitute for that which it attempted to sweep away. The palace of

---

[1] *Conversations with Stalin*, Penguin Books, London, 1963, p. 129.

marriage cannot replace the *obvenchaniye* in Church (the word for Christian marriage implies the crowning which is the central part of the ritual). The tomes of Lenin can never become a proverbial part of Russian culture, as the Bible has done. Shostakovich may be universally admired, but his music can never be a complete substitute for that of Bach.

Anti-religious propaganda, as the Soviets have propounded it, is also boring and totally without inspiration. The movement lacks great writers and Russia's best thinkers have never shown any inclination to become embroiled in it. It has adduced no new arguments since those of 1925 were obviously failing in their task. It is most revealing that when the verbal campaign was taken up with renewed vigour in 1958-9 many of the inadequate books and crude pamphlets of the 'twenties were reissued. Perhaps the main weakness is that most of the propagandists do not know the nature of the enemy. No atheist ringleader has ever dared allow those under him to study the Bible, even for the purpose of spying out the enemy's territory in order the more easily to conquer it. No one has ever clarified atheist arguments sufficiently to distinguish between the practices of the Church and the beliefs which Christians hold. The propagandist believes he is attacking God, but finds himself chasing his own tail. In desperation he turns his attention to the material side of Christianity, believing that by closing churches and threatening the liberty of the faithful he can win the battle. The present, then, repeats the story of the 'twenties, or of Nero, or of Saul before his conversion . . . and Christianity continues to be a great force in the land.

At the same time honest Russian Communists admit (though I met very few who did) that Marx left no basis for Communist ethics. He was interested in man's economic progress, making vague assertions that when the whole world has fair living conditions the problems of cupidity and crime will disappear. He did not even leave the guide of an 'interim ethic' to indicate what human conduct should be like on the road to the socialist paradise.

This is one of the reasons why there were people after the Revolution who advocated free love and other types of amorality, saying that the old bourgeois morals of the past had been overthrown and now man was free to express himself more fully. Such voices were heard for only a few years in the 'twenties and before long they were silenced. The Communist Party had soon come to realize that they could not establish order with such conditions prevailing and there was a quick return to the advocacy of the family as the primary unit of society.

Thus it is that the Party has had to fall back on exhorting the nation to follow the most conventional system of morality. At its highest, one could say that this exhibits a most remarkable Christian survival. Early in 1961 the writer, Ilya Ehrenburg, devoted a broadcast on his seventieth birthday to human values:

'We must win not only through the perfection of our machines and through our cosmic travel and prosperity, but also through our spiritual flights and the quality of human feelings, through beauty and inspiration.'[1] He went on to say that what matters about the first man to reach the moon is not only the quality of his technical achievement, but what sort of man he is.

We have here a prominent Russian urging Communists to join in the struggle against the materialistic values of the greater part of the world, a campaign which the Christian Church should be leading.

Mr. Khrushchev's new Party Programme, issued in October 1961, went beyond the materialism which was the basis of his drive for the future to include:

'Humane relations and mutual respect between individuals—man to man a friend, comrade and brother. . . . Mutual respect in the family and concern for the upbringing of children . . . intolerance of national and racial hatred.'[2]

Even more remarkable are some of the lectures on behaviour which have appeared in print. Sentences in this one by a certain Viktor Rozov would by no means be out of place in a pulpit. This is part of an article called 'What are the true values?':[3]

'They [a group of speculators] changed Soviet roubles into gold and then buried this gold in the ground. So that it should lie there! So that nothing should be done with it! What sort of sub-human behaviour is this?

'Their own most stable, most valuable currency changed into nothing! Dear friends! The most stable, the most precious, the most indestructible value is human dignity: talent, mind, moral beauty. These cannot be bought or sold for money. They have no price. It is these values that a man must guard and, by his own way of life, bravely and steadily add to them. And the worst thing that can

---

[1] *Church Times*, 3rd February 1961.
[2] *Observer*, 29th October 1961.
[3] *Literaturnaya Gazeta*, 10th June 1961.

happen is when these, the most important of all values, suffer devaluation. . . .

'Truly it is not worth it, not for two, for twenty or for a hundred million to trade one's honour and conscience. It is unprofitable! Let me quote one of the Gospel sayings: "For where your treasure is there will your heart be also".'

Such sentiments are surprising in the way they are expressed, even considering that so many Christian proverbs and expressions survive in popular speech. Mr. Khrushchev himself quoted quite frequently from the New Testament.

Many people believe that the Communist Party has been instrumental in raising the moral standard of the Russian nation, despite its lack of a theoretical basis for embarking on such a programme. If this is true, and to some extent it is, the improvement has been accomplished by the threat of savage reprisal against misconduct rather than by the example of its leaders and the reform of human nature. To the credit of the Soviet Government, something has been achieved by the suppression of all stimuli to mass eroticism and cupidity which are so common in the West through pornographic literature or advertising.

I am firmly of the opinion, however, that not so much has been achieved as the Soviet Government would have us believe. One of the reasons why one knows so little about crime in the U.S.S.R. is that no reports of it are printed in the newspapers, unless a particular offence is chosen in order to make an example of those who have committed it; then a punishment is imposed of such severity that it is calculated to deter any other would-be offenders.

For example, the Soviets claim that prostitution is not a problem any more. In fact, offenders are ruthlessly punished by being deported to Siberia. A young Russian journalist once showed me a fascinating report he had written on what happened to offenders; he claimed that the problem had still not been solved, and that there were recognized pick-up points near the centres of Moscow and Leningrad. Needless to say, this article was never accepted for publication.

While living at the University I did not notice that the standard of conduct was above what one would expect in a British institution of equal status. There was certainly some sexual promiscuity which led, in the year after I left, to the segregation of the sexes into different 'zones' of the building. On my floor alone two hundred roubles, the whole of a generous initial grant for an African and his wife, were stolen from a room, while shortly afterwards a Russian had his smart new overcoat removed. The University authorities paid the African compensation, so that 'officially' there had not been a theft.

The incidence of drunkenness is much worse than in any other country of Europe. There was a time during the worst years of Stalin's oppression when this was encouraged. Vodka could be bought from slot-machines on the streets at a very low price, and instant inebriation was probably used as a safety-valve to prevent too great a build-up of tension in the atmosphere of terror. A heavy tax has now been imposed on spirits, but the habit could not be so easily rooted out. Because there are no public bars as such, it is still almost impossible to visit a good restaurant on a Saturday evening (and often on other nights too) without being troubled at some stage by a drunk. The public reaction to drunken antics is often one of amused toleration. A drive round the streets at night can be a hazardous experience because of the number of swaying bodies trying to walk in the middle of the road.

One retrogressive step in the official legal code was the re-introduction in May 1961 of the death penalty for speculation, embezzlement and illegal profiteering. Every few weeks news comes from the Soviet Union that capital punishment has been carried out on the ringleaders of some financial racket (usually reported to be Jews). This is certainly a legal cover for resurgent anti-Semitism, but even so the new law is surprising in that it seems to be out of tune with the image of a liberal power which the Soviet Government is trying to foster. It is also surprising that English newspapers pass over these sentences so lightly. As more goods are now becoming available to Soviet citizens, the temptation to acquire money illegally in order to buy them is becoming stronger. Sometimes new temptations are the least easily resisted.

A more insidious form of immorality in Soviet society is anti-Semitism itself which is unfortunately often officially encouraged. The Government always claims it is doing no more than attacking Judaism as a religion, but many Russian Jews feel that it is encouraging irrational prejudices against Jews as people. The recent outbreak of popular feeling against African students resident in the U.S.S.R. is a similar blot on Soviet morality.

If one compares all aspects of Soviet life with their equivalents in capitalist countries, nothing illustrates better than the ethical code and its observance that 'plus ça change, plus c'est la même chose'.

The lack of a distinctive morality which is both appealing and recognizable as Marxist remains the weakest feature of applied Communism. Fulminations in the Press against the immoral conduct of Christians carry little weight, even if some of them are true, because people react with such words as, 'So what? I know dozens of Communists of whom the same could be said.' There is no sign that the standard of conduct laid down in the Gospels can be replaced in Soviet society and unless it is, the Church will continue to retain its prestige for having safeguarded this code for the world. Perhaps one of the greatest psychological contradictions in modern Russian culture is that no one can publicly admit this to be true, while at the same time nothing that is best in Russian history can be explained without it.

CHAPTER V

The Sparrow Hills

The British Council exchange group of students for 1959–60
arrived in the U.S.S.R. on the day before the epoch-making
Soviet moon-rocket reached its objective. Those of us who
had been assigned to Moscow travelled there overnight from Leningrad. The first day was a Sunday. The University was almost empty,
but those students who were there spent the whole day in a state of
intense anxiety and anticipation about the fate of the rocket, which
was due to strike the surface of the moon that night.

I went to bed about eleven o'clock and lay listening to the news as
it was relayed through the loud-speaker which each of us had in his
room. Just after midnight, at the precise moment forecast, the radio
bleeps from the rocket ceased. There was a moment's silence, then
cheering broke out all over the University. Rowdiness continued, more
or less unabated, all night.

The next morning we were summoned to see the *Pro-rector* (vice-
principal) of the University for our formal introduction to our life
there. He prefaced his short address with the remark, in which I de-
tected a tinge of sarcasm: 'I do not know which gives me more
pleasure today—the impact of the Soviet rocket on the moon or your
arrival among us'.

Moscow State University (always abbreviated in the U.S.S.R. to
the initials MGU) has a splendid situation on the southern outskirts
of the city, on a high bank overlooking a great bend in the Moskva
River. Before the Revolution this place was picturesquely called
Sparrow Hills, but its name has now been changed to Lenin Hills.

This site was chosen, significantly, for the building of a huge new
university to replace the decrepit old one—which still houses the arts
faculties—in Manège Square, near the city centre, for from here the
symbol of new learning could watch over the whole city from a

height far exceeding that of Ivan the Terrible's bell-tower in the Kremlin.

Moscow's skyscrapers were once considered by Russians as a huge leap forward in civic architecture. Now there is a tendency among more sophisticated people to disparage these six or seven grandiose manifestations. To the foreign visitor, the University, the most vast of them all, now represents the last pretentious monument to Stalin's megalomania: it was built at his command and finished in 1953, the very year of his death.

A more unattractive way of planning a new university could scarcely be imagined. Here was a superb site, which could have been imaginatively developed with piazzas and scattered buildings set in the natural woodland. It was thrown away on one massive edifice, rising from a central square of twenty stories which was flanked by four extensive residential wings, each ten stories high and capped by an enormous spire of over thirty floors for laboratories, museums and administrative rooms. The building is strictly symmetrical, and once I entered after dark, took all the correct turnings and lifts and arrived at (I imagined) my own room. The lock yielded to my key—and I was confronted by a completely strange figure. I had forgotten that the bus had stopped at the back, not at the front, of the building, and so I had arrived at the counterpart of my room on the other side of the University. There were no distinguishing marks in the long corridors I had traversed, so nothing had pointed out the mistake. Among the miles of corridors in the building I could not distinguish mine at a glance, even after living there a year.

I had a single cell in this monstrous beehive of Soviet student life. The rooms for single students were about ten feet by six, arranged in pairs, each one sharing a shower, wash-basin and lavatory with its neighbour. Inside the room itself there was only just room for a bed, table, bookshelf and built-in cupboard. Many Russians seemed to have brought their wives—and some their whole families, including grandparents and children. However large the family, they had to share one room not quite double the size of mine. It is little wonder that it was impossible to obtain statistics on the number of people who actually lived in that one building. It could not have been less than ten thousand and was probably a good many more.

This agglomeration of humanity had its complications and inconveniences. We were told on arrival that it was perfectly possible to live there all winter without ever leaving the precincts. This is strictly true—providing one's faculty was not in the old buildings in the city centre—and many Africans, not feeling able to brave the elements, did so, remaining immured in their centrally-heated tombs for months on end.

In the basements were laundries of the most primitive kind. There were shoe-repair shops, *gastronomy* (grocers' shops), female barbers for male hair and book and stationery kiosks. Sometimes a *babushka* would appear in one of the corridors with a small basket of lemons at two or three shillings each or a few dozen eggs, and wait there until her meagre wares were sold. For entertainment there was a theatre ticket agency (which never had tickets for anything except the most boring political plays and films on in town). If one wished to stay immured for one's entertainment, there was a swimming-pool (in order to use it one had to join a group and one was allowed to go only at certain specified times), a theatre where student drama groups often performed, and a large assembly hall where Moscow's best musicians could sometimes be heard.

However, the struggle for survival was sometimes intense. In planning the building it had been forgotten just how large the restaurants would have to be to accommodate such a vast number of students. Consequently, in spite of the Russian habit of dining at any time between midday and five o'clock, it was almost always impossible to obtain a meal without an interminable wait. In fact, it seemed at times as if the largest proportion of anyone's day in Russia is spent waiting. To buy one packet of tea or a tin of fish in the *gastronom* you had to join one queue to see what goods were available and at what price, then stand in another to pay for what you wanted, which gave you the right finally to queue with your ticket for your goods.

We foreigners, being well paid, soon learnt that it was best to eat either in the professors' restaurant (which was legitimate for anyone who could afford it) or in a hotel in the city. In neither case did this ensure quick service, but it did at least guarantee an edible meal. The food in the normal students' canteens was cheap, but dreadful.

Many Russians in the University, especially the girls, would prepare their own food in their rooms. There was a kitchen on each corridor containing gas stoves which could be used free of charge.

In the first year of the exchange programme the studies of all the members of the British group proceeded without major incident, though since then there have been explosions for various reasons. Each of us was put to work under a supervisor whose job was to help

132

us organize our postgraduate work. The situation was not unlike that in an English university, except that the supervisor took no personal interest in his students. Mine was B. A. Rybakov, Member of the Academy of Sciences, whom I always found helpful. He did not expect me to attend lectures, which left me free to arrange most of my time as I thought best. Officially I was engaged on studying the history of the Kievan period and in particular the conversion of Russia to Christianity, but it seemed to me that academic work for a B.D. thesis could be done at home in England, while the opportunity of meeting so many Russians might never be repeated. Academician Rybakov did not inspect my work closely, but when the day of reckoning came in May and I had to spend an hour addressing a select group from the academic board of the historical faculty, I seemed to have done enough work to satisfy them.

Moscow University cannot be considered typical of universities in the Soviet Union. Although the academic requirements are probably more or less the same throughout the country, compared with students elsewhere we were living in complete luxury. Moscow University is the only one in the whole of the U.S.S.R. where students have individual rooms (though some have to live out in dormitories for the first two of their five years)—so it is little wonder that the pressure to get in is immense.

The members of the British exchange group who were studying in Leningrad shared the fate of the average Soviet university student. They had to sleep four or five to a room, the food was worse than in the student canteens in Moscow, with no alternative other than the hotels in the city, and the sanitary conditions were unbelievable— no hot water, filthy basins, a public bath-house a mile away and toilets without doors which were nothing more than a hole in the ground. However, to compensate for this, they found it much easier to make real contacts with Russian students. Away from the doctrinal centre of Moscow, the atmosphere was much freer; there was more intellectual curiosity and less dogma. The students among whom I lived at Moscow University were hand-picked primarily for their reliability as good Communists rather than for their intellectual prowess: they were to supply the future leaders and diplomats of the country. It is little wonder that we met with difficulties.

At first, after the postgraduate who had been appointed to look after us on our arrival had carried out his assignment, I thought I would never make a single friend among the Russians. Admittedly there were one or two persons who obviously desired a closer contact with us, but although we tried to see this in the best possible light at first, not wishing to think ill of our hosts who had put us in such a privileged position, it soon became apparent that they had been detailed to keep a close watch on us. These self-styled 'friends' of ours, who were probably appointed by the leaders of the Komsomol, would appear in our rooms at all hours of the day and night.

The evidence of their activities was cumulative rather than spectacular, but when we compared notes among ourselves we were left in little doubt as to what was going on. Some of our party were interrupted by young Russians bursting into the room with the announcement that they wanted to meet us. When asked how they had known about our presence, at least two of them replied that they had just guessed that they would find a foreign student in that particular room, seeing that last year it was occupied by an American.[1]

The way I met my protector (a fourth-year economics student) was different. I had gone to the 'House of Culture' within the University to inquire about choirs and other activities. As I left, Zhenya suddenly appeared beside me and started to ask questions about England, though he had not been in the room when I was and therefore could not have known that I was English. I saw a lot of him at first. He came to my room almost every day, but we had nothing in common and conversation with him was very difficult. He did not try to indoctrinate me, but when he came to see me he would always pick up and finger every book in sight and would comment on any personal objects lying around the room. Once he found me typing a letter home to my parents which he read while it was still on the machine (although we used to converse in Russian, I suspect his English was rather better than he admitted). On another occasion I was writing up my diary (where I recorded many facts which could not be sent through the censored mail) and he seized the whole thing and started to read it. I was very annoyed and told him sharply not to—after which I saw much less of him, though he was soon replaced by another student who seemed to be fulfilling the same function. Besides this obvious scrutiny, we could not consider anything we did or said in our rooms as being private. Apart from the possibility of there being hidden microphones in the walls, our doors could be unlocked by many other keys, just as my key could be used for the

---

[1] An American exchange similar to ours had occurred the previous year for the first time.

doors of several of my friends. A common joke at the time was that of the thousands of doors in the main building of the University, one-half were permanently locked, while the other half could all be opened by the same key.

This atmosphere of discomfort and suspicion was reflected in my initial attempts to set up friendships. All the students I met seemed extremely wary of having anything beyond a nodding acquaintance with me. Later on I was told confidentially by a Russian student that at a meeting of the Komsomol held before our arrival, one of the professors had made a speech warning everyone that we might well be spies, or if not, at least be hand-picked representatives of the capitalist system. (This I considered to be a pertinent comment on the way in which our Russian counterparts in England were chosen; nothing could have been less true of the selection of our group.) The professor then told them to treat anything we said with extreme circumspection and be constantly on their guard if they met us, because we would all be out to make converts to our way of thinking.

When we arrived, the Komsomol obviously put its warning into practice and kept away from us any students who were beginning to show undue interest in the strange beings from the West. I would strike up acquaintances with students—at lectures or concerts—and would find some of them almost immediately responsive because we already had an interest in common. The relationship would progress well for a week or two, with each of us obviously finding something stimulating and different in the other's company. Then one day the student would fail to come to my room at the time agreed, or leave me standing alone at a rendezvous we had arranged in the city. Some of them I never saw again. Others I would catch sight of at a lecture or a concert sometime later, but they would either hurry off to avoid me or they would answer any question I might put to them in a polite monosyllable and excuse themselves. I took some comfort from the fact that the same thing was constantly happening to other British students; also I might well have been regarded with more suspicion than some of the others because of my religious affiliations, which I had never made any attempt to conceal from the Russian authorities.

Perhaps the most insidious pressure of all which the Communist system exerts against Christianity (and indeed against any other religion) is on young people who are known to have religious leanings. Atheism is an integral part of the educational system almost from the cradle.

135

I know a little boy, the son of a simple Christian household, who always used to wear a little cross on a chain round his neck. At the age of three he had to go to a kindergarten because his grandmother became ill and could no longer look after him while his parents worked. On the first day the teacher discovered this cross, called the child out to the front of the class and publicly ripped it off his neck. 'Borya won't come to school again dressed like that, will he, children? And we shall all report it to teacher if he does anything to shame us in future, shan't we?' Borya has never worn his cross to school since, but one evening when I was in his home he came back into the living-room crying after he had been put to bed. His mother had forgotten to put on the cross before kissing him good night, and, his father told me, he would never go to sleep without it.

When children start their proper schooling at the age of seven they are pressed on all sides to join the Pioneers. This is the most junior branch of the Communist organization, to which young Soviets are expected to belong until they begin their higher education and join the Komsomol. Its distinguishing mark is a red neckerchief, worn by boys and girls alike. Membership of the movement carries with it some genuine advantages—for instance, the camps which the organization owns and to which it sends children for a free holiday in the summer are excellent. However, a basic obligation of membership is full participation in atheist indoctrination sessions. When parents refuse to allow their children to join the Pioneers it is almost always because they want to protect them from this anti-religious instruction which is additional to that included in the school curriculum.

Children who do not conform are watched most closely by teachers and by other children. Misdemeanours, including those connected with religious practices, are judged in the first instance by a council of the child's class-mates and the sentence is finally reviewed (and usually passed) by the teacher. This system, perhaps one of the least desirable aspects of Soviet education, leads directly to the ostracism of the Christian child. In country districts it does not always work out like this, however, for sometimes those with religious affiliations out-number the others. In towns and anywhere else where it is possible to isolate Christian children into minority groups, it is quite impossible for them to enter upon any course of higher education whatsoever. Provincial institutes may number a few practising Christians among their inmates, but no believer can be selected for university education under the Soviet system. It follows, then, that Christians are regarded as inferior citizens and can never fill positions of importance in society.

Once a student is a member of a university or technical institute, the Komsomol keeps a close watch on all his activities. Church buildings are kept under close surveillance and a single visit to one by a student may arouse suspicion. A student who has been to church may be called to appear before the Komsomol committee in order to explain his action. One visit may be explained as curiosity or a desire to know what the enemy is thinking in order the better to combat him, but a series of visits, whatever the explanation, will not be tolerated. Continued disobedience after a reprimand from the Komsomol committee leads to certain expulsion from the university; though a charge of some moral offence or of failing exams is always trumped up and the practice of religion is never officially given as the reason for the action. The 'wall-newspaper' of the university publishes a vicious attack on the former student's morals or laziness and this is all the outsider sees. But the next private meeting of Komsomol members will reveal what has really happened and warn others against following the path of the expelled student.

Of all educational institutions in the Soviet Union, Moscow University attaches most importance to ideological conformity. It was not surprising, therefore, that during the first few weeks of my stay there I had the impression that the Communist Party's campaign against religion had been overwhelmingly successful. The ceaseless verbal onslaughts against Christianity to which these young people had been exposed since early childhood seemed to have gained a total victory. However, the longer I stayed there and persevered with my endeavours to get to know the students, the more I realized the difficulty of generalizing about their attitudes to the non-material aspects of life. Each reacts to the pressures and the propaganda in his own way and shows an individual lack of knowledge about the most elementary facts of religion.

I would like now to present the attitudes of various young people to Christianity. Some are students whom I met at the University; others, not members of MGU, I met in Moscow.

Within the University itself every particle of air seemed hostile to the values which for many years I had cherished as the basis of life. I had to accustom myself to being regarded as a complete outsider and a very strange person because I was a Christian. Spiritually this made life very difficult, though I have come to wonder since whether every Christian should not experience a situation like this at some time in his life.

The most favourable attitude I met with among university students was one of condescending tolerance—'You can't help being a Christian because it's part of your capitalist heritage.' The worst was an aggressive scorn which I eventually learned to ignore.

Viktor, of all the students I came to know, was the most difficult to understand. He was implacably hostile to any idea not bearing the stamp of Lenin. He was gullible, accepting without question every change in the party line. His mind was that of an automaton. There was no spark of warmth in his heart. Viktor came to my room often, but never as a friend. It was he who replaced Zhenya as my overseer. His only other interest in me appeared to be that I spoke English. He used to pursue me ruthlessly, trying to persuade me to give him lessons and offering in return an equivalent time of Russian conversation for my benefit. His English (he was a postgraduate student) was fluent, though completely mechanical and not one glimmer of personality showed through what he said. The lessons were organized down to the exact number of minutes which had to be spent on conversation, reading, grammar and idiom. I was prepared to continue the lessons only if they included conversation on topics of general and personal interest, but this seemed to him incomprehensible—'Why do you not wish to work as hard during your Russian lessons as I do during my English ones?' He constantly tried to refute facts which I wanted to explain to him about Great Britain (free education, the National Health Service and so on) and eventually I decided I could no longer stand the long tedium of our two-hour sessions, which he was always begging me to increase to double the time, and asked him not to come any more.

With Viktor, and one or two other people like him whom I met, it was always impossible to judge how far their attitude was a piece of play-acting designed to deceive both me and the Komsomol, an exaggerated pose adopted to cover inner unresolved doubts, or how far it was a genuine characteristic of the ideal Communist man. I never felt happy when challenged to defend my Christian beliefs before people like Viktor and during my last months at the University I would guiltily try to avoid mentioning religion to them at all.

These young Communists would start from a position of almost impregnable strength—they knew all the answers about religion, though to them Jesus Christ was no more than a name and they had never read a word of the Bible (except possibly chosen extracts from *Jonah* and *Genesis*). In fact all they could do was to repeat the official atheist line and I was continually struck by the way they used an identical vocabulary. If one were to judge the success of the propaganda machine solely by what they said, one would have to admit that it has been completely successful. In vain did I argue that I could prove to them that religion was not moribund in Russia by taking them to a church to see for themselves. They would not come, and their minds remained firmly closed and sealed, because they had never set foot inside a place of worship. I have to admit, to my shame, that I never found a starting-point from which to put to them any sort of case for the Christian faith.

I tried not to attach an exaggerated significance to my impressions of this type of student, remembering how the students who went to Moscow University were chosen. Some of them were probably not as fanatic as they sounded, but were keen enough careerists to know how and when to produce the right answers.

Natasha was one of the pleasantest, most beautiful and least doctrinaire Russian girls I met. She was highly intelligent and studied English, which she spoke with a most appealing accent, but with full confidence in expressing nuances of meaning. We often used to meet and discuss such authors as Graham Greene, Aldous Huxley and the 'angry young men'. Even though Natasha knew from her reading that Greene, whom she admired most of all, was a Christian, she had quite a shock when I told her that I was too. When I told her of my intention of becoming ordained she could hardly bring herself to believe it. 'When you are a Communist,' she said, 'you are working for the State, for others, for the common good. If you become a Christian you never look beyond yourself. You're going to become a priest? It's impossible. An educated person can't do that.'

During our subsequent meetings Natasha would listen to my point of view for as long as I cared to expound it, but I never succeeded in modifying hers. The whole of her education had been so fundamentally atheist that the word 'Christian' carried for her emotional overtones of hatred which she could not dispel, even though she could show friendship for me as an individual. In all our long conversations I never once brought her to a state of mind where I could begin a logical explanation of what the Christian faith meant to me. When she bumped into me in the street in Moscow two years later she was certain that I had given up my vocation, because I was

139

interpreting for a group of Englishmen and she thought that this was now my permanent work. Still, I always hoped in such instances that what I said, or even just being myself, might sow some seed of understanding which contact with other Christians might germinate in the future.

Kolya, one of my very best friends, knew all the correct answers, but when he reeled them off he would have such a twinkle in his eye that I used to love hearing him perform his little act.

'Hello, Misha,'[1] he used to greet me, 'how are you today?' and when I said that I was well, he would reply: 'That's because you've said your prayers.'

Once he agreed to meet me on a Sunday evening. When he came up to me he said very seriously: 'Have you taken your opium today?' He made this remark, and many others like it, in such a tone of voice that it was impossible to take offence—indeed his observations struck a note of gaiety which would often continue throughout our meeting.

Once he told me a preposterous joke. 'Shortly after Stalin's death a group of Jews came to the Kremlin to see Mr. Malenkov. He received them, and they asked him if they could have Stalin's body to embalm it. They were experts in the process, they said, and wanted to do him a final honour for the magnificent treatment he had accorded their race during his lifetime. "No," replied Malenkov, "you people have had one resurrection and we're not going to risk another".'

One day Kolya asked if I would take him to the Baptist Church on the next Sunday. We met beforehand and this was the first time in his life he had witnessed Christian worship of any description. Afterwards he admitted to being impressed with one aspect only—the way they prayed so fervently for their brethren absent through sickness. He mimicked the preachers and solemnly addressed everyone as 'Brothers and Sisters' for days afterwards, yet he never said a hard word about the people he had met there. Even this, I thought, was something.

Lilya represented the new wave of Russian youth. She studied at a technical institute, not having won a place in the University. Like Kolya, she believed in the future of Communism, fully admitting the defects of the present system, but at the same time she was confident that the Soviet leaders would be able to overcome them. Lilya had

---

[1] The familiar form of Mikhail (Michael).

many friends among the young poets and artists whose work circulates freely in the cultural underground. She was interested not in whether her artistic friends were writing good poetry or painting masterpieces, but in whether they were expressing new ideas. She wrote rather bad poetry herself, which she often used to read me. I used to look forward to these sessions because I always felt that I was in contact with a mind trying to untrammel itself from second-hand ideas, whether pro- or anti-Communist, even though Lilya herself did not have the technique to do justice to her originality.

She had no knowledge of religion nor interest in it, but always showed indignation when I told her of the way Communists had persecuted Christians in Russia in the years after the Revolution. I would like to know what her attitude to this problem is now, but she graduated from her institute at the same time as I left Moscow in 1960 and went off with crusading zeal to work in an electric power station in the far north-east of Siberia. Since then we have not been in touch and I have not seen her on subsequent visits to the U.S.S.R.

However much I admired Lilya's wish to be unconventional, I always thought there was something too naïvely optimistic in her attitude. She was critical of the fact that her friends could not exhibit their abstract paintings, but fully expected that all would soon change and that within a year or two she would be able to publish her own verse, though during the few months that I knew her there was never any sign to indicate that this time was approaching. It always seemed to me that she expected 'them' to change their attitude, but that she would never actively do anything to persuade them to do so. Perhaps she has now found herself with a group of like-minded people, and with the increased confidence she will have gained from successfully completing her studies, is helping to form a small cell of a genuinely more liberal society in a remote corner of the Soviet Union, far from the central Party control.

Kolya, Natasha and Lilya seemed to have developed into rounded and interesting personalities, despite the limits which had been imposed on them from the time they were born. I met them after I had been in the Soviet Union about two months, at a time when I was beginning to feel I would never make any friends. It was a case of one good friendship leading to another, for they all knew each other and through striking up a friendship with Kolya I was introduced to the other two.

There is a saying that a Russian is like an onion: you can peel the layers off him, but the more you strip off, the more you weep. I was told this before I went to Russia, without the warning that the process might need considerable perseverance. I never felt this applied to Kolya, Natasha and Lilya, but it did apply to many others, though, and when I started stripping off the layers I indeed wanted to weep. Beneath the brash, self-confident exterior of the future world-builder or cosmos-conqueror, I often found a spiritual *malaise*, which seemed to me to come from a deep-seated dissatisfaction with the drear materialism of Russian life.

Igor studied history, so I used to see him sometimes at the faculty. Our common interest in music gave us much to talk about. We used to go to concerts together and listen to gramophone records, and sometimes he would play Chopin's or Schubert's piano music for me. He enjoyed accompanying my singing, but I was just introducing him to Benjamin Britten's arrangements of folk-songs when he suddenly stopped seeing me and began to avoid me at the faculty. He had certainly been warned against any further association with me, and our most promising friendship was cut off just as it was taking root. Perhaps he had been suspect before. He admitted to me once that he used to go to church and occasionally still did, not because he believed in God, but because he was extremely fond of his old grandmother and wanted to please her by going with her when the great festivals were celebrated. While there he used to feel overcome with emotion at the magnificent solemnity of the chanting. '*Gospodi pomilui, Gospodi pomilui*,'[1] he sang to me in a low voice, his eyes filling with tears. I always regretted that our friendship stopped so abruptly, because I felt that although he would not admit that his interest in religion was anything other than aesthetic, his was at least a different attitude from those I had previously met at the University and I would have liked to have known more about him.

Mila was a teacher in one of the new boarding schools. Although she was a mature woman in her thirties, with a daughter at school, I have included her in this section because her attitude casts an interesting light on what can happen to the crusading zeal of the young Communist after it has been blighted and disillusioned by succeeding changes in the Party line. Her attitude may be typical of those who were nurtured in the Stalin-god ideology and then one day cheated at the very foundations of their belief. Such people are, of course, afraid to talk. It was on one of my later visits that I met her,

[1] 'Lord have mercy'.

and it was only when she heard that I was due to return to England on the next day that she unburdened herself.

'Since the dethronement of our god, many people of my generation have become sceptics. Here was something we could live for and burn up our energy in trying to attain it. Now we just don't believe the same way any more. Oh, yes, of course the students you met at the University were intolerant and idealistic, just as I was at that age, but they will change. It's a tragedy for our country that materialistic doctrine has ousted religion. Our cultural life is sterile, but religion is a great civilizing influence. No, I don't believe in God, but I often wish I could. I need something to fill the void in my life. I deeply envy Christian people and I've tried to believe in their God—but in vain.

'The Russian economic system which forces women, particularly young mothers, to work is thoroughly bad. I was divorced not long after I had my daughter and since then I have had a terrible struggle to bring her up. I receive only twenty-five per cent of my husband's wages as alimony, and as I have had my old mother to look after too, my life has been hard over the last few years. It's only recently that my wages from teaching have been high enough to relieve my anxiety. The three of us living in one room often get on each other's nerves. Now my daughter is growing up to be very selfish. She expects everything and just does not realize the immensity of the difficulties I have faced. I make no secret of being bitterly jealous of the lot of Western women. What is theirs by right I can never hope for, and soon I shall be too old to enjoy it even if I had it. I conceived this envy when I was working as a secretary in the French Embassy and had thousands of conversations with diplomats' wives. I was never told why I had my permission to work there withdrawn, but I'm sure it was for getting too friendly with the people I was working for.

'I would come to the West if I could, but of course with the incredible complications of travelling I shall never make it. Money would be the least of my worries. One must be resident in the same place seven or eight years; people would have to pledge their signatures that I would not be a security risk. I wouldn't do it for anyone else, so how could I expect anyone to do it for me?'

Igor and Mila are, I am certain, the potential converts to Christianity of the Soviet Union today. They are to a greater or lesser degree dissatisfied with their lives, and are groping towards some kind of fulfilment which the Communist Party, with its hollow religionless ethics, cannot offer.

I expected to spend a whole year at Moscow University without ever meeting a single Christian student apart from the foreigners there on exchanges and some of the Africans who had received a Christian schooling in their homeland before being offered scholarships by the Russian Government. Whereas the aim of the best university education in the West is to temper specialization with broader interests, to persuade the scientist to widen his scope by cultural relaxation and discussion and to lead the arts student into an involvement in world affairs, I imagine a symbolic diagram of Russian higher education as an inverted funnel. However diverse the material sucked into the base, the aim is to blast out of the narrow top a stream of 'ideal Soviet men' who will stay strictly on the courses into which they are orbited.

The chances that a Christian or a practising Jew might be ingested in the first place are slender, but if one should happen to be, through his own cunning concealment, he would almost certainly join the Komsomol at once and determine to preach for five years what, in his inmost heart, he despises. By this very act he may, despite himself, start to conform inwardly as well as outwardly to the Soviet mould. A faith unnurtured can easily wither away.

How many of the University's twenty thousand students never inwardly conform? Apart from the occasional one hounded out for a crime or some other immoral act, the official answer is 'none'. Besides, if such a person did exist, a Christian graduate from a capitalist country would be about the last person in whose company he would be seen.

It was, therefore, a considerable surprise to me when a girl of twenty-two, in her final year at the University, confided to me on our second meeting that she was a Christian. Galya had been introduced to me by an African friend, who said that she would like help with some technical English she could not understand. I have never met anyone whose whole personality seemed to be so ravaged by nerves. She stayed only a few minutes on the first occasion and never took her eyes off the printed page from which we were working. As its hieroglyphics and technical jargon didn't mean anything at all to me, I tried to veil my deficiencies by introducing some more general topics. She then started to glance nervously from side to side, as if trying to catch someone eavesdropping on us. When I started asking questions she became even more frightened and left.

I thought I would not see Galya again, but to my surprise she came

A young seminarist, Nikolai Sokolov, is ordained at Irkutsk in Siberia. Here the Archbishop begins the liturgy

back the next day saying my help with her translation had enabled her to do a good piece of work. I doubt if this could have been true, but this time her mood was quite different. She was less jumpy, though still not relaxed, but she did want to talk. I was surprised that I had said enough the first time to win her trust, but perhaps she had been waiting for a long time to find someone to confide in. We cannot realize what an immense strain it must be not to be able to trust any of one's friends. How can 'Love one another' become part of the Communist ethic, as the more enthusiastic advocates of the system say it already is, when there is so much distrust of others?

After Galya and I had discussed topics of trivial interest for a few minutes, the conversation came round to Christian names. She asked me about the sort of names we have in England, and I explained our custom of giving the child a name at baptism.

'Do you know,' she said, 'my name's not Galya at all, although that's how I always introduce myself and that's how I'm officially known here. I was baptized Marya, which I like very much but now the name has most unfortunate associations for me.' I asked Galya why this was, and she said: 'As a child I used to love going to church. I adored the feeling that I was entering a new world, one which was different from and quite superior to the world of my home, with its degrading poverty and lack of privacy. I didn't understand what the priests were talking about in their quaint old language, but from the calm look of joy on their faces I knew they were experiencing some kind of happiness which wasn't part of my world. It was such a shock to me, one day in my second year at school, when my teacher called me to her after classes and said: "The headmaster has been talking to me about you. We know you have been going to church and we think you're old enough now to know better. You had better mend your ways."

'When I got home my grandmother caused a scene, saying she would never forgive me if I obeyed. So I went to church the next Sunday. On Tuesday the following week the teacher called me up in front of the class. Do you know, I can still hear every word she said, as if it happened yesterday. "Children, what do you think little Marya has been doing? She's been going to church every week. She thinks that Lenin and Stalin aren't good enough for her. She wants God instead. She even calls herself Marya—a horrible name from the Bible—to let us all know what she believes in. Now, Marya, if I were you, for your own good I would change your name to a nice one,

145

like Nina or Natasha or Galya—one that's fit to belong to a good young Stalinist. Just do this for us to show us you mean to turn over a new leaf. Promise us you'll try to lead your parents into better ways and we'll help you to begin over again!"

'I've never really recovered. from being so humiliated in front of the whole class at school, you know. The children themselves never seemed to hold it against me, at least not after the first few days. In fact they helped to make it easy for me when I changed my name to Galya. My parents didn't help, though. They persisted in calling me Marya for years afterwards and finally stopped only when I was considering applying for university. I'm sure that later on certain pupils were detailed to watch me closely. I didn't give them much to look at, though. Do you know, since that time at school I have never set foot inside a church nor spoken to a priest.'

'And you've lost your belief in God?' I broke in.

'No. They could watch everything I did, but they couldn't read the thoughts of my heart. I soon learnt all the right answers about Marx, Lenin and Stalin and found I had an ability for scientific subjects. I got on so well that I was accepted for Moscow University, which means my teachers must have given very good reports about my conduct, too. But they didn't change what I really believed.'

Only someone who has experienced the hollow, pretentious, stifling atmosphere of the University building, as I then had for nearly four months, could appreciate the amazement I felt at this admission. 'You can't mean that you're a Christian and you've managed to hold on to your belief over four years in this place undetected?'

'Oh, it's easy if you learn how to repeat all the right answers. I've long been used to not revealing my innermost thoughts to anyone. In fact, sometimes I was at a distinct advantage. It was during my first year here that Khrushchev denounced Stalin, and I was one of the quickest to learn the new answers. I was near the top that year in the *Diamat*[1] exam. I have done very well ever since, which gives me quite a lot of prestige.'

Galya's face relaxed into a smile for the first time. How strange, I thought, that she dared say all this to me, whom she hardly knew and certainly had no proof she could trust—unless our African friend had assured her it was all right. Perhaps it goes to show that it is possible for some human beings to wear a mask constantly without acquiring

[1] A student abbreviation for dialectical materialism. This has to be studied by all, no matter what they are reading for their degree.

its expression as a permanent feature of their personality. What Galya said about her long-assumed hypocrisy contrasted sharply with her unbearable nerviness. I could not understand why she had not had a complete breakdown long ago. However, she did seem to be less on edge after she had confided in me, and I thought she would not mind telling me more.

Up to then, the whole conversation had been conducted in a cautious whisper, so I suggested going outside so that we could talk more naturally. As it was quite late in the evening, she asked me to take her to her home on the other side of Moscow. We went by Metro and arrived at one of those bleak, anonymous, tumble-down areas, so typical of the Moscow which lies beyond the sights the tourist sees.

We turned down an ill-lit side street. One would have called the unpaved road a cart-track, were it not for the fact that it separated two rows of identical buildings, all so high that their tops disappeared into the gloom above the farthest reach of the dimly burning lamps. We were accosted by a drunk who rolled out in front of us from behind a pile of rubble. Galya looked terrified and motioned to me not to speak to him. His words were so slurred that I could hardly understand what he was saying. I think he was asking for a certain number in the street. No wonder he couldn't find his way home in such a place! We turned in between two blocks, and Galya said: 'Now we can continue our conversation.' I asked her how she could believe so strongly in God, as her education had given her no opportunity to learn about religion.

'Belief is not the same as understanding. I know almost nothing about Christianity, and I've never been able to get a Bible from anywhere. Yet the belief seemed to be in me from the first and nothing has ever happened to me since which seemed to contradict it. You see, everything I have learnt as a scientist stops short where the ultimate questions about the purpose of the universe and of human life begin. What we learn in *Diamat* begs every essential question to do with religion. To be successful in this subject one just has to learn that there are many questions one must not ask.'

At that moment she broke off. There had been a noise in the street near us and I could just make out the lurching figure of the drunk again as footsteps started to shuffle up the alley-way towards us.

All Galya's anxiety had returned. We walked quickly round to the back of the block and she slipped into one of the entrances. 'Go away quickly. Please don't speak to anyone. I'll call next time I come to the Lenin Hills.'

I never set eyes on her again.

This brief acquaintance with Galya set me a problem. I had met a young Russian believer who had somehow found her way into what should have been the country's strongest bastion of militant Communism. I now had to ask myself what proportion of Moscow University students had similarly managed to hold a seed of faith against all the odds. This made me wonder what percentage of those who had made the grade for other universities were Christian, and even more important, how many young people who had not been accepted for higher education at all, believed in God.

There are no answers to questions like these, but that Galya was not an isolated example of a nest of atheism producing a fledgling Christian was proved to me just before I left Moscow in 1960. It was Kolya again who came to my room, saying he had been with two married friends on the previous evening, my name had come up in the conversation and they had said they would like to meet me.

Kolya took me directly to their flat which was not far away in one of the new residential blocks rising in their hundreds in the south-western quarter of Moscow. Tatyana and Ivan welcomed me most warmly, poured out four glasses of Georgian wine and said, 'To real friendship'. Kolya had to leave us soon and after he was gone a most expansive atmosphere seemed to spread over the room.

Tatyana and Ivan were graduates of Leningrad University, where they had met, and they had been living in Moscow since completing their studies in 1953. It was immediately obvious that they were passionately interested in everything to do with the West. They had read widely among English and American authors whose works are not published in the Soviet Union. When I complimented Ivan on his knowledge, he stood up, crossed the room to an alcove and drew the red plush curtain which had been drawn across it. I was astounded to see a number of English books and a collection of jazz records such as I had never seen before. It included virtually all the titles from the great days of jazz which were then available on long-playing records in England and America. The collection even included some records of the latest hit tunes. I expressed amazement at the completeness of the collection, not one record of which could have been bought in Moscow. Ivan said it had required great patience and very good friends to acquire it.

'Our interest doesn't stop short at jazz,' said Tatyana. 'We love classical music too, especially choral music of the great masters.' I asked her what her favourite choral work was, and she said it was Beethoven's *Missa Solemnis*. I had never heard the work mentioned in the Soviet Union before, but Tatyana said it had been a favourite of hers ever since she had heard it broadcast from Finland while she had been studying in Leningrad. 'I believe it's the piece of music', she went on, 'where the creative mind of man reaches out furthest towards God.'

I was immediately struck by the unselfconscious way in which Tatyana spoke the last phrase. I said I presumed she was speaking figuratively in talking of God in this way. 'Not a bit of it,' Ivan interjected. 'I was converted to Christianity in my last year at university and Tatyana came to share my convictions the next year, just after we were married.'

'I didn't believe that under the Soviet system anyone could be converted to Christianity while still a student—and in the last year of Stalin's life, too,' I said.

'Actually I was converted just a couple of months before he died. My interest in religion was aroused in a fairly logical way, when you come to think of it. During my first year at the University I came to think of Communism as an inhuman and intolerable system. I kept my beliefs to myself, of course, but my interest was keenly aroused by anything which they taught me was a product of capitalist deviation. Of course, that's how I first became interested in jazz. I came to religion later, purely as a matter of intellectual curiosity, thinking that there must be something in it to make it worth opposing so violently. At first I couldn't find out much about it, but then one day I met a student of my own age sitting on a bench in a park. Striking up a conversation with him, I discovered that he was from the Theological Seminary. I was impressed with his quiet sincerity, not at all the sort of trait I had been taught to expect in a seminarist. But by this time I accepted such contradictions.

'We started to meet regularly, and one day he brought me a manuscript copy of St. Matthew's Gospel. I read it carefully and was most impressed with the ethical content of Our Lord's words. It soon became obvious to me that I had discovered something here which was of infinitely greater value than any of the tomes of Marx, Engels,

Lenin or Stalin I had been forced to read at the University. The following winter I went to a church secretly one evening where a priest baptized me.'

I listened to Ivan's story with rapt attention, hardly able to believe what I was hearing. 'Are there many products of the Communist system who have turned out like you?' I asked.

'Not many,' Ivan replied, 'but I know of some others. It's a pity you are going back to England so soon. If you'd been staying longer I could have introduced you to some.'

Tatyana told me that she had become a believer simply out of loyalty to her husband at first, but had then become deeply convinced, once she had gained some knowledge of Christianity. 'Ivan told you his interest in Christianity was aroused through intellectual curiosity, but now I always tease him and say he doesn't read as much about it as I do. A friend of mine got me copies of Berdyaev and Lossky the other day and I've re-read them so many times now I almost know them by heart. Ivan has read them, too, but he hasn't spent as much time on them as I have.'

Six months earlier I would not have believed it if I had been told that there were young graduates in Moscow who had read Berdyaev.

I asked them if their religious beliefs affected them adversely in their jobs. Ivan said that they had to be very careful. There were only one or two Russians with whom they would speak as they had just talked to me. Not even Kolya was close enough to be told of their Christian beliefs. 'We simply don't dare go to church regularly,' Tatyana said. 'It's safest at Christmas and Easter when there are so many people about that you don't get noticed in the crowd. The real problem is going to arise when I have a baby. I'm expecting one in six months' time and it won't be easy to bring up a child in the faith with all the pressures it will meet in its education. Still, perhaps everything will turn out all right in the end, as it did with Ivan and me.'

On a subsequent visit to Moscow I found strangers in their flat. They said they had only recently moved in and had no knowledge of the previous occupants. I hastened over to see Kolya to find out whether Ivan and Tatyana were all right. He assured me they were. Tatyana had had her baby and they had recently had to go to Volgograd to live because Ivan's work had taken him there. I hope his information was reliable.

CHAPTER VI

Baptists and Evangelicals

WESTERN INFLUENCES

One scarcely known fact about Soviet religious life is that there are in existence over forty sects and schismatic groups, not including the former national Churches of the peripheral peoples.[1] Apart from the various branches of Old Believers, the majority are both Western and Protestant in origin. Most Western visitors interested in religion meet the Russian Baptists, but can do very little beyond this because so few of the sects are officially recognized by the State and their members live mainly in areas which are inaccessible to foreigners. When I went to live in the Soviet Union in 1959 very little had been published on the subject and I did not know what to look for in the provinces. Even if I had known, I doubt whether the time I could spend there would have been sufficient to find out much in the way of concrete facts. Most information so far gleaned about the sects comes from Soviet publications attacking them, which means that nothing is known about the quality and character of their religious life. Their very existence and their recent proliferation are, however, in themselves an indictment of the Communist system, showing how poorly it satisfies the highest ideals of the soul.

The Baptists are by far the most important of all the groups which owe their origin to Western Protestantism. The movement originated almost simultaneously in three parts of the Russian Empire—in St. Petersburg, where Lord Radstock, a prominent Plymouth Brother, made two extended visits in the 1870's and had a notable influence on the aristocracy; in the Caucasus, where a Scotsman named Melville, an agent of the British and Foreign Bible Society, prepared the

[1] See Chapter VII.

ground for conversions by Martin Kalveit, a Lithuanian Baptist; and in the Ukraine, where Lutheran and Reformed pastors, together with Mennonite missionaries, had considerable influence at the time of the emancipation of the serfs in the 1860's. In 1884 the Union of Russian Baptists was formed in the Ukraine, but it did not become legal until the proclamation of religious liberty in 1905.

At one time it seemed as if the growth of the Evangelical and Baptist faith was going to be encouraged by the Soviet régime as a means of breaking the power of the Orthodox Church and of opening up the virgin lands, the cultivation of which was so desperately needed for the success of Soviet agriculture.

The best known and most influential, though also one of the most controversial, of the Evangelical leaders of this century was Ivan Stepanovich Prokhanov[1] (1869–1935), whose ultimate aim was to convert the entire Soviet Union to his Christian philosophy. He wanted to return to the principles of the Jerusalem Christians of the first century and form communes where everything would be held in common ownership, except for the few personal belongings which each worker could keep around him. The amazing thing is that he persuaded the Communist authorities to let him found Evangelsk (otherwise called the 'City of the Sun') in central southern Siberia, not far from Novosibirsk. Prokhanov's project was to make his first commune a Christian model which the rest of the Soviet Union would wish to follow. On 11th September 1927 there was an initial tree-planting ceremony, in which the Evangelicals were joined by local Communist officials.

In the mid-1920's the Evangelicals were also permitted to publish three editions of the Bible (one complete, two partial) which totalled about sixty thousand copies in all, and in addition ten thousand copies of a biblical concordance were produced in 1928. Both the Evangelicals and Baptists could train their presbyters in Moscow and Leningrad at a time when no comparable opportunities existed for the Orthodox.

However, this brief period of flirtation between Christianity and Communism was followed by a complete change of face on the part of the State. Prokhanov's project never went beyond the tree-planting stage, for it soon became obvious that the commune would be very

---

[1] For details about Prokhanov and for most of the rest of the historical background in this and the next chapter I am indebted to Walter Kolarz, *Religion in the Soviet Union*, Macmillan, London, 1961.

similar to those which the Communists themselves had long been trying in vain to found. They feared not only that they might lose face, but also that people might flock to Evangelsk to seek refuge from official dogma or forced collectivization. Prokhanov himself escaped from the U.S.S.R. and a few years later died in Berlin a disillusioned man. Many leading Baptists and Evangelicals were arrested in 1928 and sent to labour camps, while all their special privileges were cancelled in 1929.

Since then Baptists and Evangelicals have suffered as badly as other Christians of the Soviet Union, though as with the other sects much of their missionary work has been clandestine and therefore the authorities have found it difficult to combat. They profited from the general easing of the situation towards the end of the war and in October 1944 united to form the All-Union Council of Evangelical Christians and Baptists. This did not reduce the number of sects because some congregations stayed outside the Union, but it did ensure that this one main Evangelical body was now large enough to gain strength from its new organizational unity. By 1957 the Council claimed to have 545,000 baptized members, but this number does not allow for the millions of adherents who have not yet taken the final step of undergoing adult baptism. The total number of Soviet citizens who have some connection with the Baptist Church may reach three million,[1] and there are registered communities in all parts of the U.S.S.R. For a sect which had such a brief period of legal existence before the Revolution this is a quite remarkable achievement.

THE APPEAL OF EVANGELICAL CHRISTIANITY

Alexander Solzhenitsyn's novel, *One Day in the Life of Ivan Denisovich*, contains a fascinating testimony of the evangelical zeal of Baptists in the labour camps. Without sentimentality or self-pity the author describes the details of everyday life in the camps. His objectivity and impartiality are nowhere better illustrated than in the last part, where Ivan Denisovich Shukhov has a conversation with Alyosha, a young Baptist who has been persecuted for his faith.

'Alyosha heard Shukhov's whispered prayer, and turning to him:

' "There you are, Ivan Denisovich, your soul is begging to pray. Why, then, don't you give it its freedom?"

---

[1] *Bratsky Vestnik*, No. 3–4, 1954, p. 91.

'Shukhov stole a look at him. Alyosha's eyes glowed like two candles.

' "Well, Alyosha," he said with a sigh, "it's this way. Prayers are like those appeals of ours. Either they don't get through, or they're returned with 'rejected' scrawled across 'em."

' "But, Ivan Denisovich, it's because you pray too rarely, and badly at that. Without really trying. That's why your prayers stay unanswered. One must never stop praying. If you have real faith you tell a mountain to move and it will move" . . .

'They were a luckless lot too. What harm did they do anyone by praying to God? . . .

' "Ivan Denisovich! You shouldn't pray to get parcels or for extra skilly, not for that. Things that man puts a high price on are vile in the eyes of Our Lord. We must pray about things of the spirit—that the Lord Jesus should remove the scum of anger from our hearts." '[1]

Alyosha goes on to explain that he is glad to be in prison and to have the chance of suffering for Jesus Christ. Ivan Denisovich is not, of course, converted, but it is amazing that such an unbiased account of Baptist evangelization should have been printed at all in the Soviet Union. Nothing like it has appeared publicly since the Revolution, neither in the religious nor in the Communist Press.

I was reminded of Alyosha when I met Andrei recently in Leningrad. Among the very small number of Christians I met below the age of thirty, he was the only one who was prepared to make a public show of his beliefs. If he had been ten years older he probably would have found himself where Alyosha was. In the present worsening situation he may yet follow him.

In 1962 the Leningrad Baptists had to transfer their only church, which had been situated not far from the centre, to a distant suburb of the city. Now it takes half an hour to reach it by bus No. 75 from Liteiny Prospect. The journey, however, is worthwhile, for Troitskoye Polye (Trinity Meadow) where the church nestles among the birch trees is a delightful spot. To my surprise, I found that the Baptists have taken over a former Orthodox church and converted the inside to Protestant use. The cross has been removed from the spire,[2] the iconostasis has made way for a pulpit and the gallery at the back is occupied by a choir and harmonium.

An English-speaking pastor, Anatoly Kiryukhantsev, officially re-

---

[1] Penguin ed. (translated by Ralph Parker), London, 1963, pp. 138-9.
[2] See illustration facing p. 176.

ceived me and gave me a rosy picture of Baptist life in Leningrad. He supplied all the conventional answers to my questions, and I was beginning to feel disappointed with my visit. But meeting Andrei changed all that. Just after I left the church he bobbed up beside me from nowhere, it seemed, in that strange way that only Russians do. In silence we walked very fast towards the city centre, sometimes doubling back on our tracks, and after a few minutes, when he seemed satisfied that we were not being followed, he led me into a sordid backstreet *stolovaya* (cafeteria). When we sat down he leaned towards me, head bent and eyes lowered. It was as if a dam across his tongue had been breached. Instead of the isolated monosyllables of command I had heard outside, I was now engulfed by the torrential flood of his words. Not that there was the slightest suggestion of hysteria about Andrei. His complete self-possession never allowed his voice to rise above a low whisper. Yet at the same time there was a compelling urgency in his words, as if he had much to say and very little time to do it in and as if life and freedom depended on what he told me.

I deeply regretted not being a born Russian speaker. How could I catch all he was saying without having the full rich vowels to guide my ear? I was left with an impression only of the heroic stand Andrei had made to keep kindled the fire of his passionate beliefs. My mind could not retain many details of his life in the excitement of what he was saying, even if my ear had disentangled them.

He is the only person I have ever met whose every word, thought and action is dominated by the ideal of Jesus Christ. I imagine St. Paul to have had a temperament like his, though, of course, welded to a fine education and a cosmopolitan outlook, both of which had been denied to Andrei.

His parents, he said, had taken him to the Baptist Church from his infancy and he had acquiesced in this without any particular feelings for or against the worship in which he was participating. One day his parents 'disappeared in unpleasant circumstances' (a current Russian euphemism to designate victims of the purges). His world might well have capsized, had he not met at church a very saintly and compassionate minister who taught him the consolation of the Christian message of hope and how it applied to the unhappy realities of his own life.

From this time he saw the gospel of salvation as the ideal for which he wanted to give his life. He reached the age for national service and was recruited into the army. His ability gave him the chance of doing well. He scrupulously observed the discipline and was interviewed as a possible candidate for officer training. When the questioning turned to Marxism and ideology he made no attempt to conceal his views before the board of officers, but said that his Christian beliefs made him a no less capable soldier who would be loyal to his fatherland.

As a result of this stand, he found himself not only rejected for officer training, but dismissed from the army altogether and sent back quietly, though ignominiously, to Leningrad. Since that time he has never been able to find any work in which he could earn more than the most miserable pittance, let alone embark on any course or apprenticeship to qualify him for a good job. When I asked him what exactly his work was, he replied: 'There can be nothing interesting to tell you about a job for which I get thirty roubles a month.' I was astounded that a man could earn so little: it was about the same as Olga Sergeyevna's pension, and a fifth of my former grant.

I think Andrei told me his life-story right at the beginning of our acquaintance in order to gain my confidence. He never spoke of his past again. He had been awaiting the opportunity of meeting a foreigner because he needed help.

'We young Christians here are desperately short of Bibles and other literature which would help us to strengthen and spread our faith,' he said. 'Couldn't you give me anything in this line which you have?'

Unfortunately I had to tell him that all I had left was my English annotated copy of the Bible, with the substance of two years' work pencilled into the margins, which anyway no one else would be able to decipher. I had had one or two Russian ones, but I had given them away some time before.

'Look, the whole future of Christianity here depends on getting literature from somewhere. A friend of mine met an American once who managed to get some New Testaments in for us somehow—we didn't ask how. Couldn't you possibly manage to do the same? You must know ways and means.' I told him I would do my very best, but the customs officials keep the closest watch on all literature which is imported.

His main business out of the way, Andrei went on to tell me about his views on life and the discipline of the Christian faith. I have never known anyone outside a monastic community who subjected himself so completely to a rule of life. Every day had to begin and end with prayer, he said, and no food or drink should be taken at any time without first thanking God for it and reflecting that there were millions of people in the world whose very life was being eaten away by famine. In view of this, complete asceticism was the only way for the Christian—every day he had to renew his pledge to take only such subsistence as was necessary for his continued existence. Andrei, of course, would not touch alcohol nor smoke a cigarette and he insisted that indulging in these was immoral in itself, not merely a matter of discipline.

He looked at the text of the Bible as something sacred and wholly indivisible, which it was impossible to question without being disloyal to the faith it proclaimed. He believed that modern scholarship was irrelevant to the self-sufficient word of God and that nothing beyond complete faith in the truths of the Bible was necessary to salvation. It was easy to understand the urgency with which he needed Bibles, and more Bibles. He said that if a million were deposited in Red Square, a multitude would seize every one in five minutes and the place would be left empty.

Beside Andrei, with his passionate sincerity and single-minded zeal, I felt a very second-class Christian indeed. If I did not agree with this approach to the Holy Scriptures and did not think that it was the most practical way to combat Marxism, what right had I to say so, who had not known suffering for my faith?

Andrei went on to tell me that the situation in Leningrad was growing more difficult and it was becoming increasingly dangerous for him and his friends to be seen at church. A year ago one of his closest friends had been sentenced to seven years in a camp near Michurinsk for distributing Christian leaflets. He had heard indirectly that since this time the friend had had no meat at all to eat except dog's flesh. He himself was not unduly disturbed by this. Even if he should be imprisoned he could still live as a Christian, just like his friend, and try to persuade others to do the same.

Andrei told me that for him there was one feature in the present situation much worse than the threat of persecution. There seemed to be a conspiracy among the Baptist pastors to keep quiet about the deterioration since 1959. Not one of them would admit that Andrei's friend had been silenced for Christian activity and they went further than this: they had warned the congregation never to mention to foreigners that there were restrictions on religious liberty and that Bibles and hymn-books were unobtainable. He said that not all the pastors had compromised themselves in this way, but he was very

157

dubious about the integrity of those who had been allowed to go to England to study.[1]

Kiev up to recently had four Baptist Churches, and when I was there in 1960 I had the opportunity of meeting a young pastor, Grigory Melnikov, from one of them. Though I cannot completely understand the Ukrainian language, I heard him deliver what seemed a superb sermon on *Acts* 20. 9–12 (the passage about Eutychus, who fell asleep, overbalanced and tumbled backwards out of the window while St. Paul was talking). He made a few humorous comments on those who sleep while listening to sermons today and then went on to talk of different types of sleep (both physical and metaphorical) and of different types of fall. Spiritual sleep is the most dangerous, he said, and inevitably precedes a spiritual fall, because, in a state of torpor, one loses all sense of the horror of sin.

After the service I remained behind to meet the preacher, wanting to tell him how impressed I had been with the sermon. Spontaneously he invited me to come to his home, so we left after he had telephoned his wife to let her know a guest would shortly be arriving.

The evening I spent with Grigory was one of the happiest experiences of my life and our friendship has been a source of inspiration to me ever since. To reach his flat we caught a tram which took us on a winding route far into the suburbs of Kiev beyond the Dnieper. The hot summer was only just beginning, but already every passing vehicle sent up clouds of dust from the unpaved roads and the bright-green spring foliage which had so recently appeared on the wayside trees was starting to look tarnished and mat.

The scene, when we reached our destination, was a familiar one. Roadway, pavement and courtyard were all the same texture, and the colour of bare earth. The course of the road was marked only by the double track of the tramlines which threaded a way between the towering new blocks of flats, the same colour as the ground from which they rose. Opposite the tram-stop a pocket of wooden houses stood walled in and menaced by the advancing forest of new buildings. Perhaps the planners had forgotten to order their demolition.

Grigory treated me as if the whole of his life had been a preparation for my appearance. I have never felt anything like it. He took me into his flat, apologizing for the bareness of it, but not concealing his pride and gratitude to God because he possessed, for the first time in his life, a home of his own. He was about thirty-five and until his

[1] Five pastors from Moscow and Leningrad did so in the late 'fifties.

recent marriage he had been living with his parents in Odessa. He had become a pastor there before moving to take on increased responsibility in Kiev, where he at once met Natalya, his vivacious and charming wife. She was Russian, and thanks to her, Grigory said, he spoke Russian with no trace of a Ukrainian accent. The two rooms were spotlessly clean and an incipient lustre was already appearing on their long, knotted wooden floorboards. The smaller room, Grigory explained, was used as a bedroom for himself and his wife and a playroom for their young son of two. This room, about sixteen feet long and twelve across, served as study, dining-room and living-room. The flat was much more spacious than a couple like Grigory and Natalya could have expected in Moscow. 'I'm afraid we have no lampshades yet, as we have only recently come into the flat,' Grigory explained, 'but we hope to have them soon. What do you think of my books?'

I inspected the bookcase standing against the wall. It was full of Russian literature, containing a good selection of authors from the beginning of the nineteenth century up to the present. I told him that I was most impressed by his collection, as indeed I was, but surprised that he had no theological books.

'Ah, I keep those in a special place.' He went to his desk which stood beside the bookcase and took out a new edition of the Bible (printed in America for Russian *émigrés*), two tattered pre-Revolutionary books on Christian doctrine and Church history (obviously produced for the Orthodox Church), and a paper-back in English on the Church's ministry of healing. Such is the material which a Russian Baptist minister has at his disposal and from which he has to produce a continuous flow of long sermons. That Baptist preaching should be so varied and of such high quality seems to me to represent a remarkable triumph in face of great difficulties.

Grigory took me down to the end of the room where a glass door opened on to a tiny balcony. From here we had an uninterrupted view across the river back to the golden cupolas of Kiev. 'You're very lucky to have such a lovely view,' I said. It looked wonderfully peaceful. Unfortunately, Grigory told us, in a year or two the view would be lost for the whole intervening area was scheduled for building. 'You come to the outer suburbs thinking you will be able to combine the advantages of town and country life, but before long you are engulfed in the metropolis just the same.'

In the middle of the room was a table covered with a white cloth and piled high with food. There were plates of several varieties of cooked meats, both tinned and fresh fish, two sorts of cheese, black bread and white, cake, a bowl of oranges and a saucer of sweets. It is no exaggeration that the cost of the whole spread must have come to more than Grigory would earn in a week. I was absolutely over-whelmed, but Grigory insisted that it was 'nothing' and that he was sorry his wife had had such short notice to prepare it all. Otherwise he would have given me a real Ukrainian meal and shown me what the local hospitality was really like. Grigory went out to help his wife with the preparations in the communal kitchen.

He soon reappeared, carrying a kettle and a steaming cauldron of soup. He somehow managed to clear a space for them on the table and said: 'Shall we stand for a prayer before the meal?'

What followed was no formal grace, but a long and fervent sup-plication. His intensity held me to a degree of concentration I had never known before in prayer. He prayed for Britain, America and Russia and for the leaders of the world, especially for President Eisenhower and Mr. Khrushchev, who were at that time about to meet in Paris. He mentioned all his close relatives individually before God, enumerating all their needs and asking blessing on his parents' holiday on the Black Sea Coast. Finally he prayed for me asking that God would use my life to bring increased understanding and friend-ship between his country and mine.

When we sat down to the meal, Natalya adopted a tone of gay banter, though at times, when she talked of God or his Church, her voice would at once take on a note of gravity and she would speak slowly, with increased weight on all the stressed syllables. The flow of conversation was uninterrupted, save when they broke off to press my flagging appetite into another helping of meat or fish.

Every observation Grigory made was rooted in Christian love, whether he was talking about America, the Communist Party or the Orthodox Church (a subject on which I had heard some Baptists speak with less than charity). We talked and drank tea until what came out of the pot was cold. Grigory then embarked on a monologue of which the main theme was that the Baptist Church had a great role to play in Russia's future, and with God's help the country would be reconverted to Christianity. He said he considered that every pastor had a part to play in the strategy for evangelism.

I asked him about his background. He told me he had been born of Evangelical parents who had given him and his three brothers a

Harvest Festival in the Baptist Church

thorough grounding in the Bible through daily family readings. Prayer at home became more intense in the 'thirties, when pressure on the Church increased. His parents stopped taking him to the church when he was in his 'teens, but he never felt that he wanted to do anything other than preach the gospel to those unfortunate enough not to believe in it. After leaving school he served in the army for the last two years of the war. He stayed on in Eastern Germany until 1947, when he came back and was demobilized. His parents were delighted at his decision to take a part-time job in Odessa, where he could study for the ministry in his spare time with a saintly Baptist pastor. The authorities did not object to this and his studies progressed well. He found no doctrinal difficulty in studying with a Baptist, though he had been an Evangelical Christian before the union.

The time came for me to go, but Grigory begged me urgently to stay. When eventually I stood up to leave, he said I could not go without a final prayer, and that I must offer it.

'I have never prayed in a foreign language before in my life,' I objected.

'That doesn't matter. We shan't worry about what words you use—it's the fact of your trying which is important.'

So, thrusting aside my self-consciousness, I did my best to show the couple, by thanking God, how profoundly touched I had been by the evening's fellowship. I have not the remotest recollection of the words I used.

Still this was not the end. Before I could leave, Natalya started to ply me with gifts. There was a porcelain statue illustrating a folk-tale, a wooden plate with a reproduction of a photograph of Tolstoy in the middle, a delightful photograph of the family. Then Grigory started to stuff into my brief-case such relics of the feast as were portable and some that were not. Knowing the astronomical price of sweets, I tried to persuade him to keep them for his child, but entirely in vain.

Such overwhelming generosity from people who are unable to afford it can never be repaid. It is remarkable that over forty years after the Revolution the Soviet Union can still produce young men who not only live their whole lives in accordance with the principles of Christianity, but seem much more imbued with the spirit of the Early Church than anyone I, at any rate, have met elsewhere. Communist propaganda may attack the morals of individual Baptist

161

leaders in a vicious way, but any Soviet citizen who meets a Baptist like Andrei or Grigory personally cannot fail to be impressed with the generous, outgoing attitude to others and the absolute integrity which seem to be the hallmark of those who profess this faith. A chance meeting between Andrei or Grigory and a member of the Komsomol would probably be worth more than a dozen sermons, and it is through such personal contacts that the Baptist faith propagates itself today.

THE MOSCOW BAPTIST CHURCH

Of recent years foreigners have gradually become aware of the existence of the Baptist Church in the U.S.S.R. Its delegates have been allowed to participate, side by side with those of the Russian Orthodox Church, in foreign ceremonial occasions, and in August 1962 it joined the World Council of Churches. Many distinguished guests from abroad have been received at the church in Moscow. These include Adlai Stevenson, Mrs. Eleanor Roosevelt and Dr. Billy Graham, and if you look through the visitors' book you get the impression that it is now high on the list of priorities in the tourist schedule. This is confirmed by the fact that it is even possible to find an occasional taxi-driver who knows how to find the church in Vuzovsky Maly Perulok, a sure sign that it has 'arrived', since Moscow drivers are notorious for their lack of local knowledge. It is even marked on an Intourist map of Moscow.

I had deliberately delayed my first visit there until my second month in the U.S.S.R. in order to give myself a chance to become accustomed to the most important Church of the country before looking at less typical Christian bodies. From the first time I set foot inside the Moscow Baptist Church I always received a warm and genuine welcome which quite surpassed anything else which I regularly experienced in the Soviet Union. To go there from the University was like coming from the darkness into the light. Every time I made my way up the dingy side-street to the sandy-orange coloured building, with the white mouldings of its classical façade crumbling and discolouring, I was filled with a keen sense of anticipation, knowing how the exterior belied what lay within. Each time I knew I would make more friends and learn something new about the problems of living and worshipping as a Christian under a Communist régime.

162

One of the pastors is always on duty at the front door before and during services to watch out for visitors, greet them and introduce them into the congregation. If the newcomer is a foreigner, the pastor looks for someone who speaks his language and ushers him into a seat in the front row of the gallery which is permanently reserved for such visitors. On hearing that I was from England, the pastor who first greeted me immediately sent for Ilya Orlov, who told me that he had been in England from 1956 to 1958. He had been studying at the Bristol Baptist College, and when he discovered that I was from the West of England he told me with great enthusiasm that he had preached both in Plymouth and Paignton. He took out his wallet and drew from it a newspaper cutting. It was an account of the latter occasion printed in the (to me) unmistakable type-face of the *Western Morning News*. I felt a warm breath of home.

This feeling of familiarity increased when I heard an organ playing the introduction to 'The Church's one foundation', only to be submerged at once by a thundering sea of voices. I did not want to miss any more of the service, and was shown to one of the reserved seats in the gallery.

On future visits I always felt ashamed of receiving this preferential treatment, while so many Russian women were forced to stand throughout the long service. Several times I offered my seat to some of them standing near, but they would never take it and always seemed embarrassed by my action. Eventually I found it was best to go to the service, as it were incognito, through the side entrance and stay downstairs until the end, then to meet my friends behind the scenes afterwards. Mikhail Zhidkov and Dmitry Krasnenkov, as well as Ilya Orlov, always went out of their way to speak to me and make me feel at home.

On this first occasion I was struck by the strange mixture of the familiar and the unfamiliar in what I saw and heard. All my succeeding visits reinforced this impression. If I had been expecting a pure transplant of Western Protestantism I would have to revise my ideas, for the Russian Baptist Church can be understood only as a fusion between Protestantism and traditional Russian piety. Although it is of such recent origin it now expresses the Russian mentality as genuinely as anything in the Orthodox Church. Thus the forms of worship and the interior of the Church itself are extremely familiar to a Western Protestant, while the spirit is purely Russian.

At the same time the Russian Baptists are conscious of being members of a world-wide brotherhood and they have a great feeling of solidarity with their co-religionists in other countries. This awareness of Christianity as a world-wide religion is something I rarely found among Orthodox people, who would sometimes ask me, when I said that I was a member of the Church of England, whether I believed in the same God as they do.

Physically the Moscow Baptist Church is hardly larger than a Nonconformist church in an average English or American town, which means that as the only one in the city it is far too small for the baptized church membership of 4,500. When it is empty, you would hardly recognize it as being Russian at all. From the balcony which runs round three sides you see rows of wooden benches facing the Lord's Table on which there is no cross but two burning candles. From either side of the table two low flights of wooden stairs run up to a platform about half the height of the gallery, and this is occupied during the service by the various pastors taking part. When their turn comes to speak they walk to the pulpit at the front of the platform, decorated with the fleshy leaves of a potted plant and situated directly above the Lord's Table. The platform recedes into an apse with three stained glass windows. Two of them have pale geometrical patterns and these flank the central one which has emblazoned on it the three words: *Bog yest lyubov* (God is love). At the opposite end of the church, above the main entrance, 'The Lord be with you all' is written in large letters. Above this is a clock attached to the front of the rostrum where the choir-master stands. Behind the choir are ranged the pipes of the organ, the most familiar feature of all. Take away the two inscriptions in Russian and the potted plant, and one would hardly be able to distinguish the building from its Western prototypes.

Yet when the church is full of people the atmosphere is totally and unmistakably Russian. It is not so much the physical appearance of the people as their intense devotion evident both in the prayers and in the singing which gives the service its unique stamp. It was the same quality of concentration which used to impress me so much in Orthodox worship—it is one we sadly lack in the West.

The comparison with the Orthodox service, however, ends here. The pattern of worship could hardly be less similar. In the one the main emphasis is on the liturgy, with its rich visual and symbolic elements, in the other it is on the spoken word.

The Baptist services are very simple in their outline. Three long

sermons, delivered by different pastors, are interspersed with con-
gregational hymns and anthems from the choir and at the end there
is an extended period of prayer. The whole service invariably takes
two hours. While I was in Russia in 1959–60 there used to be six
services a week, three of which were on Sundays. My first visit
happened to be on the 'Day of Unity', the fifteenth anniversary of the
union between the Baptist and the Evangelical Christians. I thought
that this perhaps explained the large numbers of people crowding
into the aisles and occupying every inch of available space by the side
of the organ and in other corners. But I soon discovered that large
numbers were the rule, on weekday evenings as well as on Sundays.
It is obvious that a very high proportion of the 4,500 members must
attend several times a week and that many others come too. A year
later the number of services was reduced to five a week, which puts
further pressure on the capacity of the building. When I asked why
one of the services had been cancelled, a presbyter told me that it was
to ease the strain on his colleagues, not because of pressure from the
Communist authorities. With eighteen, or even fifteen, lengthy sermons to be preached each week, the small band of presbyters must
indeed be extremely busy, especially as some do part-time secular
jobs as well.

Orthodox critics of the Baptist Church have often complained of
the poor theological standard of its presbyters and of the naïve
beliefs of its congregations. Even the impartial Walter Kolarz repeats
this allegation: 'The absence of any proper training of presbyters and
the dearth of literature are bound to keep the Baptist community in
the Soviet Union at a low theological and intellectual level. It will be
hard to replace the present leaders of the movement by people of
equal quality, although a handful of young Baptists have been allowed
to follow theological courses abroad.'[1]

It is difficult to agree with this judgment, although one has of
course to bear in mind that the standard in the great cities is probably
higher than in the provinces. I had heard people talk of extreme
fundamentalism in connection with Baptist leaders, but found very
little evidence of it. Members of the congregation, like my friend
Andrei, for instance, do sometimes have a rather extremist outlook,
but in the face of hostile propaganda it is no more crippling than the
belief in the miraculous power of icons which one generally finds in
an Orthodox congregation. As a result of its foreign contacts, the

[1] *Religion in the Soviet Union*, pp. 320–1.

165

Baptist Council receives many periodicals regularly from abroad, including twenty-five from the United States. This enables the pastors to keep in touch with the trends of modern theology, and on the evidence of sermons I have heard they seem to be doing this more than the Orthodox clergy. On the Day of Unity E. G. Karev, the general secretary of the All-Union Council, preached a masterly ecumenical sermon, summarizing what had already been achieved and talking of the events leading up to the unity conference with the Evangelicals in which he participated. Nor did he minimize the immense task which still lies before the Church, both in Russia and elsewhere, if it is to achieve its goal of unity. He had a detailed knowledge of what was happening with reunion schemes in other countries and the whole was suffused with a warmth of Christian love. His high standards are carried over into the younger generation by Grigory Melnikov and many other presbyters like him, most of whom have never set foot outside the U.S.S.R.

The Russian-speaking visitor to the Moscow Baptist Church is sometimes handed a copy of the *Collection of Spiritual Songs* so that he can join in the singing. Although this hymnal was reprinted in 1953 and 1956, the number of copies available must be wholly inadequate, since in this particular congregation fewer than one in twenty members had one. Most of them seemed to know all the hymns by heart, while others refreshed their memories from manuscript copies. The words of the hymns are often translations of familiar English originals, and sometimes they have the usual tunes still attached to them, though they are sung so incredibly slowly that one has to listen carefully in order to recognize them. I remember once singing 'Nearer, my God, to Thee', to the tune of *Horbury* and I did not recognize it until I had mentally translated back the repeated words of the last line. Sometimes German chorale melodies are used, and they sound very strange wedded to evangelical Russian words, even though these themselves are sometimes translations of German originals. The volume of sound is always overwhelming, its intensity moving.

I never found this last quality more strongly present than when I visited the Baptist church on 6th January 1960. It is strange to find that the Baptists use the Julian Calendar, according to which this is Christmas Eve. Many traditional Christmas customs have been transferred by the Communists to the secular New Year festivities, so I had already seen many animated gatherings around Christmas trees in the public squares and rubbed shoulders with 'Grandfather Frosts' (Father Christmases) in all the big stores. Even before this I had celebrated an English Christmas as a guest of the Ambassador at the British Embassy. I thought that after all this it must come as an anti-climax to keep the festival with Russian Christians.

However, the service was filled with the keen sense of quiet antici-pation, which one finds on Christmas Eve in England. The con-gregation's singing of 'Silent Night' remains most vividly in my memory of that evening. It was taken so slowly that one had, almost, to breathe in the middle of words, but it was remarkable how this most Teutonic of melodies had taken on a new Slavonic lease of life. It brought home to me more sharply than anything had done before how completely the Baptist faith has married Slavonic tem-perament to the ethos of Protestantism.

The choir, which used to sing two or three anthems in each service, could never equal the best Orthodox ones. There are two main reasons for this. The best Orthodox choirs are professional and re-ceive a sufficiently high remuneration to attract singers of good stan-dard, often graduates of the Conservatory of Music. At major festi-vals, for instance, members of the Bolshoi Opera take part in the services at the Patriarchal Cathedral. The Baptist choir, however, is drawn from the ranks of the committed members of the congregation. Among them are some older women, though the average age would not seem to be over forty. They practise twice a week under their choir-master, who is a qualified musician. Since they sing services on weekday evenings as well as on Sundays, they are very busy people. They sing well together, even if the middle parts are not as well defined as one would wish, but they are handicapped by the inferiority of the music which has not progressed beyond the late nineteenth-century anthem and revivalist hymn inherited from the West. While Orthodox choirs are the heirs of a great tradition, the Baptists have not had enough time, nor have they produced anyone with the genius, to form a satisfactory style of their own. I did once hear an anthem adapted from one of Mozart's masses, but most of the music is cloying and harmonically stillborn. Even the compositions of Russian choir-masters are still firmly based on the models of Moody and Sankey.

Prayer does not occupy a high proportion of the total time in Baptist worship, but when it does occur, usually near the end, follow-ing a sermon of high quality, it can be prayer of a rare intensity. This is what had impressed Kolya so much on the occasion when I took him with me to a service.[1] He regretted that Communists do not have the same solicitude for each other as the Christians here have for those who are absent through sickness.

Occasionally the mass concentration on prayer produces a kind of general tension which mounts up and up until, with the emotions of the congregation being played on, something snaps. This happened once when I was present. We had had two addresses in succession, the second of which had obviously made a profound impression on the congregation; by the time the preacher had finished, everyone was tense and somehow waiting to be led further. Even though the prayers were spoken by another pastor who had been silent up to this point in the service, he immediately caught the mood of the people. One could feel the tension rising. The atmosphere was, I imagined, like that of a revivalist meeting. An old lady behind me started to sob quietly when the prayer talked of purging us from all our deep and secret sins. She was joined by another on the opposite side of the balcony who began to whine audibly. Still the speaker continued, taking his cue from these noises to emphasize even more the abject prostration of the sinner before the judgment of God. Suddenly a young man, not far away on my left, leapt to his feet and cried out: 'Oh God, save my soul, I am a miserable sinner,' and much more too fast for me to catch. His words were partially drowned by those around him who tried to restrain him by pulling him down and putting their arms around him. For a moment the pastor tried to continue in competition with him, raising his voice still higher to make it carry above the hubbub. But soon he gave up, since the young man showed no signs of becoming calm, and then Ilya Orlov saved the day with a blast on the organ, *fortissimo*, and the whole congregation relieved its feeling by joining in with the doxology. The young man was persuaded to leave by those around him. My impression was that the pastor had deliberately played on the emotional tension of the worshippers and that if he had not, the incident would not have taken place. The members of the congregation are always eager to respond in such a way, and I have little doubt that this urge is increased by the flatness of their everyday lives.

On one occasion a Norwegian peace delegation visited the church and one of its female members was invited to address the congregation, which she did in English, so that one of the pastors could

[1] See p. 140.

translate sentence by sentence. The whole party had to leave before the end of the service. When they rose to go, all the old women took their handkerchiefs out of their pockets and waved them in the direction of the Norwegians, murmuring, 'Good-bye, good-bye'. Some women could be seen crying as they said their farewells to the visitors.

My relations with the pastors and officials of the Moscow Baptist Church became increasingly cordial during my stay, though they were always more guarded in what they said than the younger people with whom I talked. I always nurtured a hope at the back of my mind that I might be invited to address the congregation. This was a privilege sometimes accorded to members of visiting delegations, particularly if they had the 'peace' label attached to them. However, when a foreigner did address the Moscow Baptists there had to be a double safeguard. Firstly, the speaker was in the country for at most a few days, and secondly, whatever was spoken had to pass through an interpreter. I was unsuitable on both counts, and I am sure that the pastors were, from the point of view of their own safety, wise in not inviting me. I found out, too, that in the past people whose addresses might have contained inflammatory material, such as Billy Graham, had been fêted, but not asked to make any public pronouncements.

BAPTISTS AND ORTHODOX

In its official statements the Baptist Church has not been less zealous in the cause of 'peace' (Soviet version), nor less prepared to support the Government's line on international affairs than the Orthodox Church. This, however, plays no visible part in its life and worship, except in the odd prayer, nor has the Baptist Church indulged in the active intrigue in the satellite states and in the Middle East of which the Orthodox Church has been guilty since 1945.

I was depressed, however, by the frequent expression of uncharitable opinions on the part of the Baptists about the Orthodox Church. Andrei, for instance, said that most Orthodox priests were in their jobs only for what they could get out of them. I was interested to see how this accusation recurred in *One Day in the Life of Ivan Denisovich*:

' "Don't talk to me about your priest!" Alyosha said imploringly, his brow furrowed with distress.

169

' "No, listen." Shukhov propped himself up on an elbow. "In Polomnya, our parish, there isn't a man richer than the priest. Take roofing, for instance. We charge thirty-five roubles a day to ordinary folk for mending a roof, but the priest a hundred. And he forks up without a murmur. He pays alimony to three women in three different towns, and he's living with a fourth" . . .

' "Why are you talking to me about priests? The Orthodox Church has departed from Scripture. It's because their faith is unstable that they're not in prison." '[1]

It is unhappily true that in the minds of some Russian Christians the image of the Orthodox Church is tarnished by its compromises with the régime and by the reputation for simony that some priests have. Whether or not the allegations one hears are justified (and the evidence remains inconclusive, with much of it based on atheist sources), the growth of all kinds of Russian sects is a comment on the failure of the Orthodox Church to evangelize in new areas and in new ways for changed conditions. Perhaps even in places where the old faith is well organized and flourishing, people find that the sects give more scope for the individualism so sadly lacking in Soviet life. The conversation I had with Tatyana and Ivan, however, contains a firm warning against making comparisons about the appeal of the Baptist and Orthodox faiths on evidence that is too superficial.

One is tempted for instance to compare sermons in the Orthodox Church with those one hears in the Baptist Church and to emerge with a marked preference for the latter, as regards both style and content. This, however, cannot be extended into an argument for the greater vitality of the Baptist Church as compared with the Orthodox, because the sermon is little more than an adjunct to Orthodox worship, while it is the essential ingredient of a Baptist service.

Sermons in the Baptist Church are almost invariably based on the Bible, with illustrations taken from modern life. They end with applications which usually show where Christian duty lies in modern society. I never heard one which went so far as to say: 'If the Communist Government tells you to do something which your Christian conscience opposes, you must obey the dictates of the latter,' but a person who listens to the sermons regularly should be in no doubt about his pattern of conduct.

Andrei assured me that I must not judge Baptist sermons by what I heard in the churches at Moscow, Leningrad and Kiev. Many of the

[1] Penguin ed., p. 139.

most important gatherings, he said, take place out in the country. There the participants are often dispersed by the militia, but when this happens, they merely go off to another rallying point and continue there. Sermons on such occasions are distinctly anti-Communist.

The proportion of young people in a Baptist congregation is slightly higher than in most Orthodox gatherings. I estimated that usually about 5 to 7 per cent of the Baptist congregation belonged to the under-forty age group; of these, nearly half were men (in contrast to the Orthodox Church, where there were sometimes no young men at all). However, on my most recent trip to Russia, when the persecutions were already far more violent than they had been when I was living there, I thought that there were more young people present at Orthodox services; and I saw about twenty young men making their communions together at one service. At a baptism which I attended in the Baptist Church, thirty-four out of the thirty-seven who lined up for the ceremony of total immersion were women. They were all middle-aged, or older, with the exception of two girls of about eighteen who seemed to be the daughters of one of the other women. One of the three men in the group was probably their father. The women looked wonderfully serene in their flowing white baptismal robes, with caps on their heads which gathered their hair underneath them.

Comparisons, I know, are invidious, but I have often been troubled by this question: if I had a Russian friend who was a potential convert to Christianity, would I introduce him first to the Orthodox Church or to the Baptist? Obviously it would depend to a great extent on the friend himself. I would consider the question of language on the one hand, of aesthetic appeal on the other. One needs to be nurtured in Old Church Slavonic, or to study it specially, in order to understand the language of Orthodox services. The prospect of this might be daunting to the potential convert, and he would certainly feel that its use increased the strangeness of his new surroundings. By contrast, as soon as he stepped inside a Baptist church the familiarity of the language would help to assure him that Christianity is something of the present, not the barely surviving relic of the past which Communist propaganda tries to make it out to be. It is still possible, however, for an educated young person to feel that by going to an Orthodox church he is refreshing himself at the wellsprings which gave his nation its life and cultural heritage. In most instances, taking everything into consideration, I would probably advise a potential convert to go to the Baptist Church.

My view, of course, is unpopular with many Russian *émigrés* with whom I have discussed this question in England. I find support, however, in Walter Kolarz's book which expresses so succinctly the conclusion to which I had already come before reading it, that I cannot do better than to quote it. He says of the Baptists: 'They have understood better than the rest of the "religious front" how to adapt themselves to life and work under a communist régime, not so much by making peace with it, although they have done this too on a superficial level, but by challenging it on its own ground.'[1] This last phrase gives the central reason why I think a convert would, all other things being equal, draw more moral strength from the Baptist Church.

Within the U.S.S.R., relations between the Baptist and the Orthodox Churches have never been other than hostile (at worst) or coldly formal (at best). The days before 1905, when the Baptist faith was illegal and the Orthodox Church backed the Government's persecution of it, are not likely to return; but mistrust certainly exists among Orthodox clergy about recent Baptist successes, while many ordinary Baptists, for the reasons given above, have a low opinion of the Orthodox Church. At the same time, official relations between the two Churches are better than they have been. Now that both these great Christian bodies are members of the World Council of Churches, one hopes that they will have a forum where they can discuss their difficulties and differences. This may be possible at ecumenical gatherings abroad, even if it is impossible to do so formally at home. The Soviet Government is most unlikely to give any encouragement to an act of union between the two persecuted Churches, especially if it suspects that they are trying to band together against a common enemy. Abroad, it may just be possible to think about some common programme though the close surveillance which delegations are subjected makes even this unlikely.

[1] *Religion in the Soviet Union*, p. 283.

CHAPTER VII

A Glance Round the U.S.S.R.

I t lies beyond the scope of this book to deal with the multiplicity of minor sects scattered throughout the Soviet Union—Seventh Day Adventists, Jehovah's Witnesses, Molokans, Dukhobors, Imyaslavtsy, to mention only a few. On their distribution and relative importance Walter Kolarz's encyclopaedic survey is destined to remain the standard work for many years. Had it been published before I first went to the U.S.S.R., it would have been an invaluable guide. As it was I had no reliable information on where to look for minority groups, and I knew of their existence only through the occasional hostile articles about them which appeared in the Soviet Press. Consequently, when I was able to travel away from Moscow I concentrated my attention on the Orthodox and Baptist Churches, or on the most important denomination in the particular area I was visiting. I did not have enough money or time to visit the Moslem areas of Central Asia nor the Buddhists of the Buryat-Mongol Autonomous S.S.R., so I decided to confine my inquiries to the Christian religion only.

In travelling for about six weeks I was able to see something of the Lutheran, Georgian and Armenian Churches in the areas where they are strongest, but I would not claim that the time I spent on each was long enough to give me more than a very superficial impression of their life.

This chapter, then, aims at little more than giving a brief sketch of the six main denominations which have not already been discussed, in order to complete the broad picture of the Christian religion in the U.S.S.R.

THE OLD BELIEVERS

I described the Rogozhskoye Cemetery and the Pokrovsky Cathedral in Chapter I, but in a sense, although the Pokrovsky Cathedral is the main centre of the Old Believers' Sect in the capital, it is quite unrepresentative of the Church as a whole and gives no guide to its present state in the U.S.S.R. The true nature of the Old Believer is to avoid the glare of publicity and retreat into his fastnesses, where he can re-create the atmosphere of Old Russia.

Thus it is that no aspect of the Christian religion in the Soviet Union today is more difficult to penetrate, nothing is less easy to assess than the extent and the vigour of the various sects of the Old Believers. As a result of the incessant persecutions of three hundred years, the adherents of the old faith fled from all the main centres and entrenched themselves in the far-flung border areas of the Russian Empire, with the direct intention of avoiding publicity and the inquisitions of the Tsar's underlings.[1] 'Lost tribes' of Old Believers, inhabiting remote and hitherto unmapped areas of the Soviet Union, are still being discovered by teams of surveyors, but it is impossible for foreigners to visit them while the itineraries of visitors are restricted to certain well-worn paths. It is in these places, not in Moscow, that one would be able to learn about the Old Believers' way of life, but my experience, like that of almost all other foreigners, is restricted to the capital.

The largest and best organized group of Old Believers is known as the 'Church of the Belaya Krinitsa Concord' and it is to them that the Pokrovsky Cathedral in Moscow belongs. The name is that of a village in the former Austrian province of Bukovina (now in Rumanian territory) where a community of refugees took up residence after the Schism. They were given permission by the Austrian Emperor in 1844 to choose a bishop (the first time in 180 years that any group of Old Believers anywhere had been granted such a privilege). The man they chose took up residence in Belaya Krinitsa and the name has been preserved up to the present.

This is the only group which exists in significant numbers in any accessible area of the U.S.S.R. other than Moscow. Certain areas in the Urals and in the Middle and Lower Volga regions are traditionally their strongholds, but even if one gets permission to visit the main towns in those parts one would still have to go right out into the country to find the parishes in their original state and this is usually impossible.

I have never talked to anyone who has visited these places and to my knowledge the only person who has done so and written about

[1] See Walter Kolarz, *Religion in the Soviet Union*, pp. 137–46.

them is Constantin de Grunwald.[1] He travelled by rail to Kostroma, on the Volga, and made an excursion from there deep into the countryside to the village of Strelnikovo, which is inhabited almost exclusively by Old Believers. He attended their liturgy, was deeply impressed by the fervour of the participants, and only just missed witnessing both a baptism (of several children at once) and a funeral. He noted that none of the males in the community shaved and that everyone preserved the traditional dress which had not changed since the Middle Ages. He was even fortunate enough to be invited by the priest to a meal at his house with several of the parishioners.

This, of course, gives a totally different impression from the one I received at the Pokrovsky Cathedral where most of the Old Believers I saw were very old indeed—even older, it seemed, than an average Orthodox congregation. There was much fervour in the worship, but I never saw a baptism or a young person present at a service, and nothing made me think that this Church would still be flourishing in ten years time. One knows, however, that it will be, even if only through the continued activity of Kirill Alexandrovich Abrikosov.

He is the Archbishop's chief lay administrator, an active and learned man who is very ready to receive foreign visitors if they telephone to make an appointment with him. He was most charming with me and not only gave me a guided tour, with erudite commentary, of all the magnificent icons in the Pokrovsky Cathedral, but also gave me information about his sect. He insisted on speaking to me in French, for some reason, and I received the impression (comparing notes with others) that what he said to me was exactly the same as what he always says to visitors. Certainly he refused to be drawn out into any more detailed discussion.

Mr. Abrikosov furnished me with plenty of statistics. He said that the number of Old Believers in the Church of the Belaya Krinitsa Concord may be as many as one million, of whom 50,000 live in the Moscow Region. Altogether there are three hundred churches in the whole Soviet Union, but this is the only one in the capital. These are looked after by 420 priests, four of whom officiate here in the Cathedral. All the churches are in a good financial state, with the revenue coming, as in the Orthodox Church, from the direct gifts of the faithful and from the sale of candles. He added that the Cathedral itself had been further enriched because so many families had deposited their priceless old icons there for preservation during the

[1] *God and the Soviets*, pp. 161–3.

persecutions. He also told me that his church was now free from oppression for the first time since the *Raskol* itself, with the result that nothing could now prevent its growth nor halt its campaign for the re-conversion of Russia to the old faith. I asked whether they had a seminary open for the training of priests, to which he replied that today, as always in the past, an ordinand could be instructed only by the method of affiliation to a priest for a number of years.

On the question of persecution I noted Mr. Abrikosov's optimism, though I could not persuade him to elaborate on what had happened in the past. Obviously there were some grounds for his (relative) confidence. The Old Believers' lot is certainly easier now than it was under the Tsars, and I could appreciate his emotion when he said that his Cathedral had been closed and kept locked, with all its contents sealed inside, from 1854 until the granting of religious liberty in 1905. However, one knows that during the period between the Revolution and the Second World War many Old Believer bishops and priests suffered as severely as their Orthodox counterparts. When I asked Mr. Abrikosov about this, he replied that this was a thing of the past and had been due to 'misunderstandings'. A new era had been inaugurated in 1946, when Archbishop Irinarkh had received a telegram on his sixty-fifth birthday from the head of the Government Council for the Affairs of Religious Cults, a unique event in the three hundred years of the Old Believers' history. Now, he continued, for the first time they were able to have a proper constitution, they could publish an official calendar[1] and anyone could read about their faith in Melnikov-Pechersky's novel, *In the Forests*, which had had a huge printing of 300,000 copies in 1955.[2]

The situation cannot, of course, be as bright as Mr. Abrikosov depicts it. Some forms of persecution certainly persist. I remember reading in a Leningrad newspaper, sometime early in 1960, a letter from a reader complaining that Old Believers were holding services in his block of flats. They were, he claimed, disrupting the public amenities by overflowing into the corridors and blocking them, so that on one occasion a sick child had to be hauled out through the window to a waiting ambulance. In addition, this practice was making the atmosphere of the place deteriorate, because it was allowing

---

[1] Interrupted for some reason from 1951–5.
[2] As a great work of Russian literature, this could not be suppressed indefinitely. This edition was prefaced by an essay attempting to represent the author's work as an attack on the Old Believers. The large size of the printing is hard to understand even so.

'Trinity Meadow': the Leningrad Baptist Church, now housed in a
former Orthodox building

A peasant woman in Suzdal rests beside a church

children to hear naughty religious words which ought not to be in their vocabulary. If the authorities allowed the Old Believers to have as many places of worship open as they needed, such makeshift substitutes would not, of course, be necessary.

In spite of the imposing dimensions of its Cathedral, the Belaya Krinitsa sect of the Old Believers is not the one which claims most adherents in Moscow itself, for the 'Fedoseyevtsy' may have as much as twice as many. The name comes from that of their founder, Feodosy Vasiliev, though they are also known by the name of *Bespopovtsy*, which means 'priestless sect'. They have become an organized group only in Moscow itself, where their centre is in a church on Preobrazhensky Val. Even Walter Kolarz is vague about them[1] and I myself found out nothing about them while I was in Moscow.

Another group of Old Believers, the *Beglopopovtsy*, was so called because its ministry was originally supplied by priests who had run away from the official Church. They never recognized the Belaya Krinitsa Church, considering it tainted by its connections with Austrian officialdom. They have been allowed to become a recognized organization only since the Revolution, when a bishop from the 'Living Church' came over to them in 1923, to be joined seven years later by an Orthodox one.

They have a church in Moscow next door to the Pokrovsky Cathedral and I visited it on several occasions. The first time I went in and found a service in progress. It was only a tiny church, with every available space on the walls covered with icons or artificial flowers. There were about a dozen very old women making a ghastly noise in a strange chant, but with them were a boy and a girl of about nine, each paying rapt attention to the service. Later a girl in her teens came in, with whom I tried to enter into conversation, but failed. After a few moments a priest came out from behind the iconostasis and the incredible dignity of his bearing really took my breath away. He must have stood all of six feet four inches and his height was emphasized by the majestic sweep of the magenta-coloured *mantia* which swathed him from neck to foot. His auburn hair and beard flowed in waves, like a Leonardo drawing of water, curling down on to his powerful shoulders and chest. His singing voice, of dynamic power and breadth, added a last touch of authority to a superb figure.

[1] op. cit., pp. 140–2.

177

On my second visit there was no service in the church, but in no time at all a crowd of about twenty old men and women gathered round to speak to me. They were very willing to talk of their Church, telling me that they had thirty congregations in various parts of the U.S.S.R., with headquarters in Kuibyshev. This was the only church in Moscow, but it was served by two priests. They said that after the Revolution it had looked as if they would have better times and they changed the anachronistic old name to a new one, the 'Old Believer Church of Ancient Orthodox Christians'. However, the old name has stuck, and they viewed the future without much hope. They were not allowed to publish any literature to let people know about their faith and there were no young people interested in offering themselves for their priesthood, so they thought that their Church might not outlive their own generation.

What one sees of the Old Believers as a whole in Moscow does tend to make one feel pessimistic about their future; yet in their traditional strongholds their faith is a way of life and the Soviet Government is a long way from changing it. They retired from the 'realities of the modern world' three hundred years ago, so it is unlikely they will come to regard the Soviet Revolution as anything other than one more vagary of a sinful and hostile world, in the middle of which they are an island of faith. Probably anti-religious propaganda touches them less than any other Christians of the Soviet Union.

THE ROMAN CATHOLIC CHURCH

When one lives in Moscow, one does not realize the extreme importance of the Roman Catholic Church in the Soviet Union today. After the Russian Orthodox Church and the Moslem faith, it has more adherents than any other religious group, but in Moscow, as in many other parts of the Russian Republic (R.S.F.S.R.), it is the church of such a tiny minority of people that it could easily escape notice altogether. I was not fortunate enough to travel in any area where Roman Catholics form the majority of the population, so I cannot give any personal impressions of Catholicism in the Soviet Union.

The Communist Party has nearly always presented the Roman Catholic Church as its arch-enemy and as a vicious obstacle in the way of progress. The main reason for this, of course, is that the

Communist Party finds its universalist tendencies especially disturbing and regards its adherents as potential agents of Western powers; but even so, Russian distrust of the Pope cannot be explained exclusively in terms of the post-Revolutionary situation. Like so many other phenomena which persist in the present-day Soviet Union, it goes back hundreds of years—to the days of Tsarist expansion in fact. During the extended struggle against Poland, Russia's fear of Rome was associated with her hatred of the Poles, and since then the Russians have always been especially wary of Roman influence in the weak western border areas.

Despite this, there have been Roman Catholics on Russian soil since the earliest days. It is possible that there were small groups with Western allegiance in Kiev at the time of the conversion to Christianity.[1] There was a Catholic church in Novgorod when it became part of the Russian Empire in 1475, although Ivan III closed it down a few years later. In the main, however, it has remained the faith of minority groups which the Russians feared for other reasons beside their religion. An exception to this were the many trusted Roman Catholics among the Germans who helped Peter the Great to rebuild his empire and in St. Petersburg it was no more an alien religion than Orthodoxy was. By the end of the eighteenth century there were two Roman Catholic churches in Moscow—St. Louis des Français and SS. Peter and Paul.

Between the Revolution and the Second World War specific persecution of Roman Catholics living within the confines of the U.S.S.R. came in two main waves—the first right after the Revolution was directed against the Poles living in Byelorussia; the second, in 1926, was more general.

The first of these campaigns culminated in the trial of the Archbishop of Mogilev, John Cieplak, and his deputy, Constantin Budkiewicz, in 1923. Both were sentenced to death, but Cieplak's sentence was commuted to ten years' imprisonment and he was later exiled in exchange for a Polish Communist. This was the end of effective Catholic organization in the area, despite an attempt by a French Jesuit, Michel d'Herbigny, to reorganize the administration in 1926. All the people he appointed were victims of the purges.

Persecution of the small national groups of Poles and Germans during the middle 'twenties was equally severe and, like so many

[1] See M. Jugie, 'Les Origines Romaines de l'Eglise Russe', *Echos d'Orient*, 1937, pp. 257–70.

Lutherans, the Catholics suffered both for their race and their religion. Like the Lutherans, too, they were almost extinct as an organized body by 1939.

The Communist Party built up a mythology about the Pope, attempting to show that his main goal in life was the destruction of Russia. These accusations became increasingly hysterical and ill-founded and did not always find their mark. The Vatican, for its part, kept a close watch on the plight of its faithful followers in the Soviet Union. In St. Peter's, Rome, on 19th March 1930, Pope Pius XI celebrated a Mass of Expiation for the wrong done to Christians in Russia, while many Protestants and the Anglican Church associated themselves with the intention and held a day of prayer just before the Mass. There were not only howls of protest at this from the Soviet authorities, but the Patriarch Sergius issued a statement praising the Government for its tolerance and goodwill and repudiating the suggestion that there was any religious persecution in the U.S.S.R. This statement undoubtedly did his own Church much damage. The reaction of one Orthodox priest, probably typical of many, has been given earlier.[1]

The Roman Catholic Church alone received no benefit from the concordat which Stalin granted to other Churches in 1943. However, just when it seemed that organized Catholicism in the U.S.S.R. was a spent force, millions of new adherents to the faith became Soviet citizens through the 'liberation' of a large segment of Polish territory and the whole of Lithuania. The latter was the first entire country with a Roman Catholic majority to come under the sway of Communism. At the time of the first Soviet occupation in June 1940 80 per cent of its 2,900,000 population were Roman Catholics and a further 500,000 lived in Latgalia, the south-eastern part of Latvia, which was annexed at the same time.[2]

Stalin obviously had no intention of leaving them in peace. Four of the five bishops who remained in Lithuania after the 'liberation' were deported to labour camps, while of the 1,470 priests at work in 1945, only about a half were left in 1954. There are at present seminaries at Kaunas and Riga, the only sources of replenishment for the ranks of Roman clergy in the whole Soviet Union. The number of students is limited by the State (seventy-five at Kaunas, for example)

[1] See p. 56.
[2] For these statistics, as for most of the facts in this section, I am indebted to Walter Kolarz, op. cit., pp. 176–217.

THE ROMAN CATHOLIC CHURCH

and there is a strong possibility that some of them are Communist agents. Though they may provide enough graduates to allow the Church in the Baltic countries to continue its existence, it is more than doubtful whether they can replace ageing clergy in the scattered Roman Catholic parishes of Armenia and Georgia, for example.[1] A very aged priest I talked to in the Roman Catholic church at Tbilisi told me that when he died he thought that his congregation would have to carry on as best they could without a priest, possibly being led in prayer by a layman but without ever receiving the sacrament.

Despite the depredations on the clergy and the churches in Lithuania and Latgalia, it is very doubtful whether very great inroads have been made on popular faith, and demonstrations in support of Christianity are still likely to occur on feast days. On 1st July 1957, a new church, built at a cost of 350,000 new roubles given by the faithful, was opened at Klaipeda (formerly called Memel). Twenty thousand people mobbed it, attempting to gain admission for the consecration ceremony. Over the last few years some bishops and priests have been allowed to return to their homeland, either from abroad, or, as a result of the post-Stalin amnesty, after spending many years in labour camps. Though the bishops have not been able to take over their old sees, they have at least been able to celebrate mass.

Unfortunately, there are now younger clergy who are prepared to lend vocal support to all aspects of Soviet foreign policy. A particularly odious example of this was the statement made by a prominent cleric[2] condemning Anglo-French-Israeli aggression against Egypt, while at the same time making a tirade against Western distortions of the true facts about Hungary. Bishop Peter Strods, who succeeded Archbishop Anthony Springovics as head of the Latvian Catholic Church in 1958, does not go so far, but he gave Constantin de Grunwald a most rosy picture of church life in his diocese in 1960.[3]

The only existing Roman Catholic church in Moscow, St. Louis des Français, has miraculously remained open without a break for over 150 years and it occupies a remarkable place in the history of Christianity in the Soviet Union. As a result of the Roosevelt-Litvinov agreement of 1933, Fr. Leopold Brown, an American Assumptionist, was allowed to minister there for twelve years, draw-

[1] According to Bishop Strods (Constantin de Grunwald, *God and the Soviets*, p. 183) there are 1,235 Roman Catholic parishes in the whole Soviet Union.
[2] *Izvestia*, 25th November 1956.
[3] op. cit., pp. 182–4.

ing his congregation both from Soviet Roman Catholics and from the diplomatic corps. Fr. George Laberge, another American, replaced him in 1945, but was refused a re-entry permit when he went home on leave after four years. A French priest carried on for a short while, but was removed as the result of a 'petition' signed by members of his congregation and asking for a Russian-speaking priest. Since 1950 no foreign priest has been able to celebrate in St. Louis des Français, and the foreign priests Fathers Brassard, Bisonette[1] and Dion have had to confine their ministry to diplomatic personnel and hold services in their private apartments.

The present incumbent of St. Louis, Fr. Witold Bronicki, is a Soviet citizen of Polish-Lithuanian origin, who preaches in Polish, which, he claims, is the main language of his congregation. He told me that he has about three thousand parishioners, of whom a third come regularly to mass. On Sundays the church always seemed to be full, the congregation looking identical to that of an Orthodox church, but perhaps with more young children accompanying their parents. The church is centrally situated not far from Dzerzhinsky Square, so that many Roman Catholic and other tourists also find their way there.

THE UNIAT CHURCHES

It is difficult to estimate the importance and present strength of the several groups of Uniats in the U.S.S.R. In attempting to bridge the gulf which had gradually opened between Eastern and Western Christians during the Middle Ages, these people who celebrate the liturgy in their own language yet owe their allegiance to the Pope, tend to arouse both the hatred of the Orthodox and the mistrust of Catholics of the Latin Rite. The movement arose in the sixteenth century[2] and has been judged by some as an honest early attempt at ecumenical *rapprochement*, while others have written it off in harsh terms.

There is a minute Catholic church of the Slavo-Byzantine Rite on Russian soil which owes its official origin to the limited freedom of worship granted in 1905 and to the conversion to Catholicism of Fathers Zerchaninov and Susalev, Orthodox and Old Believer priests respectively. There is also a small Greek Catholic Church in Byelo-

---

[1] For a comment on Bisonette's book, *Moscow was my Parish*, see Notes for Further Reading, p. 238.
[2] For the origins of the Uniat Church, see Zernov, *The Russians and their Church*, pp. 85–8.

russia, but this is not as important as the Uniat Church in the Ukraine, which serves, or did until recently, the largest single group of Uniat Christians anywhere in the world. This Church was organized in this century by Metropolitan Andrei Szeptycki, a remarkable man inspired by the vision of a united Orthodox and Catholic Church. He died in November 1944, and within a few months a movement had arisen within the Uniat Church to agitate for union with the Orthodox Church. This design was pushed by both the Communist Party and the Orthodox, and it is certain that the Ukrainian Uniat Church was not liquidated as an independent body in any way voluntarily. The intricacies of the situation have never been documented and I know of no one who has been able to travel freely in the areas affected, but it is certain that Western Ukrainians who wish to continue their old allegiance are not able to do so, for the Uniat Church there is now illegal. However, rumours are seeping out of the U.S.S.R. which indicate that activity on a local level still continues.

INTERRUPTED BALTIC JOURNEY

To Western Protestants the Lutherans of the Soviet Union are a subject of special interest. The extreme north-west of Russia was evangelized by Finnish and Estonian pastors before it was properly colonized by the Russians themselves. Indeed the site on which St. Petersburg was built belonged to a Lutheran parish before the city came into being and there was any Orthodox population in the neighbourhood.

Before the Revolution, Lutheranism was chiefly the religion of the German minority, which, however, formed a significant proportion of the local population in certain areas. Because of this national association it suffered very severely from 1928 and was almost totally annihilated in a way that befell no other Christian church. At the Revolution there were 287 churches, looking after 1,136,000 parishioners, of whom nearly a tenth lived in St. Petersburg. By 1937 there was not a single parish which had not been liquidated nor an active pastor left anywhere in the U.S.S.R.[1] The human suffering bound up with this operation can only be guessed at and it remains the most devastating single success of Soviet atheism.

[1] For these and all other statistics in this section I am indebted to Walter Kolarz, op. cit., pp. 248–70.

It is exceedingly ironical that this campaign had hardly been completed when the Soviet Union acquired a further two million Lutherans, through the annexation of the Baltic countries in 1940. Three-quarters of the total population of Estonia and just over half of that of Latvia were Lutherans. The people had already had a short foretaste of the persecution to come during the temporary Soviet occupation in 1918–19. Then there had been a vile and open campaign against Christianity, but it did not last long enough to have a deep effect and the two countries were lucky to escape Soviet rule for the next twenty years. By the time the oppressors returned in 1940 to snatch away the hard-earned independence of the Baltic States, they had learned a modicum of civility and tact in dealing with religious problems; though this did not prevent wholesale deportations of prominent Lutheran pastors and bishops on manufactured charges of collaborating with the Germans during the wartime occupation. It is surely one of the great ironies of modern Russian history that both Jews and Christians who suffered abominably under the Germans fared little better after their 'liberation' by the Communists. The head of the Estonian Lutheran Church was deported to Vorkuta in 1951 and succeeded by Jaan Kiivit who later took the title of Archbishop. Not much is known of the circumstances of his appointment.

In Latvia, the Archbishop of Riga, Gustavs Turs, never completed his theological training. He had been allowed to take up a living in a small country parish on the sole condition that he never aspired beyond the office of parish priest. Needless to say, there was much opposition to his election as Archbishop, but those who objected were arrested.

Both men are prepared to play a full part in the Soviet Government's peace campaign and are signatories to all the necessary pronouncements. But however much they have compromised themselves, they have been allowed to continue the organization of the Lutheran parishes under their charge. Pastors must preach regularly in support of Soviet propaganda (a touchstone of their loyalty) and are under exactly the same restrictions in connection with parish life as their Orthodox counterparts, which strikes a Lutheran particularly hard; nevertheless church life goes on.

There have even been some concessions since 1954. A few selected ordinands, for instance, are allowed to train abroad. There are evening classes for others and a Latvian hymn-book has been issued in a miserably inadequate edition of five thousand copies with expurgations to remove Luther's anti-tyrannical passages.[1] The archbishops have been able to renew contact with their co-religionists in other countries, through exchanges of delegations. Even more significant, some Lutheran worship has been established in Central Asia and Siberia, the areas to which so many Germans and 'collaborators' had been sent years earlier. After the amnesties of 1953–6 released prisoners were able to form parishes, the names of two of which are known. This is a spontaneous movement, so far entirely unrecognized either by the Soviet authorities or by the Lutheran archbishops, but it does something to compensate for the seizure of Riga Cathedral and for the inadequate staffing of many parishes in the Baltic States. Attempts by the Lutheran World Federation to establish contact with the parishes in Central Asia have met with a sharp rebuff from the Soviet authorities.

I was fortunate enough to be one of the first foreigners, apart from one or two official delegations, to visit Tallinn, the capital of the Estonian Soviet Republic, after it was opened to foreign visitors at the beginning of 1960.

During my second year at Wycliffe Hall in Oxford, Pastor Kaide Rätsep, of the Estonian Lutheran Church, had come there to live while doing research on New Testament subjects. Shortly after I first arrived in Moscow I met him there again when he was on his way to England for his second year of study. He had insisted that I should visit his family if I had the opportunity of going to Tallinn. I assumed that he would not have made the invitation if its acceptance were likely to involve him or his family in any unpleasantness. Presumably, too, if the Soviet authorities were willing to let him study abroad, they had also foreseen the possibility of his foreign friends visiting his house.

It has long seemed to me one of the strangest phenomena of the post-war phase of Church-State relations in the U.S.S.R. that the Government has allowed selected individuals from the Protestant Churches to travel abroad for study. Nothing seems more totally at variance with everything else I know of the Communist attitude to religion and with the Party's confident forecast of its future extinction. I would not publicly like to hazard a guess at the Communists' reasons for allowing this freedom to selected students.

Be that as it may, I was so eager to call on Pastor Rätsep's family

[1] Kolarz, op. cit., pp. 267–8.

that I decided to go there at once upon reaching Tallinn. I deposited my case at the left-luggage office and set about locating the address. I discovered that Nömme was a suburb which had to be reached by a local train. Before the end of the short journey we were passing through thick pine woods, frequently broken by delightful clusters of Scandinavian-type houses. They were shining with new red, green and blue paint, as no other houses I had seen in the Soviet Union, contrasting sharply with the ugly suburbs of Moscow, also situated in what was formerly densely wooded country.

As an accurate street plan would be considered an item of military significance in the U.S.S.R., one can only find one's way by asking. After I had alighted from the train, several inquiries took me along a path which led straight into the woods. It was no more than a sandy track, but it eventually joined a wider one, flanked by houses with cars coming up and down it at some speed. There was no suggestion of a bound surface and the sand lay at least six inches deep on it, spurting up in a bow-wave every time a vehicle passed. Another narrow path through the woods brought me to the place I wanted. The two-storey house stood in its own small garden, separated from the next plot by a wooden fence and a strip of pine trees.

I went up the path to the bright green door and knocked. A man with grey hair put his head out of the upstairs window, and then came down to answer the door. He was able to speak only a few words of Russian, so I did not know how to explain who I was. I said 'Kaide Rätsep' and showed him the address from the back of my diary, written in Kaide's own hand. A broad smile broke out on the old man's face. He made me understand that he was Kaide's father and asked me to come in. On the wall I caught sight of a group photograph in a frame. I recognized at once the Wycliffe Hall crest and saw that it had last year's date on it. Both Kaide and I were there, so I pointed first to one and then to the other, and the old man was overjoyed.

It was a most peculiar experience to enter a house in the U.S.S.R. and discover my own photograph on the wall. It completely solved the problem of introductions. The old man said that Kaide's wife was out but I must wait until she returned. When I said I would go away and come back the next day, he jumped up and barred the door, so I gathered that he was ordering me to be their guest.

It was not long before Enid Rätsep returned to the house. Kaide had told me that his wife spoke English, but judging from the amount he knew when he first came to England I was not expecting it to be much. But Enid was bilingual, having been born in Estonia of an English mother. The family language had always been English. Ann, Enid's daughter of twelve, had also spoken English while her grandmother was alive.

Enid Rätsep was obviously overjoyed to welcome her husband's friend to the house, and she reiterated her father-in-law's invitation to stay there. I agreed, as their circumstances seemed to be fairly comfortable, with three rooms downstairs for Enid and Ann and the same upstairs for Kaide's parents.

For the next three days I could hardly believe that I was still in the Soviet Union. The atmosphere in the house was almost entirely English, with numerous objects like lampshades and bedspreads showing the country of their origin. I slept in Kaide's study, with a bookcase of English and German theology rising from behind my pillow. In the house I was able to relax completely and chat with Enid about almost anything I wished. The only topic I had decided to keep off was that of Soviet oppression. Enid steered clear of it too, and I was not sorry to let her do so, as she could scarcely have benefited by talking about it. If Kaide in England had been extremely difficult to know, his wife at home was the exact opposite.

I did not have much time in the house, however, for there was not only much that I wanted to see, but Enid insisted on organizing me to the best of her ability. The first day was a Saturday and so Ann had no school. Dressed in an English cotton frock and with a light mackintosh over it, she took me in the morning for a long walk up to a hill-top. From here one had a wonderful view of the thick woods which gradually gave way to the town. Tallinn was dominated by the hill on which stood the medieval castle, and it bristled with slender Gothic spires.

In the afternoon I went into the city, wandering about in a fairyland of Gothic doorways, guild signs, sudden vistas of higgledy-piggledy, red-tiled roofs, old wooden stairs and low stone arches completely hidden away in dark corners. Perhaps the most impressive view of all was from the castle, because it dominates the old town, reducing the maze of streets to a single plane, like a jigsaw puzzle.

Whether you look at Tallinn from far or near, you are reminded of scores of similar Teutonic towns far to the west. Indeed, Estonia has always looked westwards for cultural and economic links, if only to escape the embraces of her mighty neighbour to the east. Tallinn (formerly known as Reval) was a member of the Hanseatic League from the thirteenth century, and it is this which moulded its character, while Russian annexations during the eighteenth and nineteenth centuries and again now, seem to have touched it only superficially. Even the omnipresent Communist slogans and incentives to greater productivity do not seem to have suffocated Tallinn to the same extent as other towns of the Soviet Union. Perhaps this is because the visitor who is ignorant of the language does not notice them so much. The campaign of sovietization is probably also more subtle here, attempting to submerge nationalist feeling under a large influx of Russian immigrants. I was most surprised to find without any difficulty seven or eight places of worship open for denominations other than Lutheran. The only churches that were closed were those which had suffered severely in the war, and some of them had been rebuilt.

On Sunday I asked if I could go to Kaide's church, which Enid had pointed out to me the previous day. She did not accompany me and I arrived at the Karlikiek, as it is called, a little late.

This is the largest church of Tallinn and is a vast building, seating about 1,200 people. There was a sermon in progress when I arrived, which continued for another forty minutes. Not being able to understand a single word, I used the time to look around and observe the scene.

The Karlikiek could have been a large Lutheran church in Germany. It was extremely plain in style, with bare, unplastered walls, severe rows of seats and a huge organ at the back. The congregation filled the front part of the church, leaving row upon row of vacant pews behind. This was not a vast congregation, yet it was not a discouraging one, considering that several other Lutheran churches in the city would be holding their services at the same time. What struck me most of all was that 30 to 40 per cent of those who had assembled for worship were young people. The service continued for another hour after the end of the sermon and there was no mistaking the extreme concentration of all those taking part and the enthusiasm with which they sang the familiar German chorales. In the middle there was a beautiful alto solo from the organ loft. It was thrilling to hear this magnificent organ so well played in its true context of worship. I was told that it is the biggest in Estonia, with more than seven thousand pipes. At the end of the service the closing voluntary was 'He shall feed his flock', from Handel's *Messiah*. I felt I had come home at last.

It was virtually impossible afterwards to make any contact with members of the congregation. Most of those with whom I tried to speak indicated that they did not know Russian. They may have thought I was Russian myself (though not from my speech), and so not unnaturally tried to keep out of the way. I found a verger who spoke a few words of German, and I managed to tell him that I was a friend of Kaide Rätsep. This made some impression, but he said he was too busy to be able to stay and talk. I went through a door at the front to try to find my way to the vestry, hoping to see the pastor who had preached. But there I found the corridor tightly packed with people, mainly young couples, also waiting to see him. I asked them whether they would have to wait long, first in German, and then when no one answered, in Russian. Not a person made a gesture or an attempt to answer or to help. Obviously I was not welcome. I repeated my question in English and French, with identical results. It seemed as if they were all waiting for some private instruction and my intrusion was resented or feared.

I cannot claim that my fleeting impressions of the Estonian Lutheran Church have any substantial value. However, after nearly twenty years of German and Russian oppression, including mass deportation of its leaders, it still seems to be holding its own well. Nowhere else in the Soviet Union did I see such a high proportion of young people at a service, although of course evidence of fear and suspicion is not hard to find, and it seemed to me strange that Enid did not wish to visit her husband's church with me, nor to discuss his work at all. When I saw Kaide back in England a few months later, I told him how impressed I had been with the number of young people in his church, and he replied: 'The real situation is much blacker than you imagine. So few young people are Christians in Estonia now that there does not seem to be much hope for the future.'

I intended to leave Tallinn by air for Riga, where I wished to break my journey on the way back to Moscow. I thought it would be a good idea to spend a short time there to compare my impressions of Lutheranism in Riga with those already gained in Tallinn.

As I was due to leave the airport, a very unpleasant experience brought me out of my euphoria with a sharp reminder of the fact that I was still in the Soviet Union. I had completed the baggage formalities ten minutes before departure time. I then joined a knot of people on the tarmac, waiting to walk the few steps over to the aeroplane. I was day-dreaming about the perfect weather and how agreeable the flight was going to be, when I felt a hand on my shoulder. A man in the uniform of the civil airlines said: 'Excuse me, I would like a word with you.' He took me back inside the building and into an office, where he asked to see my documents. These I showed him and he took them away. A moment later he returned with a man in plain clothes, wearing an Intourist badge in his lapel, who told me very brusquely that I would not be able to travel on the plane. I was quite taken aback for when I bought my ticket the day before no questions had been asked. I tried to argue, but of course with no result. The official told me that it was absolutely forbidden for foreigners to leave Tallinn by any way other than the train to Leningrad. 'When I was in England', he continued, 'I was under severe travel restrictions and was several times refused permission to go to parts of the country which I wanted to visit. At least we let you go where you want, even if it is not always by the means you want.' Although I argued, there was obviously no point in trying to make him change his mind, so I accepted a refund on the price of my ticket, though he refused to give me back the taxi fare which I had spent to come out to the airport.

This foiled my intended visit to Riga. To go there by train via Leningrad would have involved an immense detour. After three days, during which I had for the first time felt free in the Soviet Union, I had suddenly been reminded of the fact that below the surface surveillance is no less close in the Baltic States than elsewhere.

GEORGIA

The Caucasus, much of which lies within the Georgian Soviet Socialist Republic, is one of those areas of the world which can most truly be described by that over-used adjective 'romantic'. The hinterland behind the north-eastern shore of the Black Sea was a region of mystery and legend to the ancient world, and it was here, according to Greek tradition, that Prometheus was bound and that the Argonauts came to seek the Golden Fleece. For the Russians, the great range of mountains is linked with the magnificent descriptions of them in the works of Pushkin and Lermontov.

The Christian history of Georgia is a long and distinguished one. St. Andrew the Apostle is supposed to have preached in the coastal area of Abkhazia, while the official conversion took place under the Iberian King Miriani after St. Nino had been martyred for her faith in 330. A cross associated with her can still be seen in the Sioni Cathedral in Tbilisi. All Georgians are extremely proud of the antiquity of their Christian tradition—a girl at Tbilisi University said to me, 'The reason why the Georgians are so much more civilized than the Russians is because they have been a Christian race longer.'

In the twelfth century Georgia blossomed out into a great Christian kingdom, with a large area of northern Asia Minor under its domination. Many fine churches were built during this time and others which had existed since the fourth or fifth centuries, enlarged. A fine literary tradition grew up, making the classical Georgian language an instrument of beauty and a fine vehicle for the liturgy. Despite intermittent pressure from the Golden Horde, then from the Persian and Turkish Empires, the Georgian Orthodox Church retained its independence right up to the nineteenth century.

At the end of the eighteenth century misfortune set in. The expanding Russian Empire set its eyes on Georgia and a century of subjection, broken by sporadic nationalist uprisings, followed. Independence was proclaimed in 1917, but it was precarious and destined to be short-lived. The Russian army invaded the territory early in 1921, and on 25th February a Soviet republic was proclaimed in Tbilisi.

The history of the Church was inextricably bound up with political history from the beginning of the nineteenth century. When the Russians first crushed the Georgians, the conduct of the Russian Orthodox Church acting in allegiance with the State was despicable. Catholicos[1] Anthony II was deposed in 1811, breaking a succession of nearly fourteen centuries, and a drastic campaign was initiated to russianize the Georgian Church. The new head was styled 'Exarch' and he was subservient to the Holy Synod in St. Petersburg. The first one was a Georgian, but his sixteen successors were Russians. An attempt was made to replace the classical Georgian of the liturgy by Old Church Slavonic, though this was only partially successful. All this was indeed a betrayal of the ideals of Orthodox Christianity, which had pioneered the concept of the national church from its earliest days.

Even the liberal reforms and the right to religious freedom granted in 1905 did not secure the independence of the Georgian Church, despite an impassioned appeal by the country's nobility to the Viceroy of the Caucasus, backed by Bishop Kirion. Independence was finally

[1] The title of the heads of the Georgian, Armenian, and some other Eastern Churches, equivalent to 'Patriarch'.

won in 1917, though the Russian Orthodox Church did not formally recognize it until 1943. The Georgian Church owes much to the first Catholicos reinstated in 1917, Leonid Okroperidze, who stood firm in his office during the Soviet *coup d'état* of 1921, but he unfortunately died in a cholera epidemic in August of the same year.

The lot of the Georgian Church during the years of Soviet terror was a bitter one. The second Catholicos, Ambrosius Khelaya, made a great stand for his people, demanding a free plebiscite to decide their future. He was arrested and tried for treason, then thrown into prison. The sentence was in fact more lenient than might have been expected from the Communist-instigated demonstration of workers demanding his death which had taken place during the trial. The stigma of his bravery attached itself to the Georgian Church and during the 'twenties and 'thirties it was identified with everything that was bourgeois and anti-Soviet and subjected to a constant barrage of propaganda and appalling persecutions. The man who organized this terror was Beria, a native of Abkhazia and head of the Georgian secret police. The League of Militant Atheists had a higher membership per head of population than anywhere else in the Soviet Union, and this was the only area in which it increased during the 'thirties. During these years Kallistrat Tsintsadze, who had been elected Catholicos in 1932, tried, in an incredibly difficult situation, to reach a *modus vivendi* with the Communists, and to put a brake on the persecutions by becoming a spokesman for Soviet foreign policy. He lived to see years of greater security and tolerance as a result of the diversion created by the Second World War. On his death in 1952 he was succeeded by Melchisedek III who was followed by Ephraim II in 1960.

Today there are only about one hundred Georgian Orthodox Churches open out of 2,455 before 1921. Of these, eleven are in Tbilisi. There are eight bishops, but only five of them administrate dioceses which actually exist.[1] But if the statistics look grim, as indeed they are, it is due only in part to the Soviet Government's anti-religious campaign.

The Church had already lost much standing before the beginning of Soviet rule, because of its subservience to the Holy Synod and the priesthood, as a class, had already become synonymous with the oppressor. This explains the high degree of success with the anti-

---

[1] These figures are found in Walter Kolarz, op. cit., p. 105, and they agree closely with those I obtained from a priest in Tbilisi.

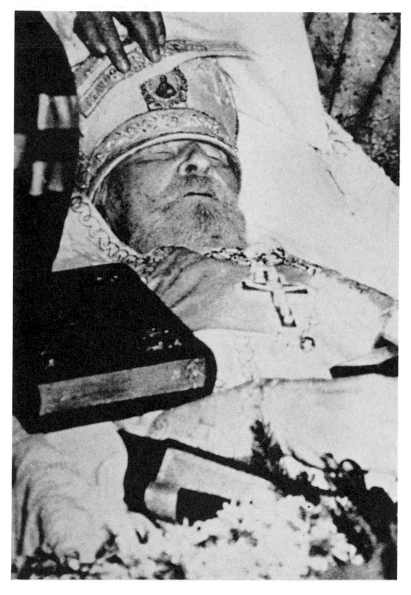

Death of Metropolitan Nikolai. The hand of the Patriarch blesses the man who had been expected by many to succeed to the highest office

religious campaign encountered in Georgia, for much of the youth of the country had already become disenchanted by the Church. Stalin's own early career was typical of that of many of his fellow-Georgians. Born Soso Dzhugashvili, he was the son of a peasant woman who wished her son to enter the priesthood and sent him to study at a seminary in Tbilisi. But the Church could not hold even its ordinands, and Stalin, like many others, defected to Communism.

I have seen round that seminary in Tbilisi where Stalin studied. It is now the Georgian National Museum and the spirit of Christianity has finally fled from it altogether. The memory of Stalin was still revered in Georgia when I was there in 1960, even though Mr. Khrushchev's first denunciation of him had long since cleared away all signs of such adulation in other areas. The University was at that time the only one in the Soviet Union still called after him, and a young man there asked me whether they still worshipped him in my country, a question which seemed to reveal a lot about Georgian attitudes. One of the first sights which met my eyes when I entered Georgia across the mountains was a church which had been desecrated. On the outside wall were splashed in huge whitewashed letters the words in Russian and Georgian: 'Praise to great Stalin'.

I stopped in the old city of Mtskheta, which was the capital of Georgia from the second to the fifth centuries A.D. It has long since dwindled to a place of minor importance, but still preserves a number of magnificent churches dating from Georgia's Golden Age. The whole of this area contains some of the great treasures of Byzantine architecture which have never been adequately photographed or described in an English publication. I particularly wanted to see the imposing Jvari monastery, perched high on a hill the opposite side of the River Aragvi, not only because it was built in the eighth century, but also because it is the scene of one of Lermontov's most famous poems, *Mtsyri*.[1] However, in attempting to cross the bridge to reach it I was arrested by a Georgian soldier who marched me off at the point of a bayonet. Fortunately the incident had no unpleasant consequences.

Despite this experience, the atmosphere in Georgia is unbelievably genial after Moscow. The Georgians themselves were originally a Mediterranean race, and the name of their capital, Tbilisi, which means 'warm springs', somehow reflects both the climate and the temperament of the people who live there. It was difficult either to

---

[1] Georgian for 'novice'.

walk down the spacious tree-lined main streets or to wander through the narrow alleys of the old quarter without attracting the attention of local people who would come up and start a discussion quite spontaneously. Many people in Tbilisi are virtually bilingual because the country has been in such close contact with Russia for a century and a half.

Children were especially uninhibited. They would ask to be photographed and if I agreed their parents would line them up in a suitable position for me to do so. To the first group I attempted to distribute a few remaining British postage stamps which I had in my pocket, but I immediately found myself surrounded by an uncontrollable mob increasing in size every moment. Fair distribution was impossible, even with the help of a policeman who obligingly came over to see what he could do. After the last stamps had gone the children refused to leave me, and I felt like the Pied Piper for an hour afterwards, walking round the streets with as many as fifty children following.

Another group insisted on taking me into their cathedral and showing me the tombs and monuments. Such an incident would have been unthinkable in Russia. When we came out they stuffed my pockets with sunflower seeds, which they love to chew, and then one boy of about ten initiated a collection of kopecks among his friends so that he could run off to buy me an ice-cream.

I was not in Georgia on a Sunday and so had no opportunity of making any observations about congregations. Students whom I met at the University were perfectly prepared to discuss religion, and though no one among them said he practised it, they were all extremely proud of the part the Georgian Orthodox Church played in the country's cultural development in the Middle Ages. I did attend some weekday services, where there were no young people present at all. The people there, too, were ready to talk and discussed the past persecutions quite openly. I gathered that the stand taken by the first two Catholicoi of the Soviet period had inspired many to fight for their religion and it may well be that the nadir of the Church's fortunes is already well past. One old woman told me that she had lost a husband and two sons during the persecutions of the 'thirties, but that a third son was now doing fine work as a priest at Kutaisi.

I met three priests and they all told me that the main difficulty now is that the opportunities for training priests are too few. Sir Kenneth Grubb visited the one seminary after the World Council of Churches meeting in Odessa (February 1964) and found that a West German

Professor of Theology was on the staff there. Some ordinands are sent to the Seminaries in Russia. The liturgy is still celebrated in Russian in many churches, although in others the two languages alternate.

For the moment, its independence is still the greatest strength of the Georgian Church. The people are intensely conscious of their national character and heritage and the Church is the institution which can best guarantee the survival of both. In fact, many races (Russians, Armenians, Jews, Kurds) live side by side in the city of Tbilisi and each tends to be grouped around its own church, synagogue or mosque. By this means they perpetuate their separate identities.

Taking all things into consideration—the former subservience of the Georgian Church to the Russian and the known strength of the atheist movement in the 'thirties—I did not find the situation as bad as I had expected. However, the Soviet Government has good reason to mistrust Georgian nationalism and if the Church should take the obvious course of serving as a rallying point for it, its future will certainly not be easy.

ARMENIA

The memory of my visit to Soviet Armenia is dominated by the incomparable beauty of Mount Ararat. Its twin peaks, Great Ararat rising to 16,945 feet and Little Ararat to about 13,000 feet, look all the more impressive because they are completely isolated, rising sheer from a plain three thousand feet above sea-level. This was the highest mountain known to the ancient Mediterranean world and became associated with a rich and evocative mythology. The Armenians have always considered it their holy mountain and have jealously guarded all the stories about Noah's Ark and the legends which are attached to it. For centuries the smooth volcanic dome of its upper heights was considered inviolable, and although a German conquered its 'secret top', as the monks used to call it, as long ago as 1829, it still preserves its air of sacrosanct mystery. This is true whether one sees it in the sharp clarity of sunrise, its upper slopes tinged with pink, or under the midday glare when a heat mist obscures all but its outline.

The mountain is now completely inaccessible from the Soviet side. The closely guarded Turkish frontier runs between the capital, Yerevan, and the first slopes of the mountain. If you travel along the main railway line from Leninakan to Nakhichevan, which hugs the border for many miles, you see that the whole area is bristling with frontier guards. Even foreigners cannot enter or leave the U.S.S.R. across this frontier. Tragically, the mountain itself is divided, for the peak of Little Ararat is in Persia, whose frontier with Turkey runs over the col between the two peaks.

Armenia has an even more glorious Christian history than her northern neighbour, Georgia, though a more tortured one. The traditionally held belief that St. Thaddaeus and St. Bartholomew preached there cannot be proved, but it is certain that by the middle of the third century there was a settled Christian community in Armenia, because Eusebius[1] records that Dionysius, during the reign of Decius, 'wrote to those in Armenia . . . whose bishop was Meruzanes'. The evangelizing of St. Gregory the Illuminator was so successful that in 301 (or 303) King Tiridates III was baptized and became the first monarch to accept Christianity as the official religion of a whole nation. He had been anticipated only by the small city-state of Edessa and he took this step more than a decade before Constantine did the same for the Roman empire. This is something of which all Armenian Christians are extremely proud.

Gregory was ordained and made bishop at Caesarea, but there is no evidence to show that the Church he built up in Armenia was not independent from the first. His family supplied the first succession of patriarchs for more than a century. The Armenian Church, however, remained in close touch with the Christians of Jerusalem and there were Armenian monasteries on the Mount of Olives from very early times.

During the fifth century, the Armenians were engaged in a prolonged 'Holy War' against the Persians, the outcome of which did much to cement the religious and political unity of the country. However, it prevented them from taking part in the Council of Chalcedon in 451. As a result they did not consider the assembly representative of the Christian world and refused to accept its acts, which included the definition of the two natures of Christ. The Armenian Church has therefore been branded as Monophysite ever since. It has never accepted this designation, because in the expanded version of the Nicene Creed which it uses come the words: 'By whom he took body, soul and mind and everything that is in man, truly and not in semblance', which certainly seems to preclude Mono-

[1] Book 6, section 46.

196

physite beliefs. After 451 Armenian replaced Greek as the language of the Church and from then until quite recently relations between the Armenian Church and the main body of the Orthodox Church have been tenuous. It is only in the last few years that Armenian and Greek Christians alike have come to realize that their continued separation is due to little more than a historical accident, and there are now moves afoot to bring the two great Churches closer together.

In Armenian history, as in Georgian, it is impossible to separate Church and State, and during sixteen and a half centuries we see them working hand in hand to preserve Christianity as the rallying point of a nation continuously threatened on all sides, often conquered, but always re-emerging with its great traditions intact.

The happiest time of recent centuries was from 1829–77, when, in contrast to what was happening in Georgia, the northern part of Armenia prospered under Russian rule. After that, however, there was a struggle between Turkey and Russia—with occasional futile British intervention—for this territory, the culmination of which was the terrible series of massacres at the hand of the Turks, one of the worst atrocities of modern times. They occurred in 1894, 1909 and 1915, and the last was the worst. It was then that about one-third of the total Armenian population in north-eastern Turkey were put to death and a further third deported. It is little wonder that these events are still a factor of enormous importance in the minds of modern Soviet Armenians when they come to consider political questions.

When, in December 1920, Armenia was proclaimed a Soviet republic, the Church had already been divided into two jurisdictions, those of Cilicia (Sis) and of Echmiadzin. This resulted from the mass emigration of Armenians following the earliest Turkish persecutions. The Catholicos of Cilicia lives at Antilyas, near Beirut, the centre of a strong Armenian community in the Lebanon and the Catholicos of Echmiadzin lives twelve miles from Yerevan. The latter has control over communities in the Balkans, Western Europe and America as well as his own, while most of the others look to the Antilyas. The Catholicos of Echmiadzin has always had the primacy of honour, though for an Armenian Echmiadzin does not carry quite the weight which Rome does for a Catholic or Constantinople for an Orthodox, because the ecclesiastical centre shifted about so often during the vicissitudes of Armenian history and the Catholicos governed his Church from at least seven other centres.

The Catholicos of Echmiadzin was destined to play an important diplomatic role in Soviet foreign policy, because of the possibility that he might influence Armenian communities in several countries abroad, but this did not prevent the Church from being subject to intense pressure from the Party.

There were persecutions during the 'twenties and a 'Reformed Church' was formed in imitation of the 'Living Church' of Russia. It lacked popular support and so only had a short life, but a considerable number of police agents infiltrated into the hierarchy.[1] Of much more use to the Soviet Government was the way in which Catholicos Khoren I secured the acceptance of the new régime by many Armenians abroad. He became Catholicos in 1932, but had already wielded considerable power during the last years of his predecessor's office. In return for his support of the Soviet régime, Khoren I extracted a promise from the Government that Echmiadzin monastery and several other churches should remain open. He was not, however, entirely successful in his campaign to gain the allegiance of those overseas. For instance, the American Armenian community was split in its loyalty and this culminated in the murder, on 24th December 1933, of Archbishop Levon Turian in Holy Cross Church, New York. Who or which faction was responsible for this crime has never been clarified.

Khoren I himself was murdered, it is believed,[2] by the N.K.V.D. in 1938 at the height of the terror which their activities brought to the U.S.S.R. It was the policy of Yezhov, the head of this organization, to exterminate anyone who could conceivably cause the slightest threat to Stalin's authority. Fearing a repetition of the popular demonstration of nationalist feelings which had attended the enthronement of Khoren I, the Communist authorities put off the election of a successor for a time, then the outbreak of war gave them the excuse to postpone it indefinitely. However, the Soviet war effort could not do without Armenian support and one of the sops offered to the people was the first reprinting in Soviet times of the novels of Raffi, a nineteenth-century Armenian writer whose historical novels might be calculated to whip up popular feeling against a foreign invader. This may have accomplished its aim, but there must have been many

[1] See G. A. Agabekov, *Die Tscheka an der Arbeit*, Stuttgart, Berlin, Leipzig, 1932, pp. 154–60. The author was a secret police agent who defected in 1930 and he has written a fascinating account of the methods of the organization to which he formerly belonged.

[2] See evidence in Walter Kolarz, op. cit., p. 156.

people, too, who read them with the Russians in mind as the oppressors.

Kevork Cheorekchian was acting head of the Armenian Church during the war years. He spent much effort in encouraging his people to support the Soviet military effort and was rewarded in 1945 by being summoned to the Kremlin and shortly afterwards was able to stand for election as Catholicos. Kevork VI immediately won new concessions. He consecrated ten new bishops, six of whom were to serve in sees abroad, opened a theological seminary at Echmiadzin and started up the publication of a new theological journal to replace *Ararat*, the old one which had not appeared since before the war. In return he supported the Soviet Government's appeal to all Armenians abroad to return to the homeland where, it was promised, they would be guaranteed full political and religious freedom for the first time since before the massacres. To all, especially to relatives of those who had suffered at the hands of the Turks, the temptation to go back must have been strong, but many percipient spirits in exile saw the danger and warned that this was just another Soviet attempt to beguile the eyes of the world. Others listened to Kevork VI and later regretted it.

He died in May 1954, in his eighty-eighth year, and was succeeded in September 1955 by Vazgen Balgian. Vazgen I's appointment was obviously a political one, although it was ostensibly made by the vote of an Assembly which was supposed to be representative of the Armenian clergy and people. He was Rumanian by birth and education and already had a record of collaboration with the Communist authorities there. He had held a junior position up to this time, being only forty-seven years old and in the fifth year of his episcopate.

By 1954 the number of open churches in Soviet Armenia had dropped from 491 in 1920 to 38,[1] the result of a ruthless attack on Church life which followed the pattern by now familiar to us. After his election Vazgen I, instead of tackling this immense problem on the home front, immediately left on a mission, the purpose of which was to delay the election of a new anti-Soviet Catholicos of Cilicia. In this he failed, but his brave effort seems to have impressed the Government. On his return Mr. Bulganin received him and granted him the privilege of opening more churches and restoring four ancient monasteries which were to be returned to the Church. The money for this was to come from Armenian communities abroad who wished to contribute. When I was in Echmiadzin in 1960, Vazgen I was again

[1] Statistics from Walter Kolarz, op. cit., p. 167.

away, this time on a four-month journey in Western Europe and the Americas to canvass for increased support for his Church.

I had had my first encounter with the Soviet Armenian Church while I was still in Tbilisi. I found one of the Armenian quarters by accident and before I had time to go into the church a group had gathered round me. The main spokesman was a priest in mufti, Father Hagob, who had studied at the seminary of Echmiadzin and had been sent to Tbilisi shortly after graduating five years before. He seemed quite uninhibited and ready to talk at great length, but I had to warn him that the person standing beside me was from Moscow University. This was Viktor[1] who had stuck to me all day, with the intention of 'keeping me out of trouble' as he put it, and I had been quite unable to shake him off.

I was very much struck by the way in which the whole group accepted Father Hagob as their spokesman and seemed to talk to him entirely naturally, as indeed he did to me. This, in a group of men and women not one of whom was over thirty, seemed to me remarkable. I cannot imagine that it could happen in Russia. He told me that, of the original thirty-eight churches in Tbilisi, only this and one other were left.

I travelled to Echmiadzin filled with awe at its great place in history (it had been the capital at the time when Armenia officially became Christian), yet remembering that I had already been disappointed by the atmosphere of many places of Christian antiquity in the Soviet Union.

It was a torrid day in June 1960 and the contemplative aura of the monastery's tree-shaded enclosure enfolded me from the moment I set foot inside it—it was a unique experience. The complex of buildings now comprises a beautiful small cruciform cathedral, founded by St. Gregory the Illuminator, but many times transformed and enlarged; the seat of the Catholicos situated on the western side of the quadrangle; and a monastic refectory and cells, part of which is now occupied by the seminary. The ensemble is surrounded by walls thirty feet high which were built in 1958—and even they do not succeed in spoiling the overall effect.

The first person I met was a student at the seminary who had been born into the Lebanese Armenian community and had felt the call to return to his ancestral country. 'The needs of my people here now are so great that I shall stay to serve them,' he said. He told me his name

[1] See p. 138.

was Vardan, after the great prince who had led his people in the Holy War against Persia. We spent a long time talking and were only interrupted by the eavesdropping of Viktor, whom I discovered listening to our conversation concealed behind an alcove while Vardan was showing me over part of the monastic buildings.

Vardan told me that at that time there were forty students at the seminary. In the past few were ordained after their period of study had finished, but of the five graduates in the upper group the previous year, four had taken this step, while this year all five had decided that they would do so. I also met Deacon Ioannes, who, Vardan assured me, was an excellent teacher, completely conversant with all the latest theological trends outside the U.S.S.R.

Vardan took me to vespers in the cathedral. It was a Saturday evening and I was sorry that the service lasted only forty minutes—quite the shortest I had attended in the Soviet Union. The chanting sounded more oriental than anything I had ever heard in a church before. There were people of all ages present, including a number of students from the seminary. Most interesting of all was a lorryload of young Pioneers who were disgorged from their vehicle, red neckerchiefs flying, and shepherded by an adult straight into the church. I was sure that they had been brought merely to 'observe' the strange rites of the Christians, but the fact remains that they seemed captivated by the strange music and colourful scene. Every one of them followed intently what was going on, without a trace of irreverence. At the end of the service the whole congregation moved up to the front to kiss a Bible which was being offered to them by a priest and one of the children followed.

I left Echmiadzin feeling encouraged as I had rarely felt before in the Soviet Union. While there are teachers of the calibre of Deacon Ioannes and students with Vardan's dedication there must be a great future for Christianity in Armenia. It was a welcome contrast to the political manœuvres of the Armenian catholicoi. Echmiadzin appeared to me to be a place wholly intent on the worship of God and the training of future priests.

CHAPTER VIII

New Perspectives

CHRISTIANITY FOR EXPORT ONLY?

In lecturing to church gatherings in different parts of England and talking to many Americans on the subject of Russian Christianity, I have noticed that pro-Communist propaganda on the one hand and anti-Communist propaganda on the other have caused a great deal of confusion in people's minds, completely obscuring the real situation of the Church in the Soviet Union. I hope my account will already have shown how absurd and unfounded is the picture presented by the worst sort of cold-war agitators who seek to portray the Russian Church as a mere tool of the Soviet Government, but this chapter is a warning, and I believe a very necessary one, against recent Kremlin ecclesiastical tactics.

The Communist Party is concerned to project two entirely opposed images of Christianity. The first, for export only, attempts to depict the Soviet Union as a liberal country where everyone, Christian and Communist alike, does and thinks as he feels and the Church as a full participator in the international relations of the new, de-Stalinized State. The second, strictly for home consumption, represents Christianity as being the essence of everything bourgeois, decadent and dissonant with the country's glorious future, to be restricted by every possible 'administrative measure'.

The first picture is accepted in its entirety by a very small number of people in England and even fewer in America, most of whom have been invited to the Soviet Union at the country's own expense on delegations sponsored by organizations of the extreme left wing. But apart from this minority, a disturbing number of Christians in the West, including many who have visited the U.S.S.R., seem too ready to accept at face-value the Russian Orthodox Church's assurances about its own internal freedom. They note that it is allowed to send and receive foreign delegations freely; some are fêted themselves when they visit the Soviet Union as guests of the Church.

The interchange of delegations is an essential part of the Kremlin's propaganda and, as we saw in Chapter II, the range of these contacts has broadened considerably in the last few years. Great capital can be made out of receiving the head of a foreign Church with pomp or of sending a representative to a foreign enthronement or assembly. Mr. Khrushchev is supposed to have picked up the idea of inviting Russian metropolitans and archbishops to formal receptions for visiting heads of state from President Tito during his visit to Yugoslavia in 1955. The venerable figure of the eighty-seven-year-old Patriarch, carrying on his shoulders the timeless associations of Russia's past, is a most useful person in this respect. England was recently reminded of this when he paid his first visit in September 1964.

In recent months there have been signs that the mask of hypocrisy is at times being dropped. The Soviet Government has started to think that the interest foreign tourists have been showing in Christianity is unhealthy. Zagorsk has been struck off the list of showplaces for visitors. When a group of ordinands from St. Stephen's House, Oxford, made an unofficial visit to the Soviet Union in September 1963, they were told that all tourists these days prefer to go to a clock factory rather than to Zagorsk. Before leaving London the group had specifically asked that the monastery should be the first priority on its itinerary, but after several days of arguing in Moscow they finally persuaded Intourist to let them go for just one hour. Of course, once they arrived there it was impossible to make them leave within the stipulated time, especially as they were cordially received by the authorities of the Theological Academy.

In April 1964 I visited the Soviet Union for twelve days as a tourist, and we were scheduled to see the Pioneers' Palaces in Moscow and Leningrad on the two Sunday mornings. The group objected the second time and the visit did not take place. This kind of childish stratagem to prevent tourists from seeing the vitality of church life is surely too naïve to succeed. The Intourist guide in fact told one member of the tour that all churches now hold their only services on Tuesday evenings.

Soviet hypocrisy in religious matters can be very obviously seen in the field of literature. In 1956 the Orthodox Church was allowed to publish its first edition of the Bible since the Revolution. It came out in fifty thousand copies—just over two for each of the parishes then

203

existing. Many of these, however, never reached the parishes at all, but were presented to members of visiting delegations or exported to foreign Churches and libraries.

The monthly *Journal of the Moscow Patriarchate*[1] can be obtained only with the greatest difficulty in the Soviet Union, and I could do so only by applying in person to the Patriarchate. I never saw a copy on view or on sale inside a church, the total number of each issue printed has never been revealed and since 1953 there has been no indication of price inside. Most probably the majority of Orthodox believers never set eyes on it, for large quantities of each number are sent abroad. The House of St. Gregory and St. Macrina, the Orthodox centre in Oxford, regularly receives far more than it needs. Even though the Moscow Patriarchate has repeatedly been informed of this, the supply continues, presumably at the Government's insistence, and with the purpose of impressing the freedom of the Russian Church upon English people.

The inordinate discrepancy between the benign image and the grim reality was sharply brought home to me by one incident. In February 1960 there was a Soviet Book Exhibition at the Royal Festival Hall in London, the counterpart of a similar British exhibition in Moscow two months earlier. The British had deliberately excluded any books of political or religious significance which might have given offence to Communists—despite which the Russians still banned more than a dozen volumes after they had arrived in Moscow. The titles included in the Soviet Book Exhibition had been chosen for a very different reason. The aim was not to avoid giving offence to the English by disseminating an unwelcome ideology, but simply to produce the most favourable impression possible of freedom in the U.S.S.R. There were many fine art books which had been produced only in very small editions and which one never saw on the shelves of Russian book-dealers, because they sold out on the day of publication. There were others which had never been in the bookshops at all. In this category was the considerable section of religious literature in the Exhibition. Admittedly there was no variety among these books; they consisted solely of Bibles, periodicals, service and hymn-books for various sects and in the different languages of the Soviet Republics, but the selection still gave the impression that a considerable number of religious publications are available in the U.S.S.R. and that all denominations have the literature they need to perform their worship.

[1] See p. 65.

Completely excluded from this shop-window was all the multiplicity of anti-religious publications so widely disseminated in enormous editions throughout the country.

I went to the opening of this exhibition, as I was visiting England for a short time in the middle of my year in Moscow. On the return train journey I took with me two complete Bibles in Russian and a few small copies of the four Gospels in a new Russian translation. When the train entered the station at Brest there was a customs examination. I had a whole carriage to myself, having been on my own ever since Warsaw. Two officials, a man and a woman, could therefore give me their undivided attention for the two hours or more which it takes to change the coaches on to wheels of a wider gauge.

In twenty minutes they had thrown everything out of my cases on to the floor and the four beds of the compartment, emitting at intervals cries of gleeful triumph as they found books about Russia and going into something approaching ecstasy at each one connected with religion. They made a special pile of these and started to walk off with them to the customs shed. I tried to stop them, but in the end had to give way.

In the customs shed I was told that all the religious literature would certainly be confiscated. I asked why, if they displayed Russian Bibles in London, there was any harm in my taking some into the U.S.S.R. They replied: 'We have plenty of our own here—good ones. What we want to keep out is your inferior ones published in the West.'

What is the use of arguing with anyone who makes such statements? I settled for the return of the other books of mine which they had taken. While I was arguing with the customs officials in their shed I noticed a young woman who seemed rather distressed at what was going on. When I left the room to go back to the train she offered to help me carry some of the books. She told me she lived in Brest and worked for the railway, and had been in the customs shed to clean it. Half-way back to my carriage she burst into tears. 'They're brigands, these people,' she wept. 'Can't you tell your Embassy what they have done? I have seen such things happen before and I know they'll take the books into the yard and burn them. And our need of Bibles is so desperate!' The girl let me return to my compartment only after she had made me promise that I would organize a protest in England about such barbarous conduct.

In July 1964 news came from Russia that there was going to be a literal export of Christianity from the Soviet Union. The Government announced that it was prepared, for the first time since the Revolution, to allow Russian monks to settle on Mount Athos. It does not take a cynic to see that this will achieve the dual purpose of making a propaganda point about freedom of religion and of reducing still further the already very small number of monks still active in the Soviet Union. Similarly, it seems a little strange that the Russian Orthodox Church has recently been able to build a splendid new church on the shores of the Sea of Galilee, near Tiberias, where there is no congregation to fill it, while there are huge industrial cities within the Soviet Union where there are no churches open at all.

RECENT PERSECUTIONS

'On Sundays and sometimes on weekdays, too, the churches in Moscow and other cities are packed to capacity with worshippers. This proves that the Orthodox Church is flourishing in the face of the pressures which have been put on it.'

This is the sort of comment that is made by countless tourists and even members of some church delegations when they return home to the West after a visit to the U.S.S.R. It is true that no one who attends a Moscow church on a Sunday morning could fail to be impressed by the vitality of the worship, but at the same time it is surprising how easily people, after such experiences, are lulled into facile deductions about 'vast numbers of Muscovites who regularly attend worship'.

Here is the picture as I saw it in 1959–60. After spending most of my spare time for several months visiting all the churches which I could locate in Moscow to find out exactly which were open for worship, I confirmed to my own satisfaction that the usual figure quoted of about thirty-five within the city itself was approximately correct. It was very difficult to locate many of them, as the Patriarchate would not give me a complete list and the best Intourist map of Moscow is hopelessly inadequate. I found about eighty more which were either derelict or being used as offices, cinemas, laboratories, bookstores or even, in some cases, as living-quarters. Many disappeared completely after the Revolution. The great Cathedral of Christ the Saviour, in which the Council of 1917 took place, was blown up in the early 'thirties and now a swimming-pool occupies the site.

Moscow has a population of six million. If we add five churches of other denominations to the thirty-five Orthodox, we arrive at a figure of one church per 150,000 people, approximately. This compares with 657 churches for 1,854,000 people in 1917, or one for just under three thousand. In a London suburban borough of a hundred thousand people one would expect to find almost as many churches, chapels and tabernacles as in the whole of Moscow. On seeing a church there packed with, say, two thousand people, one can make two assumptions: firstly, one in every seventy-five people living in the geographical area served by the church is present (though the distribution of churches in the city is uneven); secondly, the Soviet authorities allow fewer churches to be open than the needs of the people demand. One parish priest cannot perform the ministrations required by such a large number of parishioners.

That the number of churches is inadequate is confirmed by articles which appear from time to time in the Soviet Press criticizing Christians for holding religious gatherings in private apartments. These articles always choose to overlook the fact that the responsibility lies principally not with the people concerned, but with the Government for failing to allow enough official places of worship to be open.

In 1959 the situation in country districts was more precarious than in Moscow. The number of churches open in the whole of the U.S.S.R. was said to be approximately twenty thousand, a figure much less adequate than it might at first seem to be, because the distribution was so unequal, with a much thicker sprinkling in the west and in the Ukraine than elsewhere.[1] Information about the real state of affairs is most difficult to come by, as foreigners are rarely allowed to visit out-of-the-way places.

When I visited the old town of Yuriev-Polskoy in 1960, I was immediately confronted by an old man who asked me as I stepped off the bus whether the churches were open in my country. I explained to him that there was no religious persecution in England, to which he replied that in this town of twenty thousand people there was not a single church open.

I asked him what Christians did. 'There is one church,' he said, 'in a village twenty-five kilometres away. Some of us manage to get to it on foot or on horseback occasionally in the summer, though only on Sundays and feast-days. Of course, during the winter the journey is quite out of the question.'

[1] See pp. 60–1 and statistical table, p. 234.

This was not an utterly remote part of the U.S.S.R., but only a hundred miles from Moscow; nor was it a new industrial town, where one would not have been so surprised to find that there was no provision for Christian worship. It was an old and famous town in the middle of an agricultural district which contains some of Russia's most distinguished architecture. In various trips through the countryside I passed many scattered villages, each with its church in the centre. Very rarely did I see one which was neither derelict nor in use as a store for agricultural implements.

It was always depressing to see a great work of Christian architecture no longer used for worship, betraying the vision of those who built it. Great cathedrals in Novgorod, Leningrad, Moscow, Pskov, Kiev, Suzdal, among them some of the finest buildings ever erected, now stand idle or are open only as museums to extol the craftsmanship, but to ridicule the beliefs, of those who built them. It is little wonder that when I accompanied a party of Soviet visitors on a tour of London and took them into St. Paul's Cathedral, I could not persuade them that this was a 'working' church, as they put it.

If the state of affairs seemed bad in 1959–60, it is very much worse now. It is difficult to pinpoint any one reason why after a lull lasting several years following the death of Stalin, the situation should suddenly plunge headlong for the worse—and this at a time when the Soviet Government was redoubling its efforts to appear as the model of enlightened democracy which underdeveloped nations would wish to follow. Nor can a precise date for the beginning of the deterioration be given. It almost seems as if the Moscow Patriarchate was persuaded to publish *The Russian Orthodox Church, Organization, Situation, Activity*[1] in 1958 in order to soften world opinion in preparation for the final attempt to finish with religion inside the U.S.S.R. By the time I was living there the persecution was already under way, but so secretly was it being carried on that I did not become really aware of what was happening until shortly before I was due to leave.

The closure of more churches was the first indication that all was not well. News began to appear regularly in the Soviet Press of buildings which had been commandeered for various reasons. Perm Cathedral closed in February 1960 on the pretext that the large crowds attending it were causing traffic jams. Riga Cathedral was seized soon after because it was supposed to be too important a national monument to remain in the hands of a 'sect' (the Lutheran

[1] See p. 72.

208

Church). The fine old church of *Nikola na Dvorishche*[1] in Novgorod was turned into a museum allegedly because of its historical importance, while the Bishop was given another much smaller one to serve the whole of the town. A similar fate awaited countless parish churches and Nikita Struve[2] estimates that by the summer of 1962 seven thousand had been closed. In Byelorussia over a third of the 930 churches open in 1962 have been closed since then.

Kolya, my friend from Moscow University, told me recently that he was on a holiday in a Siberian village in the summer of 1962. The peasant-woman with whom he was staying came home from doing her shopping one morning in a highly agitated state. She had passed by the church and seen a crowd gazing at a huge new padlock on the main door. Pinned above it was a hand-written notice: 'This church will be closed until further notice as its fabric has been declared dangerous.' Later she had met the priest who told her that he had arrived for his morning service to find himself barred from his own church. He had been summoned to the headquarters of the local militia and simply told that his church no longer functioned. When he went round to some of his most faithful parishioners later to try to collect twenty signatures requesting that a new place of worship be provided, he found that they had been threatened with the loss of their jobs if they continued their religious activities.

Kolya told me he was ashamed that such things could happen in the U.S.S.R. and that in his opinion only legal methods should be applied in combating religion. Officially (according to the law of 8th April 1929) any religious association of twenty or more people has the right to a place of worship, and Kolya believed that a village church should be closed down only if there genuinely were no longer the requisite number interested in it.

Very recent news[3] indicates that the situation in Moscow itself, which had been reasonably constant since the end of the Second World War, has taken a dramatic turn for the worse. On 7th July 1964 the Church of SS. Peter and Paul on Preobrazhenskaya Square was closed. News began to circulate among Christians that it was going to be destroyed to make way for an extension to the Metro. Even the time of the projected act of barbarity became known. On Friday night, 17th July, a crowd of old people began to assemble near

[1] cf., p. 77.
[2] *Les Chrétiens en U.R.S.S.*, p. 260.
[3] *Russia Cristiana Ieri e Oggi*, Nov. 1964, among other journals, reported this.

the church. They found police cordons blocking the entrances of the several streets leading into the square. Estimates of the total number present vary, but probably there were upwards of ten thousand there. Some people broke through the police cordons and somehow managed to install themselves inside the church. Once there, they waved copies of the Soviet constitution in the faces of the angry militia, trying to prove that it guaranteed religious freedom, and refused to obey their instructions to leave. According to many eyewitnesses, there were still people inside when the church was detonated at four o'clock in the morning. Now all that remains is an open space with boards round it, through the chinks of which can be seen the twisted metal of the former cupolas and spires.

That such an act could be committed in Moscow at the height of the tourist season is almost unbelievable. I had thought that the Moscow churches, at least, would survive with impunity, but now, according to rumours circulating in the parishes of the capital, the authorities plan to close a further fourteen, four of which will be physically annihilated. However, this cannot be accomplished without arousing world opinion against the Soviet Government. Opposition among Russian Christians, too, is likely to reach flash-point. Already it is being said in the parishes that Khrushchev summoned the Patriarch to the Kremlin in June 1964 to tell him that these churches were to be closed, but that it must be done with the Church's connivance. Alexis is supposed to have replied: 'Close my churches by force if you will, but you will have to take my head from my shoulders before you use my authority to take the crosses off the cupolas of our churches.'

Greville Wynne, the British businessman imprisoned by the Russians, has provided further concrete evidence of religious persecution. He writes of his prison in Vladimir:[1] 'On the other side were some elderly women, very badly dressed; in the winter it was pathetic to see them wrapped up in newspapers and rags. Like most women in Vladimir, they had been convicted of "religious crimes" like trying to run a Sunday school. Later, when I was in a cell in which there was a crack in the window glass, through which I could see, I watched another group of women pass by on their way to the showers, chanting prayers and hymns and making the sign of the cross.' This pathetic description reminds us of the early days of Christianity in the Roman empire, but at the same time one feels a glimmer of hope in knowing that their bravery has not gone unrecognized. This hope

[1] *Sunday Telegraph*, 27th September 1964.

is encouraged when Wynne tells us he was able to help them by smuggling to them a picture of the dedication of Coventry Cathedral.

I have already referred to the closure of four out of the eight seminaries which had been opened after the war.[1] Legally, it is a simple matter for the Soviet Government to deal both with these and with the monasteries, because when the law was passed in 1929 there were none in existence and so no mention of them was made. Their reopening after the war was never written into any legal code, and the authorities did not hesitate to evoke the letter of the law in order to gain their ends. It should also be noted here that the drop in the number of Soviet students who are allowed to train for ordination is partially masked by the admission of more foreign students; for example, six Ugandan Orthodox students and one Kenyan entered the Leningrad Seminary in September 1963. Even so, taking into account the impressions of several people, I wonder whether the total number of theological students in Leningrad is as high as the 160 which the Church itself claims. Formerly, students who were ordained before the end of their training could be exempted from military service, but now many are being called up in the middle of their courses. Others are refused residence permits if they should happen to be natives of towns other than that in which the seminary is situated. The correspondence course in theology which was such a notable and influential feature of the Leningrad Seminary was quietly dropped in 1960.

The situation of the monasteries and convents is even more critical. The existence of all of the sixty-seven which were open in 1957 is gravely threatened—indeed the majority have already returned to their pre-war desolation. The case of the Monastery of the Caves at Kiev has already been mentioned,[2] but more is known about the threat to the great monastery at Pochaev, in the Ternopol district of the Ukraine. Two documents[3] were smuggled out of the Soviet Union in the form of letters addressed to the 'President of the foreign relations department of the American Churches' and to Mr. Khrushchev himself. These letters present an astonishingly detailed picture of persecution in action. The monastic victims, as well as some of the local Communists responsible for the outrages, are given by name. Here is a summary of the main points which occur in the two appeals.

[1] See p. 93.
[2] See pp. 18–19.
[3] Full text printed in Struve, op. cit., pp. 263–7.

The local authorities have been arresting and searching pilgrims who visit the Monastery, confiscating their possessions and driving them in lorry-loads deep into the forest, dumping them there without any money. Anyone found giving shelter to a pilgrim is heavily fined. The authorities have forcibly removed most of the older monks into mental hospitals, while many of the younger ones have either been dumped in the forest under threat of imprisonment if they return or else conscripted into the army, even though some were medically unfit. Others again have had to go into hospitals where doctors have insisted on a course of injections as a treatment for dysentery. The outcome of this treatment is more than dubious in many instances. The health of all of them has been seriously impaired and probably some have been murdered.

The first appeal made to me personally in connection with the new persecutions was when I was in Odessa in June 1960, and this was what made me aware of how serious the situation was becoming. I called at the Mikhailovsky Convent and met a charming young nun of about thirty who told me that the continued existence of her community was being threatened by the Government. The nuns' main income was from needlework. They could make vestments and altar-cloths for churches, from the proceeds of which they bought their food. Now the Government had secretly declared such financial transactions illegal, so the sisters were being offered the alternative of going out to work in industry or of starving.

She went on to say that there are many priests in the Soviet Union who are far worse off than the nuns. Apart from some in prison, there are many whose living conditions are beyond belief. One priest whose church had been seized by the militia was sent to work in a textile factory. He was put in charge of a machine before he understood it properly and jammed his hand in the mechanism in the first week. As a result of the accident his hand had to be amputated and he was then declared unfit for work. Having been in 'gainful employment' for less than a week, he was not eligible for a pension. Now he could be seen around the town where he had formerly been the parish priest begging surreptitiously behind the back of the militia. They had caught him once or twice and forced him to give up the few kopecks he had managed to glean from Christian well-wishers. However, one old lady used to bring a loaf of bread each evening to the barn in which he had to live.

Another sister took me out into the garden to show me one wing

212

of the convent which was now being used as a military hospital. She told me that they could still ease the situation by converting their flower-beds into vegetable patches. I was probably the last foreigner to walk in this garden while it still belonged to the convent, for it was soon commandeered by the hospital as a place where the patients could sit or exercise themselves when they were convalescing. In 1962 the Mikhailovsky Convent ceased to exist.

Recent information suggests that just one or two convents have managed to keep open by sending the nuns out to work as ordinary citizens during the day. They return to pray, meditate and sleep in their old surroundings at night. Most, however, have shared the fate of the Mikhailovsky Convent at Odessa.

I heard some arresting information about the Ovruch Convent in the Ukraine from a tourist who happened to be in the vicinity with his car in 1961, just after the events described. This was renowned as one of Orthodox Church's most venerable convents. It had been re-opened in 1947, after nearly thirty years of closure, during which much of the fabric had gone to ruin. Just when it had returned to something like its former splendour, as a result of the unstinting work of 140 nuns living there, many of whom were quite young, the chairman of the local town council suddenly appeared there. He demanded that the nuns abandon the entire premises within twenty-four hours. The town, he said, was in need of more workers in its brick factory and here was an untapped labour force. Next day the militia appeared to carry out the order at gun-point. Those who were too old to work were turned out on to the streets to beg if they had no homes to return to. Most had no right to a pension because they had not been engaged in productive work. Those who were fit for manual labour were pressed into the toil of the children of Israel in Egypt.

The persecution of individual church leaders and of parish priests over the last five years has been no less violent than the collective fate of the Pochaev monks.

Whatever the truth about the death of Metropolitan Nikolai,[1] his enforced retirement from office makes him the most eminent victim of the new wave of persecution, but he is no more than one among many. Andrei Sukhenko, Archbishop of Chernigov and Nezhen until 1961, was arrested in that year and sentenced to eight years' imprisonment on the double pretext that he had engaged in religious propaganda among a group of miners and that he had eluded taxa-

[1] See p. 81.

tion. It seems that the Soviet authorities could not make up their minds which calumny to bring down on the head of this highly revered cleric, and to an independent observer two accusations are weaker than one. In fact, he lost his liberty for refusing to allow a large number of parish churches in his diocese to be closed down. For the last year and a half he has been in a prison at Mikun in the Komi Autonomous Republic, near Arkhangelsk. The Archbishop of Kazan, Job Kresovich, was sentenced to three years' imprisonment in 1960 for an even more diverse catalogue of crimes. In reality he was condemned for the same reason as Archbishop Andrei, but he was released at the end of his sentence. Now he lives under house-arrest in Lvov and is unlikely to be permitted to officiate again. A certain Bishop Venedikt has just died under house-arrest in Kishinyov and rumours are circulating that he was murdered.

The tragedy of those priests and other churchmen who have lost their work because of the closure of the church or institution in which they served is a very great one. Some of those who have been evicted have also become renegades—for instance, one of the guides at the Monastery of the Caves in Kiev was a seminarist before his institution closed down, and his new atheist line, strangely coupled with a detailed knowledge of the Monastery, has given offence to many foreign visitors there. Such people, however, are in a small minority, even though the greatest pressure has been put on all clerics to renounce their faith. There are now thousands of priests without parishes and theological students without seminaries at large in the Soviet Union. Even though I knew something of their situation from what I had heard in Odessa in 1960, this was not brought home to me in a personal way until the unforgettable meeting I had with Archimandrite Kasyan, a monk of fifty-three who had been on the teaching staff of the Stavropol Seminary before its closure.

I called one day at a little church just off Gorky Street in Moscow. It was quite empty, except for this one man dressed in an old grey coat who was standing there praying. He came up to me at once to talk.

He told me that he had been ordained secretly just before the war, taking the name of Kasyan. Although he had never had the chance to live in a monastery, he had considered himself a monk during the time he spent fighting at the front against the Germans. After being demobilized he found that there were now some monasteries open, so he joined the one at Pskov. He was able to follow the Leningrad

Seminary's correspondence course in theology, which he did so successfully that he was invited first to become the abbot of a small new monastery which had just opened in the Crimea and then to transfer to the staff of the Stavropol Seminary not far away as the Professor of Dogmatics. After the Seminary was closed, he went back to his monastery, but all the monks were evicted from there six months later.

Archimandrite Kasyan could not stay in the Crimea because his residence permit was quite simply withdrawn. He went straight back to Pskov, but no permission to live there was forthcoming either. He thought of taking over a parish and showed me a letter authorizing him to celebrate the liturgy which his bishop had given him when he left the Crimea. However, when he presented this document to the bishops of several dioceses which he visited looking for work, the answer was always the same: 'Our parishes are fully staffed and we have no vacancies.' The Archimandrite told me it was obvious that the Communist authorities had included him in a list circulated to all bishops giving the names of all those banned from officiating. For a bishop to have offered him work would have been to run the risk of almost certain arrest.

Archimandrite Kasyan's situation was becoming impossible. He had no money and was living on the charity of various friends in the dioceses where he had been seeking work. He decided that this could not continue, and in despair, following a grave crisis of conscience in which he weighed the chances of his ever being allowed to exercise his office again, he shaved off his beard and presented himself to the local authorities for work. He happened to be at Novosibirsk at the time, where he had been staying with a priest who had been a friend of his for some years.

An official of the town council said he was glad that the Archimandrite had at last come round to the right way of thinking and had decided to offer himself for gainful employment after so many years. He himself could provide work if certain conditions were observed. Firstly, the ex-monk must keep himself clean 'like any good Soviet citizen' and dress unobtrusively; secondly, he must work at a stipulated place; thirdly, he must live in accommodation which would be provided for him, or his permission to live in Novosibirsk would be withdrawn.

Archimandrite Kasyan was not happy about the conditions, but saw that the only alternative to accepting them was to go and beg on the streets ('Which many other former priests and monks in my situation have been reduced to doing,' he added). The first condition was not too difficult to keep, although he lived in a state of penury during the first few months while he was saving money to buy a new suit. The second had reduced him to a state of spiritual desolation, the like of which he had never before known in his life. He had to do the roughest manual work in a hydro-electric station. At first he was detailed to clean the floors in the installation rooms, then he was sent outside to help in the digging of a new dam. He said he did not despise manual work in itself, of course, but his thoughts kept flying back to the marvellous contact he had had with young seminarists until recently and the chance he had possessed of moulding the characters of these men who were dedicating their lives to the service of God. Now he knew he would never do this again, unless Soviet policy should change dramatically. This, at any rate, was something to pray for.

The third condition proved almost intolerable. He had to live in a one-room slum, for which a rent was charged which was quite exorbitant by Soviet standards. After a monastic cell this was no hardship in itself, but he had neighbours next door and in the flat above, none of whom he could trust. In the first week one man of about his own age came to his room to bid him welcome to the new apartment. Archimandrite Kasyan saw him eyeing the icon-corner which contained the few treasured possessions he owned, but the conversation did not turn to religion. Next day he heard footsteps on the stairs and the sound of angry agitated voices. There was a knock on his door. When he opened it three women, accompanied by four tough-looking men, stood outside. One woman said: 'You can't disturb us here by your prayers and religious activities, you know.' The Archimandrite objected that all his prayers had been silent and that what he did in his room was his own affair, upon which the four men pushed him aside and strode into the room. One took a knife out of his pocket, flicked it open and tore a great gash into the wood of his precious seventeenth-century icon of St. John the Baptist. Another took a smaller representation of the Virgin and Child, threw it on the floor and scoured out the two faces with the nails in the heel of his boot. The other two men held him by the shoulders while this was going on and the four women hooted with laughter. Their derision was harder to bear even than the desecration of the precious possessions upon which his whole life had been centred since leaving the seminary.

216

I listened in amazement to all that Archimandrite Kasyan was saying. When I started to commiserate with him he told me that he did not want my sympathy, but he did want to feel that his Church was being supported by prayer in the free countries of Europe—and this must be prayer enlightened by full knowledge of the real situation.

Evidence that lay people are suffering from the persecutions no less than their spiritual leaders is accumulating steadily. In the autumn of 1963 an appeal was brought out of the Soviet Union addressed to the 'Eastern Patriarchs of Jerusalem, Antioch, Constantinople and others'. It was signed by a few Christians in the western part of the Soviet Union on behalf of 'parishioners and pilgrims of the Orthodox Churches throughout Russia'. There is no doubt about its authenticity. This pathetic document comes straight from the heart of a suffering Church. Not only is its construction bad, with afterthoughts added here and there as they occurred to the writers—or perhaps as they heard news of further barbarities—but also the style is obviously not that of a well-educated person. Some of the facts (about the Pochaev Monastery, for example) were already known, but the letter confirms them. When the appeal was received in Western Europe it was sent to those to whom it was addressed. After that, however, a conspiracy of silence seemed to descend on it for a time. It made very little impact in the Western Press, either through indifference or from a mistaken fear that publication would increase the danger of further reprisals being taken against Russian Christians.[1] For some reason which I quite fail to understand I was personally refused permission from several quarters to see the whole document. Because of the scant publicity it has been accorded, because of the concrete details it gives and because it shows how ordinary lay people are reacting to the present treachery of the Soviet Government, I consider it worthwhile to quote some lengthy extracts.

'Since 1959 the Antichrist in Russia has been persecuting the Orthodox Church dreadfully; at first children of school and preschool age were forbidden to serve as acolytes to bishops anywhere in Russia, even in Moscow, on the orders of Kuroedov.[2] . . . The

---

[1] The best publicity in England came from the *Church Times*, 22nd November 1963, which printed some extracts from it. The whole Russian text (leaving out a few names of renegade priests) was finally published by *Posev*, the Russian émigré newspaper, on 8th May 1964.

[2] The replacement of G. Karpov by V. Kuroedov as President of the Government's Council for the Affairs of the Russian Orthodox Church was one of the early signs of the Party's change of heart about religious matters at the beginning of the new wave of persecutions.

prices of icons and candles and other goods for sale to the parishioners at the candle counter were lowered to cut off the income of the church [in Minsk] and bring about its closing. The same year the Archbishop's church and the Kozyrevskaya Church were closed and demolished.

'. . . The mockery has gone so far that the *Oblast* Representative, Lavrienko, stands next to the door of Minsk Cathedral spying on children. If he finds any in the Cathedral, he tells the verger, and this servant of Antichrist collars the children and knocks their heads against the wall.

'This is what happened to Tolik, the son of the widow Sviridovich, who did not want to leave the church. . . . Tolik's mother is Sofia Sviridovich, once a partisan fighter, who sacrificed her health to her homeland, and who, today, is very ill. Sofia Sviridovich herself is very devout; she attends the Orthodox Church and takes her children there. She gives her children a religious upbringing and throws her home wide open to pilgrims. For this, Sofia Sviridovich and her children have been cruelly persecuted. First, the investigator Shimarov came to her house, took all the icons from the walls, collected all her religious books, all the transcribed prayers, took her last sheet from the bed and tied all the sacred things in it, intending to carry off everything, including Sofia Sviridovich herself, though at that time her children were ill. But when the investigator tried to take her to the prosecuting attorney's office, her children began to scream and pull their mother back. Hearing their cries a neighbour interfered and prevented this barbaric act. After all this mockery, people came to Mrs. Sviridovich's house in the middle of the night, banged on her door, ripped the hook off the corridor door and began to break down the door of the room. When the frightened children again began to scream, they vanished like evil spirits. After all these unsuccessful attempts to seize her, she was followed in the streets, but her children always accompanied her and the plan to seize her secretly in the street was foiled. In addition to all this mockery, the Government agents, Kovalev and Lavrienko, repaired to Sviridovich's house to seize her children and place them in a boarding school. Lavrienko said to Mrs. Sviridovich: "Today they build boarding schools for religious children, with high walls, to isolate them completely from their parents and to prevent any communication between them". Following all this persecution of Sofia Sviridovich by the Antichrists, she has vanished without a trace in order to save her children.

'. . . For a whole year the parents of Minsk pleaded with the civil authorities not to drive their children out of church and not to prohibit them from taking Holy Communion. Some went personally to Moscow to plead before Kuroedov. They appealed to Brezhnev, to Khrushchev and to *Izvestia*, but all the pleadings were disregarded by the Moscow authorities.

'We appealed to the Patriarchate and to the Patriarch himself. The Patriarch gave instructions that the children receive the eucharist and that they attend church services, but the Minsk clergy had submitted to Antichrist and did not carry out the orders of the Patriarch. . . .

'. . . The same year [1963] the Minsk and Grodno Government representatives hounded those who applied to enter the religious seminary at the Zhirovitsy men's monastery. The persecution consisted in visits by the agent to applicants for entrance into the seminary who did his best to intimidate them. As a result nobody entered the seminary. . . .

'. . . In June 1963 a Pochaev monk asked permission to spend the night [in the monastery]. His name is Father Serapion, whose surname in the world was Kashirets. He is ninety-seven years old. When he was on his way to the monastery of the Holy Assumption at Pochaev he was seized by the militia and subjected to questioning for a whole week and finally they ordered him to leave Pochaev. He went to the Prior of the Pochaev Monastery, Archimandrite Bartholomew, showing authorization from the Patriarchate to live in the monastery with his brethren.' The document goes on to say he was not allowed to enter the monastery, in spite of his pitiable condition.

'We cannot pass in silence over the barbarous mockery of Father Yosif, the [former] Prior, known in the world as Yakov Varnavvich Golovashok. He is seventy years old. In September 1962 Father Yosif was half beaten to death by the godless executioners. They stuffed his mouth with rags to keep him from crying out. He was sent to a mental hospital, but God was merciful and he was released. After the mental hospital, Father Yosif returned to the Pochaev Monastery, but the local police did not give him a residence permit for the monastery and ordered him to leave Pochaev. Father Yosif found an asylum in the village of Malaya Ilovitsa, in the Kremenets District. . . .

'In order to exterminate the Orthodox faith and to speed up the closing of the churches, the Government is secretly training its godless Communists as priests. They appoint them as heads of churches and cathedrals and make them bishops and priests. Other priests, from weakness, have become the servants of Antichrist.' Here follows a list of clergy, including an archbishop and two bishops, who are stated either to be 'a complete servant of Antichrist' or to be guilty of 'fully carrying out the orders of Antichrist'. . . . 'Most of our clergy do not fulfil the traditions of the Apostles, but the orders of Antichrist. The Antichrist prohibits sermons in the churches. The clergy that do uphold the traditions of the Apostles are the objects of persecution by Antichrist and by those priests who have submitted to Antichrist.

'The Orthodox Church is in great danger. The Antichrists may well convert the Orthodox Church into a heretical Church. Antichrist will think nothing of changing the symbols of the faith. There is a rumour that this is under way. . . . Our true pastors, the monks of the Pochaev Monastery, in spite of the terrible mockery by Antichrist, have not, and will not, abandon their monastery. They strengthen the weak faith of us, sinful and unworthy servants of the Lord, by their courage and patience. Like sunshine they warm us with their prayers. . . .

'This summer [1963] on a holy day, the priest of the city of Gorny in the Mogilev *Oblast* was conducting the liturgy; during it the godless ones shouted "fire"; the people were frightened and ran in panic. Five people were trampled to death; fifteen were seriously hurt and are now in hospital; the priest, who is guiltless, is now on trial.'

This sensational document has been followed by three more in a similar vein which have just been released as this book goes to press. One gives further factual material on individual persecuted clergy and the names of closed churches; another is a desperate appeal to U Thant by the mother of one of the former Pochaev monks, in which she begs for his release from prison; the third, possibly the most interesting, sets out the spiritual torment of a mother trying to bring up Christian children in a Communist society. Against this written evidence and the story of Archimandrite Kasyan which I have recounted, one must set statements made by Russian church leaders denying that there have been any physical measures taken against the Orthodox Church in recent years. Archbishop Kiprian[1] has denied that there is any conflict at all, but more important is an interview with Metropolitan Nikodim published by the French Communist newspaper, *L'Humanité*, shortly after an inter-confessional meeting held in Paris in March 1964 designed to make known and to give

---

[1] See pp. 74–7.

publicity to the concrete facts about recent persecutions of Christians in the U.S.S.R. Here are some extracts from what the Metropolitan said.

'In our country there are a good number of unbelievers who oppose religion as a system of ideas. . . . The atheists would like everyone to be atheists, and our vocation as Christians is to testify to Jesus Christ to the whole world, so that everyone may be touched by God's word and may become his disciple.' He went on to deplore such campaigns as the recent Paris meeting, because they 'increase international tension . . . and the participants are not well informed about the life of our Church[1] . . . and speak in erroneous generalizations. . . . It also happens that our brothers from the West, seeing in our Church forms of religious life, means of expressing the faith and attitudes towards society which are totally different from their own, *are confused and seek to interpret these differences as the result of an outside pressure on the Church—an indication of her "non-liberty"*.[2] But the forms of church life among us have evolved along different historical lines from those of the West. They are our traditions, and we firmly hold to them.' Metropolitan Nikodim ended by asking that reports of intensified anti-religious propaganda in the U.S.S.R. should be interpreted not as religious persecution, but as a 'struggle of ideas'.

At the same time *Tass*, the Soviet Government's news-agency, published a statement by Metropolitan Pimen of Krutitsky and Kolomna in which he said: 'Russian Christians have no reason for anxiety, as the right to profess any religion or no religion at all is guaranteed in Article 124 of the Soviet Constitution.'

I have presented documentary evidence from both sides and the reader can make up his own mind where the truth lies. It is necessary, however, to pause for a little longer over the character of Metropolitan Nikodim.

There has been much speculation about his spectacular rise to fame. He was born Boris Rotov in a village of the Ryazan district in 1929.[3] He became a monk in 1947 and took over a village church in the Yaroslavl diocese two years later at the age of twenty. The next year he became Rural Dean of Uglich and two years later he took over the post of secretary to Archbishop Dmitry of Yaroslavl and Rostov. He had been following the Leningrad correspondence course in theology

---

[1] One of them was Nikita Struve!
[2] Italics mine.
[3] For some of the details of Nikodim's early career I am indebted to Struve, *Les Chrétiens en U.R.S.S.*, pp. 143–4.

and finished it in 1955 by writing a diploma thesis on the Russian Mission in Jerusalem, Israel. As a result of this he was posted to the staff of the Mission in the next year and became its head in 1957. I have talked to both Christians and Jews in Jerusalem who still remember with anger the proud way in which he used to be driven round in a luxury car provided by the Soviet Embassy. In March 1959 he was recalled to Moscow to become the administrator of the Patriarch's office.

It was soon after this that I first met Archimandrite Nikodim, as he then was, and we talked on more than one occasion. From his insignificant appearance and cheeks pink with boyishness and immaturity I did not begin to guess the brilliant career which was then lying just ahead of him.

Nikodim was consecrated Bishop of Podolsk in July 1960, being at thirty-one the youngest bishop in Christendom. Yet almost immediately he succeeded Metropolitan Nikolai as head of the Foreign Relations Department of the Moscow Patriarchate. Just a year after his consecration he was elevated to the office of Archbishop of Yaroslavl and Rostov, nominally holding the title of the diocese where he had formerly served as an assistant to Archbishop Dmitry, though in fact continuing with the work he was already doing in Moscow. In August 1963 a further promotion made him Metropolitan of Leningrad and Ladoga. He had attained supreme power in the Russian Orthodox Church (the Patriarch has for long been a mere figurehead) at an age when most English clergy are just settling into their first living.

Nikodim's rise has been as meteoric as the simultaneous fall in the fortunes of Russian Christians has been cataclysmic. His career waxed in inverse proportion to the waning of Metropolitan Nikolai's, all of whose former responsibilities he had now taken over. Is there a connection between the ascent of the one and the decline of the other? Is Nikodim climbing on the shoulders of a Church already beaten to its knees? Or are the words I have just quoted ('Our vocation as Christians is to testify to Jesus Christ to the whole world') an expression of a deep Christian conviction trying to make the best of a bad job? Evidence is lacking and it is quite stupid to make hasty judgments based on circumstantial arguments.

On 16th December 1964 a press conference took place in the Russian Church in Geneva, attended by journalists from all Swiss and many other prominent European newspapers. Here Bishop

Antony of Geneva made public three documents (see also p. 220). The British Press was almost silent (*The Times* devoted twenty lines to the subject, couched in the most general terms) and all newspapers except *Le Parisien Libéré*[1] and *Posev*[2] avoided quoting the severe criticism of the Metropolitans Nikodim and Pimen contained in one of the documents. The writer of this document bitterly resents that they have denied the fact of persecution in the U.S.S.R., but she expresses the deepest gratitude for the support that Russian Christians are now beginning to feel from abroad.

None of these allegations proves anything, except that, considered together with the extract from the document printed on pp. 217–20, there is a grave mistrust of their church leaders among some parishioners and junior clergy. However, this should serve to put us all on our guard. Whether they like it or not, this is the man with whom individual Churches and the W.C.C. must principally deal in their attempts to bring the Russian Church closer into the world-wide Christian fellowship—and there is some evidence for saying that he does not enjoy the full confidence of his own Church.

THE WORLD COUNCIL OF CHURCHES

Before attempting to assess how the contacts between the Russian Orthodox Church and the W.C.C. are likely to work out in practice, let us have a brief look at the history of these relations.

During the height of the cold war years the Russian Orthodox Church joined with the Soviet Government in condemning all institutions in which America played any part, and the W.C.C. came in for its full share of opprobrium. Particular capital was made out of the role which John Foster Dulles played in the movement during its early days. At the same time, individual Christians in the U.S.S.R. were thirsty for increased contacts with their brothers in the West,[3] but during Stalin's lifetime, with his pathological xenophobia, there could be no question of this happening. However, by 1958 the 'thaw' had taken such effect that even the Church benefited from it and an official meeting with the W.C.C. could take place. Representatives from both sides gathered in Utrecht from 7th–9th August. The Russian party was represented by Metropolitan Nikolai, Bishop Mikhail

---

[1] 18th December 1964.

[2] 7th January 1965 (where the three documents were published in their entirety).

[3] So John Lawrence claims—'East and West—the New Opportunity', *The Ecumenical Review*, April 1962, p. 329.

of Smolensk, Mr. A. S. Buyevsky and Mr. V. S. Alexeyev (interpreter); the W.C.C. delegates were Dr. F. K. Fry (Chairman of the Central Committee), Metropolitan James of Melita and Dr. W. A. Visser 't Hooft.

Five main points were on the agenda:

1. The Russian Orthodox Church and the ecumenical movement;
2. the problem of Christian unity and the defence and strengthening of peace;
3. the attitude of the Russian Orthodox Church to social and political questions;
4. the W.C.C. and the One Church;
5. the common concern of the Churches for religious freedom.[1]

The first three points were proposed by the Moscow Patriarchate, the last two by the W.C.C. The discussions proceeded with reasonable warmth, although Metropolitan Nikolai expressed some serious reservations about the W.C.C.'s political activities and the lack of a sufficiently firm dogmatic basis. However, a programme of further co-operation was proposed and agreed upon, including the interchange of delegations. These increased contacts bore rapid fruit. Archpriest Vitaly Borovoi and V. S. Alexeyev spent a month in Geneva in the summer of 1959 studying the organization of the W.C.C. at its headquarters, and then followed on to Rhodes for the Central Committee meeting from 19th–29th August. Here they were joined by Metropolitan Nikolai who made a speech of such enthusiasm for the cause of unity that it seemed to all that the Russian Orthodox Church would soon apply for membership.

After mentioning that all Christians continue to pray 'Our Father' even in their separation, Metropolitan Nikolai went on:

'We Orthodox cannot but sympathize with the measures taken by the World Council of Churches and directed towards the solution of many social problems of our time. The fight against social untruth because of our realization of the truth of Christ, the efforts to help the under-developed countries, the condemnation of colonial policy and race discrimination—all this is worthy of the active support of all Christians in accordance with the demands of the Christian conscience.

'Our common moral task is the struggle to stop the nuclear weapons tests and to achieve their complete abolition. Therefore we

[1] *Current Developments in the Eastern European Churches*, No. 1, January 1959.

Orthodox entirely share and support the efforts of the W.C.C. towards this aim.

'In the meantime, I think it necessary to express the hope that the social concern of the W.C.C. will not overshadow the main task of the ecumenical movement, which aims at the unity of faith that is divided by differing interpretations. We Christians must stand above the political contradictions of our time and give to the divided peoples an example of unity and peace, brotherhood and love, removing ourselves from all self-sufficient isolationism and unfriendly relations to each other.'[1]

It is hardly surprising that these last words brought the Metropolitan an ovation. A W.C.C. delegation went to the U.S.S.R. in December 1959 and on 30th March 1960 Geneva received a formal application from the Russian Orthodox Church for membership.

It was not, however, the old team of Metropolitan Nikolai and Bishop Mikhail, whose influence had undoubtedly been a decisive factor in achieving this goal, who were there to share the world's joy when the Russian Orthodox Church was finally admitted to membership of the W.C.C. at its Third General Assembly held in New Delhi November–December 1961. Not only was their disgrace by this time complete, but by a supreme stroke of irony Metropolitan Nikolai died on 13th December, just a week after the Assembly had finished its work.

The act of joining made headlines in the world Press, though few correspondents knew what to make of this delegation of five young bishops headed by one of thirty-two, a few priests and the lay entourage which is inevitably present at every such event. Then, and subsequently at ecumenical gatherings, the behaviour of the Russian delegation was discreet, but when asked in a Press conference about the State's attitude to his Church's joining the W.C.C., Archbishop Nikodim replied: 'The Church is completely free from State interference, and it is necessary to say that we are quite independent in our inner life. Therefore it is not possible to speak of State approval or disapproval of our Church's action in joining the Council.'[2]

I understand from those who were at New Delhi and tried to engage members of the Russian delegation in private conversation that it was very difficult to do so, except in the presence of the laymen whose function is often dubious. On these occasions there seem to be

[1] *Current Developments in the Eastern European Churches*, No. 4, October 1959.
[2] *Church Times*, 24th November 1961.

several men present who have a morbid fear of leaving the other delegates alone in the presence of non-Russians for a single moment. When Nikodim came to London for the enthronement of the Archbishop of Canterbury in June 1961, he and Bishop Antony Bloom, the head of the Russian Orthodox Church in Western Europe (now Archbishop), wanted to have a private conversation in the hotel where the Russians were staying. A Baptist minister who was also in the Russian delegation tried his best to prevent this and kept on coming back to the room at five-minute intervals. He suggested, among other things, that it was already past bed-time and twice had to be told quite sharply to go.

Despite Archbishop Nikodim's assertion to the contrary, without the approval of the Soviet Government there could have been no question of the Russian Orthodox Church becoming a member of the W.C.C. The Communist Party always hopes to gain something somehow from the participation by Soviet citizens in an international movement. What did it hope to gain here? There are, I think, three answers to this question, in ascending order of importance:

1. An insight into a world-wide movement which the Soviet Government has a nagging feeling may just possibly be important. If so, they hope to find out why it is and where it will lead.
2. An influence over the W.C.C. which would be beneficial to the cause of Communism.
3. The approval of the Christian world for the Russian church leaders. By projecting them into the limelight the Government would be able to carry on the persecution inside the U.S.S.R. unscathed.

No one would wish to suggest that the Russian Church itself approves these aims, still less that all its delegates are Communist agents, but the possibility must always be borne in mind that the State is using the Church simply for what it can derive from it to help its own ends. How far have these points which I have enumerated been realized by subsequent events?

It has certainly not been difficult for the Communist Party to gain an insight into the Ecumenical Movement. A permanent representative of the Russian Church is resident at the Geneva headquarters of the W.C.C., which ensures that news of any important Christian developments anywhere in the world goes straight back to Moscow. Every Christian must applaud the achieving of this aim. The higher the esteem in which the Soviet Government holds the W.C.C. for its ability to influence world opinion the better. Russian Christianity will probably gain much more from this representation than Soviet Communism.

The question of Russian Communist influence on the W.C.C. is a much more complex one. It depends mainly on whether one believes there are any Communist agents included among the more influential people who represent the Russian Church. John Lawrence wrote of the New Delhi Assembly: 'So far experience does not suggest that Russian church-people come to ecumenical meetings in order to play politics and, if they did so, it would be seen through at once.'[1] I am doubtful whether this statement has so far been borne out in practice. The W.C.C. is so far playing safe in withholding any information which might disprove what John Lawrence wrote, though from what an outsider can glean one gathers that there have been difficulties. Nikodim, for instance, keeps on insisting that the W.C.C. play its part in the peace forum, particularly by supporting the Prague Conference devoted to the subject. This it has resolutely refused to do, in spite of such strong persuasion. Nikodim has been asked on more than one occasion why he insists so strongly and has always replied: 'By supporting such causes we gain standing in the eyes of our Government.' It is surprising that he has never said that it must be a basic Christian concern to further the cause of peace in the world.

Discussion of political issues can in no sense be excluded from the agenda of W.C.C. meetings. When the Central Committee met in Paris in August 1962 there was a resolution tabled calling on the Ghana Government to reconsider its decision to expel the Anglican Bishop of Accra and the Archbishop of West Africa for accusing the Young Pioneers (national youth organization) of 'godlessness'. The Rumanian, Hungarian and Russian delegations tried to hold up the passage of the resolution. Archpriest Vitaly Borovoi argued: 'It is quite clear we must defend personal and religious liberty. But we must also stand for the development of these countries in Africa.' His amendment, which was defeated, would have called on the Churches of Ghana to co-operate completely 'with the peoples of Ghana in the building up of a new society on the principles of complete national independence and State sovereignty, liberty and social justice'.[2]

That the delegations should hold different points of view in open

---

[1] *Ecumenical Review*, April 1962, p. 331.
[2] *Church Times*, 24th August 1962.

discussions on such topics is probably beneficial to the movement, but when I hear of political pronouncements made by members of Russian Church delegations I always think of a conversation which I had with Archimandrite Nikodim in the early part of 1960, around the time when the Russian Church was applying to join the W.C.C. We were talking about the Ecumenical Movement in general terms and I asked him what specific contribution he expected the Russian Church to bring to it. Instead of giving me an answer about the richness of the Russian liturgy which ought to belong to the heritage of the whole Christian world, instead of saying it would bring a whole new stream of Christianity into a movement which up to then had been mainly Protestant, he started to talk of the value to Western Christians of the social experience they would gain from the Soviet Union. They would have a new opportunity of seeing an ideal social system at work. I quickly changed the subject, but in view of later developments I now wish I had pursued it further.

The third point—to gain the interest of the world in the Russian Orthodox Church's external contacts as a cover for darker deeds at home—is by far the most serious. However, I need only point out here how triumphantly the Soviet Government has succeeded in this aim. In the world-wide coverage which the New Delhi Assembly received in the Press, the most prominent position was almost everywhere occupied by pictures of the Russian delegation. For allowing the Church such freedom the Soviet Government gained immense good will on all sides. The Soviet Embassy received the delegation with a conspicuous display of lavishness. Hardly anywhere in the world was there an isolated voice raised to point out the contrast with the bleak state of affairs within the U.S.S.R.

I do not wish to paint a one-sided picture of the significance of the Russian Church's action in joining the W.C.C., for there can be few Christians in the Soviet Union who did not welcome this step forward. In many, particularly those who were well informed, I found evidence of spiritual elevation as they speculated about the possibilities for the future. Priests and theological students should now have a much better opportunity of catching up with twentieth-century theology, while all Christians will, I hope, gain a feeling of solidarity with those in other countries as they become increasingly aware of Christianity as an active force in many different parts of the world. Even though many people are at present very badly informed about the religious situation in other countries because of the lack of a church press as we know it, a greater hope should filter down to those who are being persecuted.

The first time that the W.C.C. met on Soviet soil was in February 1964 at Odessa, when a meeting of the Executive Committee took place. The Russian people were informed of this through a short article in *Izvestia*. It is rumoured that a pilgrimage set out from the western Ukraine to the south to present a petition to the delegates. The people involved were intercepted and arrested.

The Russian Church could not openly admit it, but it may even hope to learn something about presenting the Gospel in a secular society by comparing its own problems with those of the industrialized nations of Western Europe.

Finally, the fact that when the Orthodox Church joined the W.C.C. it was followed in August 1962 by the Lutheran Churches of Latvia and Estonia, the Russian Baptist Church, the Georgian Orthodox and the Armenian Apostolic Churches, may make possible a genuine ecumenical movement within the Soviet Union itself.[1]

Taking all these possible benefits into consideration, one wonders whether the Soviet Government may have given away more than it intended by allowing the Russian Churches to enter fully into the Ecumenical Movement. Certainly the situation holds most interesting possibilities.

One further point which should be mentioned here is the undoubted benefit the W.C.C. itself has received through having a very large Orthodox Church as a full member. The World Council is now as well balanced as it can be until the Roman Catholic Church applies for membership. Even more important, the Western world is no longer likely to be caught up in a Protestant-Roman dialogue and believe this to be the whole of the Ecumenical Movement. Points of reference right outside will save the debate from becoming stereotyped or intransigent.

In summing up one can only say that present relations between the Russian Orthodox Church and the W.C.C. are very delicately balanced. It is difficult for someone not at the centre of the Ecumenical Movement to know all the inner tensions, but one can guess at some of them. If the W.C.C. suspects the Russian Church of political motivation in its ecumenical attitudes, it can hardly say so bluntly. This would bring a storm of protest from American Christians and a showdown would follow, which would destroy a straw of hope for

[1] cf., p. 172.

millions of persecuted Christians. The W.C.C. does have a policy of strengthening the Churches in Eastern Europe, by intervention with governments as well as by offering spiritual and moral encouragement, but I am not sure that as much is known of this as it ought to be. Perhaps the very difficult situation which the W.C.C. experienced as a result of its support of the Hungarian Revolution in 1956 has led it to be cautious in its public pronouncements. In one sphere I would like to see less caution.

There is in the Geneva headquarters a department called the Desk for Documentation concerning Eastern European Churches. Since January 1959 it has been putting out a regular bulletin entitled 'Current Developments in the Eastern European Churches'. It is divided into two main sections, the first of which gives news culled from the official publications of the Churches in Communist countries, mainly listing delegations which they send or receive; the second gives a digest of the anti-religious propaganda which has recently appeared in the secular press, mostly taken from Soviet newspapers and periodicals. One could read through the twenty-six numbers which appeared up to May 1964 and remain totally unaware of the one 'current development' of supreme significance since the first number was published—the new persecutions to which Christians in Russia are now being subjected. To read about the volume of anti-religious propaganda is not a substitute for learning the real facts of the situation. I am not suggesting that the main function of 'Current Developments' should be to document persecutions, but at least it should ensure that the emphasis is not always in the same direction. In the introduction to the May 1964 number we find the words: 'In the East of Europe the Churches continue as before, *co-existing with anti-religious trends*.'[1] Bearing in mind the documentary evidence of persecutions which had become available a few months before this was written, one would not have thought that this last phrase was very judiciously chosen to describe the situation. Even to report the Eastern European church press without elucidation may produce a misleading impression, for the bald statements often found there usually require an informed commentary to make sense to a Christian reader in the West.

I believe that by adding impartial comment on church news from Eastern Europe and replacing some of the large amount of dull and stereotyped atheist propaganda with personal impressions of Russian

[1] Italics mine.

church life, the W.C.C. could restore the balance. At the same time it could perform an inestimable service in really attempting to give Western Christians the opportunity of understanding the difficulties and the consolations of their counterparts under Communist governments.

Anyone who is passionately concerned, as I am, to see the great day draw closer when Christian unity will be established, must insist that ecumenical progress can be based only on full truths, not on partial ones; on deep knowledge of the real situations and problems facing Churches which are trying to unite, not on idealized pictures.

SOLIDARITY AND PROTEST

I hope that this book has succeeded not only in arousing interest in the Russian Church, but in causing positive concern for a vast number of persecuted Christians. To think for a while about what is happening in Eastern Europe puts our own problems into perspective and should help us to get our priorities right. We seem to spend so much time squabbling about matters of secondary importance and do so little to support Christians who need our help urgently.

Some take the attitude that any publicity about the real state of affairs in the Soviet Union is likely to make the situation for Christians very much worse. This may have been true in Stalin's time, but it is emphatically not so today. There has been every sign in the last few years that Khrushchev's Russia is sensitive to world opinion. Many examples of this could be quoted from the political sphere, but I will confine myself to two from the religious.

The story of the Pochaev Monastery did not make much impact in the British Press, but on the Continent many consciences were aroused. There is good evidence that as a result of the public protests in the West the persecution of the monks was not brought to its logical conclusion—the monastery was not closed. Some thirty monks have been allowed to remain in residence as a conciliatory gesture towards world opinion. If we allow their situation to recede into a forgotten limbo, one night a lorry will come and take away those who are left. It will be done swiftly and quietly, so that it is all over before public opinion can be mobilized again.

Before the Passover on 27th March 1964 it was announced in the Moscow Central Synagogue that no unleavened bread would be available for the feast, so members of the congregation were advised to bake theirs at home if they could. Immediately the Jewish organizations of the world sent out protests, as a result of which one bakery was rented to Jews for the purpose. This was hopelessly inadequate to cope with the needs of about thirty thousand families, but at least it was a step in the right direction. Even a token action like this on the part of the Soviet authorities is far better than if nothing at all happens because the world received the news in silence.

Unfortunately, the reason for our silence is often not fear of causing reprisals, but indifference. Of all the concrete evidence of religious persecution in the U.S.S.R. which has come to light in the last four years, only one solitary incident has hit the headlines in the British Press. This was early in January 1963, when a group of Christians belonging to an unidentified evangelical sect suddenly appeared in Moscow to stage a protest.[1] There were thirty-two in all, including men, women and children. They came by train from Chernogorsk, near Krasnodarsk, in southern central Siberia. When they arrived in Moscow they made their way straight to the American Embassy, where they forced aside the Russian militia who guard it and addressed a pathetic and hopeless appeal to the American diplomatic staff. They complained that they were not allowed to hold services and that their children were being taken away from them and sent to boarding schools in order to be removed from the religious influence of their homes. They mistakenly believed that the Americans could arrange for them to leave the country and begged for political asylum at the Embassy. The American Ambassador, however, after listening to their complaints, was of course forced to hand them over to the waiting Soviet authorities.

Does it always need such a defiant and self-sacrificing gesture to stir our consciences? It seems to me that our organs of publicity in Western Europe have much to answer for, if they confine their reporting of Russian Christianity to accounts of the itinerary of the latest church delegation to pay a visit from the Soviet Union. The persecution which is at present trying to eradicate organized religion in the U.S.S.R. is the greatest stain on the record of a nation which has many admirable qualities and infinite potential. It must be declared in the strongest terms that the world disapproves of its attitude towards religion and that it is unlikely to be accepted into the family of civilized nations until it changes it. The Soviet Government would like to have a phantom Church—one which has no members at all

---

[1] See *The Times*, 4th January 1963.

within the U.S.S.R., but which has powerful international connections which can be used to support Soviet strategy. We must make it known that we see through this and are not impressed.

Only by such fearless action is there a chance of persuading the Communist Party to drop its neurotic attitude towards Christianity and to abandon the outmoded nineteenth-century slogan that 'religion is the opium of the people'. By doing so Communists might come to see that there is a place for a free and flourishing Church in a liberalized society. If at some time in the future the Soviet Government should seek to become democratic, the true support of loyal Christians could stabilize it, and the faithful would no longer have to pray in secret for the overthrow of a godless system.

APPENDIX

Statistics for the Russian Orthodox Church[1]

	1914	1939	1947–57	1962	1966	1973
Dioceses	73	?	73	73	73	73
Bishops in diocesan service	163	about 4	74	63	63	64
Parish clergy	51,105	some 100s	about 20,000	14,000	10,000	?
Churches	54,174	some 100s	about 18,000	11,500	7,500	7,500
Monasteries and Convents	1,025	Nil	67	32	16	12–20
Monks and Nuns	94,629	?	about 10,000	5,000	?	?
Church Academies	4	Nil	2	2	2	2
Theological Seminaries	57	Nil	8	5	3	3
Pre-Theological Schools	185	Forbidden by law				
Parochial Schools	37,528					
Hospitals	291					
Homes for Aged	1,113					
Parish Libraries	34,497					

[1] Reprinted from Trevor Beeson, *Discretion and Valour*, Collins Fontana, 1974, p. 53 (with kind permission).

Notes to the Second Edition

Writing today, one might have found a different solution to the problem of protecting one's sources. At the time it seemed right to transpose various incidents and views given by Soviet citizens and to use fictitious names for my unofficial contacts. As far as I know, none of them suffered because of the book and some have now even left the Soviet Union since the limited emigration became possible. Recently the whole atmosphere surrounding contacts in the Soviet Union has become less furtive and a growing number of people are prepared to be quoted by name. This is not a freedom "granted" by the KGB, but one seized by people who are determined to see basic changes in Soviet society.

A growing number of people desire urgently to make their uncensored voice heard. A democratic (usually called "dissident") movement has emerged, disunited, but openly calling for the most far-reaching changes in Soviet society. Although its concrete achievements so far have been few (except in persuading the Soviet Government to allow some emigration), it has profoundly affected the psychology of the intelligentsia. The Church has been active in this from the beginning. Individuals and sometimes large groups from among Russian and Georgian Orthodox, Baptists, Pentecostals, Adventists, Catholics of both Eastern and Latin Rite have come very nearly to the point of formulating a common cause in their dissatisfaction with Soviet laws on religion and their discriminatory implementation.

After the fall of Khrushchev at the end of 1964, the closure of churches ceased abruptly. There followed a year in which the churches had much greater latitude, while the new leadership of Brezhnev and Kosygin established itself. The decade from 1966 has seen the emergence of a new *status quo*, with much less physical violence against believers generally, but a continuing tight control over church life, with the imprisonment of numerous outstanding figures who, either locally or nationally, have tried to broaden the frontiers of religious liberty by such actions as petitioning the Soviet Government for changes in the law or insisting on organizing some form of religious education for their children. Keston College, an organization keeping careful records on religious life in the Communist countries, had about 150 names on its list of known religious prisoners at the end of 1976 (available from Keston College, Keston, Kent). There are, of course, others who are not known.

The hesitant suggestion in the foregoing pages that some young people may have an increasing interest in religion dates this book more surely than anything else. Since it was written massive and conclusive evidence has emerged that the system, whether it uses persuasion, education or force, has been totally unable to control this. There are innumerable examples of young people whose curiosity has become a deeply-rooted commitment to the faith. But perhaps this book dates the origin of this major development and reveals some of its roots.

So much for general reflections. Here are notes on a few of the textual changes that I would have made if I had rewritten the book.

Page 67. The Soviet "support" for the Prague Christian Peace Conference was evidently not full enough. Too much control was left in Czech hands for the taste of the Soviets, who seized it and threw out the key figures after the invasion of August 1968. It is no longer the "valuable forum" it was. Virtually all the responsible western support has been withdrawn. It is now a naked instrument of Soviet foreign policy, which manages nevertheless to influence numerous churchmen from the Third World.

Page 73. Contacts with priests have become much easier in recent years.

Page 75. The official exchange rate in December 1976 was £1 = 1.20 roubles.

Page 93. The seminary at Lutsk did in fact close in 1965. The other three seminaries and the two academies have remained open and in 1973-74 were reported to have 1196 students between them: Moscow 302, Leningrad 177, Odessa 117, Correspondence Course 600 (*Religion in Communist Lands*, Vol. 2, No. 3, 1974, pp. 4–8).

Page 105. For a study of developments in the Russian Orthodox Church from 1960–68, see my book *Patriarch and Prophets*.

Page 122. Osipov died in 1967, reportedly a disillusioned man.

Page 158. Several more students have been allowed to study in the

West since. The authorities also allowed the institution of a theological correspondence course in 1968. There has also been a limited edition of the Bible and of the Baptist hymn book. Andrei is the prototype of those younger and independent spirits who were already, but unknown to me at the time of writing, breaking away to form a movement independent of State control under the inspired leadership of men such as Georgi Vins (now serving a ten-year sentence, his second period of imprisonment since this book was written).

Page 171. The judgment at the bottom of this page was made after long hesitation and thought. As I expected, it resulted in much criticism. After many years of reflection, I would not now repeat it. Young people have been joining all the denominations, coming in thousands both to the Orthodox and Protestant churches. Different traditions suit different temperaments, while a Lithuanian will naturally become a Roman Catholic.

Page 180. Subsequently the authorities severely limited the number of theological students at Kaunas. It dropped to 24 in 1965, but has picked up since to 53 in 1975–6.

Page 181. The Lithuanian Catholic movement for religious freedom which began in the late 1960's has become the most cohesive of all such developments. The authorities closed the new church at Klaipeda in 1960. Bishop Strods subsequently died, to be replaced by Bishop J. Vaivods (1964).

Page 182–3. The section on the Uniats is the most inadequate in the book. Virtually nothing was known of their present situation at the time of writing, but there is now considerable evidence that they continue as a massive illegal movement.

Page 184. Archbishop Kiivit retired for health reasons in 1967, at the age of 61, and was succeeded by Alfred Tooming. Kiivit maintained a more independent stand in relation to the authorities than his Latvian opposite number, Turs, and the Estonian Lutheran Church is correspondingly stronger than Latvian counterpart. Archbishop Turs was succeeded by Peters Kleperis in 1968 when he retired at the age of 78, but after the sudden death of Kleperis, Janis Matulis was elected Archbishop in February 1969 by the Latvian General Synod.

Page 185. The Lutheran World Federation finally made such contacts in 1976. Dr. Paul Hansen reported about 30 registered and hundreds of unregistered Lutheran parishes in Siberia and Central Asia.

Page 192. Ephraim II died in 1972. His successor, David V, has proved a highly controversial figure. Criticism of him personally and the manner of his election has called forth a vocal "renewal" movement within the Georgian Orthodox Church (see *Religion in Communist Lands* Vol 3, Nos. 4–5, July–Oct. 1975, pp. 14–23; Vol. 3, No. 6, Nov.–Dec. 1975, pp. 45–54, and Vol. 4, No. 1, Spring 1976, pp. 49–50; Vol. 4, No. 4, Winter 1976, pp. 48–51).

Page 203. Visits to Zagorsk rapidly became standard again. On my last visit to Moscow in February 1975 I was able to revisit the seminary and all tourist groups can choose to visit the monastery, if they so wish.

Page 206. The Rev. Raymond Oppenheim, formerly Episcopalian Chaplain in Moscow at the American Embassy, has provided the precise number of Orthodox churches open in Moscow and its environs in the 1970's: 44. Therefore the destruction of Moscow churches discontinued completely after the incident described on pp. 209–10 and the fall of Khrushchev.

Page 211. See note to p. 93 (above) for statistics on theological students. The authorities reduced the number of Russian Orthodox monasteries to 6 and convents to 13 by the mid-1960s, since when the figure has remained constant. The full story of the heroism of the Pochaev Monastery is told in *Patriarch and Prophets*, pp. 74–84, 87–8, 97–116, 173–5.

Page 217. Archimandrite Kasyan's words are the keynote of the requests to the outside world subsequently made by thousands of Soviet believers – for "prayer enlightened by full knowledge of the real situation".

Page 220. The word *samizdat* was unknown when I wrote this page. The flood of unpublished documents has since carried thousands of examples to the West, ranging from appeals of a few sentences to lengthy books. Most are in typescript, but the Baptists produce some of theirs on a clandestine printing press.

Page 222. My questions asked about Nikodim (now Metropolitan) were erroneously taken as judgments on him by some commentators. I still feel it necessary to ask the questions; evidence for an adequate answer is lacking even now. He became a President of the World Council of Churches in 1975.

Page 226. Archbishop Antony Bloom has subsequently questioned the Moscow Patriarchate in public over its attack on Alexander Solzhenitsyn. He later relinquished his oversight over the Russian

Orthodox parishes in Western Europe, but remains a member of the Moscow jurisdiction. These pages on the World Council of Churches seemed inflammatory to some at the time of publication. Now, perhaps, they appear less so. There are many questions here which have still received no satisfactory answer.

Page 230. *Current Developments in the Eastern European Churches* no longer exists and nothing the WCC publishes has replaced it.

Page 232. The success of subsequent Jewish protests in claiming the right to emigrate is too well known to need underlining here.

The 'unidentified" evangelicals turned out to be Pentecostals. Their leaders were severely repressed after this incident, but several of them have resumed their activities vocally since, leading even to a strong demand for the right to emigrate (granted so far only to a handful of families).

Notes for Further Reading

1. THE ORTHODOX CHURCH (general)

Lossky, V., *The Mystical Theology of the Eastern Church*, London, 1957.

Meyendorff, J., *The Orthodox Church: its Past and its Role in the World Today*, New York, 1963.

Ware, T., *The Orthodox Church*, London, 1963.

Eastern Churches Review, The House of St Gregory and St Macrina, 1 Canterbury Road, Oxford, OX2 6LU.

Sobornost (journal of the Fellowship of St Alban and St Sergius), St. Basil's House, 52 Ladbroke Grove, London, W11 2PB.

2. RUSSIAN CHURCH HISTORY

Ammann, A. M., *Storia della Chiesa Russa*, Turin, 1948.

Anon (a spiritual daughter), *An Early Soviet Saint: The Life of Father Zachariah*, London, 1976.

Dunlop, J., *Staretz Amvrosy*, Oxford, 1975.

Fedotov, G. P., *The Russian Religious Mind*, Cambridge, Mass., 1946 (paper-back, New York, 1960).

Fedotov, G. P., (ed.), *A Treasury of Russian Spirituality*, London, 1950.

Frere, W. H., *Some Links in the Chain of Russian Church History*, London, 1918.

Pascal, P., *Avvakum et les Débuts du Raskol*, Paris, 1938.

Pascal, P., *The Religion of the Russian People*, London, 1976.

Zernov, N., *Moscow, the Third Rome*, London, 1937.

Zernov. N., *St. Sergius, Builder of Russia*, London, 1939.

Zernov, N., *The Russians and their Church*, London, 1945.

3. CHRISTIANITY AND COMMUNISM

Berdyaev, N., *Le Marxisme et la Religion*, Paris, 1947.

NOTES FOR FURTHER READING

Garaudy, R., *From Anathema to Dialogue*, London, 1967.

Gardavsky, V., *God is Not Yet Dead*, Harmondsworth, Middlesex, 1973.

Klugmann, J. & Oestreicher, P. (eds.), *What Kind of Revolution? A Christian-Communist Dialogue*, London, 1968.

Machoveč, M., *A Marxist Looks at Jesus*, London, 1976.

MacIntyre, A., *Marxism and Christianity*, London, 1971.

Oestreicher, P. (ed.), *The Christian Marxist Dialogue*, New York, 1969.

Rogers E., *A Commentary on Communism*, New York, 1951 (revised edition published as *A Christian Commentary on Communism*, London, 1959).

West, C. C., *Communism and the Theologians*, London, 1958.

4. GENERAL CHRISTIAN SITUATION IN THE U.S.S.R.

Beeson, T., *Discretion and Valour*, London, 1974.

Bociurkiw, B. and Strong, J. (eds.), *Religion and Atheism in the U.S.S.R. and Eastern Europe*, London, 1975.

Bourdeaux, M. and Murray, K., *Young Christians in Russia*, London, 1976.

Bourdeaux, M., Hebly, H. and Voss, E. (eds.), *Religious Liberty in the Soviet Union. W.C.C. and U.S.S.R.: a post-Nairobi Documentation*, Keston, Kent, 1976.

Bourdeaux, M., Gerstenmaier, C. and Matchett, K., *Religious Minorities in the Soviet Union*, London, revised ed., 1977.

Kolarz, W., *Religion in the Soviet Union*, London, 1961.

Marshall, R., Bird, T. and Blane, A. (eds.), *Aspects of Religion in the Soviet Union, 1917–1967*, Chicago, 1971.

Szczesniak, B., *The Russian Revolution and Religion*, Notre Dame, Indiana, 1959.

Glaube in der 2. Welt, Zürichstrasse 155, Küsnacht, Zürich, CH-8700.

Religion in Communist Dominated Areas, 475 Riverside Drive, New York, N.Y. 10027.

Religion in Communist Lands, Keston College, Heathfield Road, Keston, Kent, BR2 6BA.

5. THE RUSSIAN ORTHODOX CHURCH IN THE TWENTIETH CENTURY

Anderson, P., *People, Church and State in Modern Russia*, London, 1944.

Bourdeaux, M., *Patriarch and Prophets: Persecution of the Russian Orthodox Church*, London, second ed., 1975.

Curtis, J., *Church and State in Russia*, (*1900–17*) New York, 1944.

Curtis, J., *The Russian Church and the Soviet State, 1917–50*, Boston, 1953.

Fireside, H., *Icon & Swastika*, Cambridge, Mass., 1971.

Fletcher, W., *A Study in Survival – the Church in Russia 1929–1943*, New York, 1965.

Fletcher, W., *Nikolai*, London, 1968.

Fletcher, W., *Russian Orthodox Church Underground*, Oxford, 1973.

Simon, G., *Church, State and Opposition in the U.S.S.R.*, London, 1974.

Spinka, M., *The Church in Soviet Russia*, New York, 1956.

Struve, N., *Christians in Contemporary Russia*, London, 1967.

Timasheff, N., *Religion in Soviet Russia, 1917–42*, New York, 1942, London, 1943.

Zernov, N., *The Russian Religious Renaissance of the Twentieth Century*, London, 1963.

The Russian Orthodox Church, Organization, Situation, Activity, Moscow, 1958 (in English).

Journal of the Moscow Patriarchate, Box No. 624, Moscow G-435, U.S.S.R.

Russia Cristiana, Via Martinengo 16, 20139 Milan, Italy.

Vestnik Russkogo Khristianskogo Dvizheniya, 91 rue Olivier-de-Serres, 75015 Paris, France.

6. External Relations of the Russian Church

Fletcher, W., *Religion and Soviet Foreign Policy 1945–1970*, Oxford, 1973.

Meyendorff, J. (ed.), *Les Relations extérieures du Patriarcat de Moscou* (*1945–51*), Notes et Études Documentaires, No. 1624, Paris.

7. Other Churches of the U.S.S.R.

Bourdeaux, M., *Religious Ferment in Russia*, London, 1968.

Bourdeaux, M., *Faith on Trial in Russia*, London, second ed., 1975.

Bourdeaux, M., *Land of Crosses: the Lithuanian Church Today* (in preparation).

Bourdeaux, M. and Howard-Johnston, X. (eds.), *Aida of Leningrad*, London, 1972.

Brandenburg, H., *The Meek and the Mighty*, London, 1976.

Ciszek, W., *He Leadeth Me*, London, 1974.

Durasoff, S., *Pentecostals behind the Iron Curtain*, New Jersey, 1972.

Grant, M., *Vanya*, Eastbourne, 1975.

Gutsche, W., *Westliche Quellen des Russischen Stundismus*, Kassel, 1956.

Hebly, H., *Protestants in Russia*, Belfast, 1976.

Kahle, W., *Geschichte der Evangelisch-Lutherischen Gemeinden in der Sovetunion 1917–1938*, Leiden, 1974.

Rothenberg, J., *The Jewish Religion in the Soviet Union*, New York, 1971.

Rowe, M., *The Pentecostalist Movement in the U.S.S.R. – A Historical and Social Survey*, Ph. D. thesis, Glasgow University (in preparation).

Scheffbuch, W., *Christians under the Hammer and Sickle*, Michigan, 1974.

Vins, G., *Three Generations of Suffering* (tr. by Jane Ellis), London, 1976.

La Situation de l'Eglise arménienne, Notes et Études Documentaires, No. 2239, Paris, 1956.

Sovremennoye Sektantstvo (Vol. IX of *Voprosy Religii i Ateizma*), Moscow, 1961.

Soviet Persecution of Religion in Ukraine, World Congress of Free Ukrainians, Toronto, 1976.

Bratsky Vestnik, A.U.C.E.C.B., Postbox No. 520, Moscow.

Index

Letter from His Holiness Patriarch Aleksiy to Doctor Arthur Michael Ramsey, Archbishop of Canterbury, Primate and Metropolitan of All England

"Your Grace, beloved brother in Christ,

In June last year, the newspaper *Church Times* which, as you know, plays a significant part in forming public opinion in the Church of England, printed three extracts from a book published at that time, *Opium of the People*, by Michael Bourdeaux, a priest of your Church. The subject matter of these extracts, consisting of accounts of the author's conversations with people he met by chance during his stay in our country, portrays in a distorted manner our country's attitude to freedom of conscience; it falsifies and misrepresents the position of religion and church life in the USSR.

I am sure that Your Grace will understand the astonishment we felt on seeing that such a serious newspaper, for such we used to consider the *Church Times*, had allowed its pages to be used for insulting statements about our Church. Our astonishment was mingled with indignation at the lack of responsibility shown by those in charge of this publication, for their action—unworthy as it is of churchmen and especially of representatives of the religious press—is contrary to the traditional brotherly spirit of relations between the Church of England and the Russian Orthodox Church, nor does it contribute to the development of ecumenical contacts between our Churches.

I would be very grateful to Your Grace if you would bring this my letter to the attention of the editors and publishers of the *Church Times* newspaper, in the hope that they will not behave like this again in future.

Our brotherly love to you in Christ our Saviour,
ALEKSIY, Patriarch of Moscow and all Russia"

15 March 1966